P9-DSZ-475

DATE DUE

MY 24 00			

DEMCO 38-296

The Other Mirror

**Recent Titles in
Contributions to the Study of World Literature**

The Other Mirror

Women's Narrative in Mexico, 1980–1995

Edited by
KRISTINE IBSEN

Contributions to the Study of World Literature,
Number 80

GREENWOOD PRESS
Westport, Connecticut • London

ion Data

The other mirror : women's narrative in Mexico, 1980–1995 / edited by
Kristine Ibsen.
    p.   cm.—(Contributions to the study of world literature,
ISSN 0738–9345 ; no. 80)
    Includes bibliographical references.
    ISBN 0–313–30180–8 (alk. paper)
    1. Mexican fiction—Women authors—History and criticism.
2. Mexican fiction—20th century—History and criticism.   I. Ibsen,
Kristine, 1961–   .   II. Series.
PQ7133.O86   1997
863—dc20   96–30580

British Library Cataloguing in Publication Data is available.

Library of Congress Catalog Card Number: 96–30580
ISBN: 0–313–30180–8
ISSN: 0738–9345

First published in 1997

Greenwood Press, 88 Post Road West, Westport, CT 06881
An imprint of Greenwood Publishing Group, Inc.

Printed in the United States of America

♾™

The paper used in this book complies with the
Permanent Paper Standard issued by the National
Information Standards Organization (Z39.48–1984).

10 9 8 7 6 5 4 3 2

Copyright Acknowledgments

The editor and publisher gratefully acknowledge permission to use the following sources:

Esquivel, Laura. *Like Water For Chocolate*. Copyright Translation © 1992 by Doubleday, a div. of
Bantam, Doubleday, Dell Publishing Group, Inc. Used by permission of Doubleday, a division of
Bantam Doubleday Dell Publishing Group, Inc.

Esquivel, Laura. *Like Water For Chocolate*. © Seventh Dimension Entertainment Company Inc.
1993. Published by Corgi, a division of Transworld Publishers Ltd. All rights reserved.

Mastretta, Ángeles. *Mexican Bolero*. Translation by Ann Wright. London: Viking Press, 1989.

Anderson, Danny J. "Displacement: Strategies of Transformation in *Arráncame la vida* by Ángeles
Mastretta." *Journal of the Midwestern M.L.A.* 21.1 (1988).

Ibsen, Kristine. "On Recipes, Reading, and Revolution: Postboom Parody in *Como agua para chocolate*." *Hispanic Review* (Spring 1995).

CONTENTS

ACKNOWLEDGMENTS

Extracts from Laura Esquivel *Like Water for Chocolate* © Seventh Dimension Entertainment Co., Inc., 1993, appear by permission of Bantam Doubleday Dell Publishing Group, Inc. in North America and Corgi, a division of Transworld Publishers, Ltd., in the English Commonwealth. Excerpts from Ángeles Mastretta *Mexican Bolero* © Riverhead Putnam, 1989, appear courtesy of the author. Earlier versions of "Displacement: Strategies of Transformation in *Arráncame la vida*" and "On Recipes, Reading, and Revolution: Postboom Parody in *Como agua para chocolate*" were published in the *Journal of the Midwest Modern Language Association* 21.1 (1988) and *Hispanic Review* 63.2 (Spring 1995), respectively. They are reprinted here with permission.

I would also like to thank the contributors to this volume for their patience through several drafts and revisions and for the friendly dialogue that has ensued as a consequence. I am also indebted to the following people for their helpful comments and technical assistance at various stages of this project: Maureen Ahern, Mercedes Barquet, Robert Blake, Robert Burke, Mercedes Casanova, Verónica Cortínez, Jacqueline Cruz, JoAnn DellaNeva, Jean Graham-Jones, Bárbara Jacobs, Carolyn Jamison, David Klawiter, Elena Urrutia, Hugo Verani, and Jennifer Warlick. Special thanks to Jodie McCune and Nina Pearlstein, our editors at Greenwood, to editorial administrator Maureen Melino and to copy-editor Carol Blumentritt. Acknowledgment and thanks are also due to the Faculty Research Program and the Institute for the Study of Liberal Arts at the University of Notre Dame, which enabled me to complete this project.

itself to resist traditional authority.[4] This alliance, Masiello contends, has two central goals: first, to permit an alternate vision of history and, second, to establish the terms for a new solidarity (53). In this sense, women's literary production is not so different from that of any other group writing from the margins of authority; indeed, women's narrative has often considered sexual inequity as corollary to political, economic, racial, and class oppression (Shea 53, Castillo 57–58).[5] Although the exclusion of women from mainstream literary activity historically has dictated to the woman who writes a different circumstance from that of her male counterparts (Miller 15; Robles II.121–124), there is not one single monolithic response of "women writers" to the structures of official ideology.

In her discussion of how canons are developed, Mary Louise Pratt points out that since the "criteria used to determine literary value are themselves constituted in ways that reflect structures of hegemony in society . . . [t]exts by members of subordinated or marginal social groups . . . will always appear to lack 'sufficient caliber to merit inclusion' if they are read through the codes of interpretation and value that produced the exclusionist canon in the first place" (11). Thus, although critical neglect of women's narrative can be, and has been, reflective of readers whose experiences lie outside the space of the text, equally or more relevant today is how "practices of reading" influence notions of literary value. Readers trained on canonical texts, Pratt suggests, may be "unequipped to evaluate texts by subordinated or excluded groups. They will invariably misread such material, dislike, dismiss it as illegible or (more likely) trivial in content and form" (11). Often forced to contend with a critical and academic establishment that questions her authority before she even begins to write, the woman writer's relation to her reading public may be experienced as necessarily ambivalent, as she negotiates the delicate balance between anticipated reader expectations and responsive textual strategies (Smith 50).

Susana Reisz contends that "feminist" literature may encompass any discourse that "expresses dissidence using discursive strategies that propose to subvert patriarchal logic from the specific interests of women" (202, my translation). This widening of the parameters of "feminist" discourse may allow for the flexibility to include works such as *Como agua para chocolate* and *Arráncame la vida* as subversive—if not overtly feminist—novels. As I suggest in my essay (chapter 9), texts such as *Como agua para chocolate* may subvert the canon by taking the domestic space as their central focus, a topic conventionally outside "serious" literature, since it hinges on discourses associated with women's values and experiences. Other novels, such as *Arráncame la vida*, use the domestic space to show how power conflicts in the private sphere may intersect with—and reflect upon—hierarchical structures in society at large.[6] Of concern here, then, are two fundamental and interrelated issues. First, if, as Reisz suggests, the use of conventional resources is an intentional means of subversion, how successful is the text in achieving such subversion? Second, does such an undermining of traditional resources also work to weaken social structures in general, that is, do such "women's novels" carry out a transgressive politicization, or are they merely reinforcing popular sentiment? Clearly, traditional critical resources may not always be effectively employed in the study of women's literature, since this kind of writing may be significant in ways other than those that typify the literary canon. On the other hand, there is a danger in *privileging* such "female discourse" to *counter* that of male writing, since this may lead to the valuation of certain aspects of femininity that not only confirm the standard view of women writers as of secondary importance, but, possibly, represent a stereotypical view of women antithetic to social progress.

One of the fundamental characteristics of "postmodernity" has been the integration of popular and private discourses into literature. Jean Franco considers the separation between private and public discourses particularly relevant to the discussion of contemporary women's writing, since in such a division notions of literary value may preclude the female experience of the private, which often hinges on expressions of the domestic, the banal, and the routine ("Going Public" 74). This facet of female experience may be expressed through the integration of private discourse: the epistolary form utilized by Bárbara Jacobs in *Escrito en el tiempo* (1985), for example; the journal kept by Susana, the narrator in María Luisa Puga's *Pánico o peligro* (1983); the letters and yearbook dedications incorporated by Rosa Nissán in *Novia que te vea* (1992); or with discourses specifically associated with women, for example, the serialized sentimental novel and recipes that Esquivel uses to frame *Como agua para chocolate* and the allusions to *boleros* in *Arráncame la vida*. Linda Hutcheon has shown that women's writing may underline the problem of sexual difference by establishing a level of enunciation that lies outside the patriarchal order. In this kind of text, the marginal gains value, what is "different" is valorized in opposition both to elitist, alienated "otherness" and to the uniforming impulse of mass culture (130). As Danny Anderson points out in relation to Mastretta's *Arráncame la vida*, this parodic undercurrent serves as a means of "critical revision" of Mexican history. Anderson's analysis of Mastretta's novel (chapter 2) focuses on the strategies employed by the author to displace the official versions of history. Although many characters Mastretta evokes are drawn from historical figures, the fact that the author removes them from their original context and fictionalizes them provides her with "greater freedom in exploring the dynamics of both public and private power relations" during the 1930s and 1940s. Although *Arráncame la vida* contains explicit manifestations of violence, it does so through the eyes of Catalina, who understands and relates the machinations of power from a perspective based on feelings and direct experience. Likewise, in *Como agua para chocolate* revolutionary battles are mentioned but considered secondary to Tita, whose sphere is limited to the home. By setting a novel in a specific and easily recognizable historical context but focusing on aspects of reality not presented by official history, such novels affect a subversive re-reading of history through the perspective of the periphery.

Anderson notes the subversive power of humor as a means of questioning the established order in *Arráncame la vida*, a factor also emphasized in chapter 3 by Dianna Niebylski in her analysis of Mastretta's collection of stories, *Mujeres de ojos grandes* (1990). Niebylski points out that the author's decision to locate her characters—both in her novel and in her stories—in a period in which such conduct was particularly aberrant "has the effect of highlighting these women's daring, unorthodox behavior." Furthermore, Niebylski demonstrates that Mastretta has parodically reinscribed the stereotype of the "fallen woman" by presenting their sexual transgressions as humorous: "The aunts of Mastretta's stories not only defy the boundaries of convention—and certainly of respectability—practically without a trace of guilt or regret, but their socially reprehensible and morally dangerous behavior is treated as comic rather than tragic by the author." Female protagonists may also transgress the private/public dichotomy by setting out their own territory in the linguistic realm: in *Arráncame la vida*, Catalina expresses her individuality through the appropriation of vulgarized language and profanities that run counter to the language expected of someone of her gender and social position. Issues of language also figure in Yael Halevi-Wise's study of *Como agua para chocolate* (chapter 10). For Halevi-Wise, the novel may be read as a "trajectory towards freedom and self-expression"; and indeed, the novel clearly associates Tita's coming of age in terms of verbalization: from her begrudging adherence to her mother's demands to complete silence following her first rebellion, and, finally, the declaration of freedom from her mother's influence and the free rein she gives her passion and her voice at the novel's end. As Halevi-Wise points out, Tita's primary means of communication is through the preparation of food, and this form of expression is based, precisely, on the integration of *feelings* in her culinary creations. Tita's culinary expertise is shown to be a means of coming to terms with her inability to express herself freely and the starting point for the written document she composes, a recipe book/diary that integrates her life story.

Although Susana, the narrator of *Pánico o peligro*, conforms neither to the traditional marriage plot nor to the domestic space, the process of self-realization she undertakes and, particularly, her relation to language is expressed along remarkably similar lines. In chapter 12, Florence Moorhead-Rosenberg demonstrates how Susana seeks to "resist being the victim of linguistic colonization" by reformulating an alternate linguistic space in which subjective commitment is more valid to her than the abstract rhetoric of her intellectual friends. Susana's notebooks relentlessly track the details that constitute her daily routine as a working woman. By making everyday existence the theme of literature, official discourse is also questioned. Moreover, as Moorhead-Rosenberg observes, by freeing herself from the bonds of language, Susana asserts an independent identity, no longer defined by others, so that by the end of the novel she has attained not only "an empowered space of equilibrium; a space from which she is able to define her own position of subject and hence take control of her life" but also a "blueprint for an authentically feminine/feminist linguistic space."

The incursion of social reality in fictional texts has a long history in Spanish American letters and is by no means a practice limited to women writers. In her analysis of Cristina Pacheco's documentary fiction, Linda Egan examines the relation between Pacheco's narrative strategies and her implied audience, concluding that by emphasizing subjectivity and "feminine" sensibility, her exposé of the lives of the underclass in Mexico may actually reinforce the notion of women as victims (chapter 11). Although Pacheco's presentation of the suffering of marginalized populations of Mexico City clearly suggests social criticism, Egan finds that readers's reactions may be "limited by her choice of narrative mode, which offers the sole recourse of empathy or indifference." Moreover, Egan affirms, the fact that most of the texts in the seven collections analyzed center on the experiences of women "reinforces the rigidity of her emblematic world of misery," since they reproduce and elevate the image of women's capacity to suffer in silence.

A similarly ambivalent reaction may be experienced by readers of Elena Poniatowska's biographical novel *Tinísima* (1992, English translation, 1996), since the character "Tina Modotti" seems to be largely the product, both professionally and politically, of the men she has loved. Indeed, as Beth Jörgensen notes, passages on the men in Modotti's life seem to dominate the narrative in much the same way as they overpower Modotti herself. Both Jörgensen and Charlotte Ekland note the significance of the novel opening with the events surrounding the assassination of Modotti's lover, Julio Antonio Mella, since this episode may seem to cast Modotti in the role of victim. On the other hand, it is clear that the hybrid nature of the novel subtly subverts narrative conventions. *Tinísima*, as Jörgensen reveals, is a hybrid text not only in the sense that it "moves across the fluid boundaries between fictional and factual discourses" but, more specifically, through the inclusion of photographs—both those by Modotti and those for which she modeled—used as a source for Poniatowska's vision of the protagonist (chapter 5). Edward Weston's photographs of Modotti that appear in the first section of the novel, while accentuating her sensuality, also suggest passivity, since she usually appears with her eyes closed or her face turned away from the camera; the first photographs by Modotti herself are portraits of her lovers. Later photographs, which illustrate her break from Weston and toward political commitment, serve not only as an alternate source for Poniatowska's vision but also, as Jörgensen suggests, "a clear correspondence of purpose and sympathy between Modotti's photography and Elena Poniatowska's chronicles of contemporary Mexican society."

Ekland also discerns a shift between the first part of *Tinísima* and its final denouement. In her close reading of the early chapters of the novel, Ekland posits a process of becoming in which narrative strategies parallel the progression of Modotti's life story. In the first part of the narration, the identity of the protagonist is not yet defined; rather, Modotti appears as a "subject in process," continually evolving and changing. This is reflected at the discursive level by "discontinuity, disruptions and shifting perceptions," multiple narrative voices that leave the reader with "no single, irrefutable version of the facts" (chapter 6). In contrast, the second part of the novel, in which, perhaps not coincidentally, Poniatowska was able to exercise more creative license, suggests to Ekland a "meaningful (i.e., coherent and consistent) identity." Ekland further distinguishes a tension in the novel between the intimate and cyclical perception of time associated with women and the chronological progression imposed by society; a tension reflected in the text by the contrast between the protagonist's erratic and often repetitive path of memory, dreams, and emotion, and the linear progression of history emphasized in particular by the precise dates that precede each entry in the novel. By presenting the character of Tina Modotti from multiple perspectives, Poniatowska's novel challenges the public/private dichotomy, suggesting a dual vision that runs counter to the binary logic of official discourse.

Binary oppositions are further challenged in Carmen Boullosa's historical novels, *Son vacas, somos puercos* (1991) and *Duerme* (1994). Boullosa's use of androgynous and bodiless narrators in these novels serves not only to ambiguate gender roles but to reassess conventional hierarchies during the conquest and early colonial period in Spanish America.[7] In her study of *Son vacas, somos puercos*, Cynthia Tompkins compares the original version(s) of the voyages of Exquemelin to Boullosa's novel, demonstrating that the novel is a "paradigmatic case" of what Hutcheon has termed "historiographic metafiction" (chapter 7). Although she retains the presence of a national figure, Boullosa rewrites history from the perspective of the periphery: African slaves, indigenous people, homosexuals, and women. As Tompkins illustrates, the reinscription of historical discourse in Boullosa is further ambiguated by the fluctuation of narrative perspective among different subject positions that negate bodily presence. The disembodiment of the narrative voice, underscored by the graphic description of acts of violence—torture, rape, cannibalism—to which the body is submitted, results in a "fluid transition between subject positions" that undermines "dichotomies such as victim/victimizer, active/passive." This weakening of conventional notions of reality is accentuated by the deformation of temporal and spatial coordinates that opens the figurative space to the implied reader.

For Tompkins, the "most subversive level of 'otherness'" in *Son vacas, somos puercos* lies in the recovery of female voices and, particularly, in the "multiplicity of levels in which the term 'woman' is deployed." This is illustrated most dramatically in the episode of the cross-dressed female sailor, a figure that foreshadows the radical inversion of sexual—and cultural—stereotypes deployed in *Duerme*. In chapter 8, Salvador Oropesa's essay demonstrates that *Duerme*, like *Son vacas, somos puercos*, is rooted in historical documents, the cases of women who dressed as men to gain access to the colonies. Intertextual resonances may also be detected from Golden Age literature, specifically, in the topic of honor and the picaresque. As with the earlier novel, *Duerme* challenges categories of binary opposition through the deferral of a unified subject: the protagonist, Claire, is able to bridge—and thereby negate—classifications of gender, race, and class according to the clothes she wears. Oropesa's reading suggests a correspondence between Claire and the presence/absence of a Mexican national identity: The fluctuations in Claire's social position are highlighted, again, by graphic images of violence that mirror the scars of violence in the Mexican historical process. The negation of Claire's body when she is raped by European men, Oropesa concludes, contrasts with the recuperation of her physical presence through the sexual act with another woman. Here, the national allegory comes full circle as Claire compares her female body to an open wound, in what may be considered a subversive recontextualization of Octavio Paz's well-known association between the figure of "La Chingada" and Mexican identity.

The incorporation of reality into fiction is made more problematic by the integration of autobiographical elements. In itself a transgression of normative social scripts, female writing about self is further complicated by the fact that women's literature is often assumed to be autobiographical, an accusation that has frequently been a pretext for the exclusion of their work from the canon. In Sabina Berman's *La bobe* (1990) and *Novia que te vea* (1992), by Rosa Nissán, these divisions are explored by tracing the life-stories of women who are doubly marginalized, as women and as Jews. In chapter 13, Darrell Lockhart's analysis shows that novels such as those of Nissán and Berman question both conventionally accepted definitions of postrevolutionary national identity and the more universally oppressive gender roles. Arguing that Jewish identity is based on difference, Lockhart maintains that Jewish literature may be inscribed within the wider tendencies of postmodernism, since this circumstance "implies an active process of self-identification on the part of the Jewish writers as not only being different, but using that difference to their advantage." At the same time, these novels share certain characteristics with other novelizations of the immigrant experience in that they draw a distinction between the younger generation, which identifies most strongly with their adopted homeland, and the immigrants, who resist assimilation to Mexican society. The issue of language is also fundamental to these novels, since they incorporate Yiddish, Hebrew, and Ladino words and phrases into the Spanish text: a discourse strategy Lockhart associates with Bakhtinian notions of dialogism. Through the use of multiple languages, the hegemony of official discourse and the canon is further challenged, here from a cultural perspective rather than one based on gender.

The immigrant daughter's coming of age is also represented in Elena Poniatowska's semi-autobiographical *La "Flor de Lis"* (1988). In this novel, the protagonist Mariana, like Oshinica in *Novia que te vea*, seeks to distance herself from the subordinate position of woman represented by her mother and destined to be continued by her sister and, as Jeanne Vaughn suggests, asserts an alternate "measure of desire" outside the "contemporary Oedipal social contract" (chapter 4). As was the case with *La bobe* and *Novia que te vea*, *La "Flor de Lis"* traces a search for self that simultaneously challenges and affirms the notion of a Mexican identity. What makes Poniatowska's novel particularly suggestive, Vaughn contends, is the connection between questions of female sexuality and those of national identification, since the object(s) of Mariana's desire radiate simultaneously toward her Mexican-born mother, Luz, and the country Luz represents and rejects: postrevolutionary Mexico.

Nearly all of Bárbara Jacobs's narrative intersects with autobiography, and in fact, her novel *Las hojas muertas* (1987; translated as *The Dead Leaves*, 1993) may be included in the line of semi-autobiographical immigrant narratives. In the case of *Escrito en el tiempo*, analyzed in chapter 14 by María Concepción Bados-Ciria, the notion of genre is challenged by a text that consists of letters written, but never sent, to the editor of *Time* magazine. Bados-Ciria's essay examines the means by which Jacobs translates the autobiographical in a form that registers, simultaneously, the private discourse of the letter and the public expression of the essay. The topics of Jacobs's "letters"—based on articles and reviews that had appeared in the pages of the magazine—allow the author to "represent herself as an identity shaped by the various readings that comprise her cultural and literary baggage." At the same time, however, the private domain is retained by the insertion of autobiographical and, sometimes, emotional elements into her commentary. As Bados-Ciria affirms, the epistolary form, "inscribed historically as a feminine literary genre and officially degraded for being the carrier of amorous and private discourses," is transformed into a "public critique of the dominant culture" represented here by *Time* magazine. Essays by women have conventionally been ignored by critics and excluded from the canon (Pratt 10). By appropriating a genre to which few women are admitted and then personalizing it, Jacobs's text, like many of those discussed in this collection, challenges the binary absolutes of the patriarchal order.

According to conventional notions of gender, edified by those in power and manifested in literature, woman's place has always been created, delimited, and defined from outside, as she assumes the role of man's symbolic Other, the mirror in which he sees himself reflected. Some twenty-five years ago, Rosario Castellanos challenged women to cease defining themselves with male experience as the frame of reference, to reject "those false images that the false mirrors offer women in the closed galleries where their lives transpire" (20). It is precisely this uncharted terrain that the authors discussed in this volume have sought to map out. Whether by appropriating, inverting, or rejecting outright the canonical versions of femininity, these texts seek an alternate space in which creative women may set forth possibilities for the future.

NOTES

1. Narrative may be considered apart from other genres of writing since women of privilege were permitted and, indeed, encouraged, to cultivate poetry and private discourses such as diaries and letters. It is important to note, however, as does Sara Sefchovich, that usually these texts were not intended for publication but, rather, seen as innocuous pastimes (I.13). Indeed, as Margo Glantz notes, it was not until the 1950s and 1960s that a significant body of narrative by women was afforded serious attention within academic circles (609). Aralia López González provides a useful overview of women writers in Mexico in her "Narradoras mexicanas: utopía creativa y acción" that includes texts from the early twentieth century; Jean Franco's *Plotting Women* discusses Mexican women's writing since the colonial period, as does Marta Robles's *La sombra fugitiva*. For a discussion of narrative by Mexican women in the nineteenth century, see Nora Pasternac and Ana Rosa Domatella's critical anthology.

2. To attempt a complete list of women who have distinguished themselves in the narrative genre would be nearly impossible; a partial list of contemporary authors whose work is *not* discussed in this volume would likely include Josefina Vicens (1911–1988), Elena Garro (1920), Rosario Castellanos (1925–1974), Inés Arredondo (1928–1989), Amparo Dávila (1928), Luisa Josefina Hernández (1928), Margo Glantz (1930), María Luisa Mendoza (1931), Julieta Campos (1934), Angelina Muñiz Huberman (1936), Beatriz Espejo (1936), Aline Petersson (1938), Esther Seligson (1941), Brianda Domecq (1942), Silvia Molina (1946), Sara Sefchovich (1949), Ethel Krauze (1954), Carmen Leñero (1959), and Rosa Beltrán (1960).

3. Asked if she considers herself a "woman writer," Carmen Boullosa alluded to the negative connotations currently implied by such a term: "I'm not a woman writer. I don't write romance novels, I don't write novels where the domestic space is important, for me what matters is language, literature" (Ibsen 53, my translation). For examples of the negative critical response to Laura Esquivel's *Como agua para chocolate* see chapter 9 in this text; her second novel, *La ley del amor* (1995, translated as *The Law of Love*, 1996) may prove to be equally controversial. Nonetheless, misogyny is clearly only one of the factors contributing to the hostile critical reception of these novels in Mexico. Literary production cannot be divorced from the complex set of socio-economic and political elements that operate in Mexican society.

4. Aside from the obvious association between "author" and "authority," my use of the term "authority" is conscious of the division between *authority* and *power*. As Michelle Zimbalist Rosaldo has pointed out, everywhere men have some *authority* over women, they have "a culturally legitimated right to her subordination and compliance. At the same time . . . whether or not their influence is acknowledged . . . [women] exert important pressures on the life of the group. In other words, in various circumstances male authority might be mitigated, and perhaps rendered almost trivial, by the fact that women . . . may have a good deal of informal influence and power" (21). The exercise of power by women is often represented or read in the same way men in society in general consider such manifestations: as manipulative, disruptive, illegitimate, or unimportant.

5. Many trends characterized—and criticized—as "women's writing" during the last two decades, such as the integration of popular culture and peripheral discourse, are affiliated with the wider set of literary tendencies associated with the equally debated term of "postmodernity." More specifically, the use of autobiographical elements and the reinscription of historical discourse seen in several of these texts also forms part of a generalized trend in contemporary Mexican literature.

6. I am thinking of the often repeated association between *machista* patriarchy in the home and political authoritarianism in general but in equal measure women's movements such as the *Madres* and neighborhood cooperatives where women seek to protect their family and home from its violation by the outside forces of repression.

7. Boullosa attributes the prevalence of androgynous characters in her novels to a "lack of sexual identity" resulting from socially imposed restrictions that prohibit open acceptance of the body (Ibsen 62).

REFERENCES

Ahern, Maureen, ed. *A Rosario Castellanos Reader: An Anthology of Her Poetry, Short Fiction, Essays and Drama*. Austin: U of Texas P, 1988.

Castellanos, Rosario. *Mujer que sabe latín*. México: SepSetentas, 1973.

Castillo, Debra. *Talking Back: Toward a Latin American Feminist Literary Criticism*. Ithaca, NY: Cornell UP, 1993.

Franco, Jean. "Going Public: Reinhabiting the Private." *On Edge: The Crisis of Contemporary Latin American Culture*. Ed. George Yúdice, et al. Minneapolis: U of Minnesota P, 1992.

Glantz, Margo. "Criadas, malinches, ¿esclavas?: algunas modalidades de escritura en la reciente narrativa mexicana." *América Latina: Palavra, Literatura e Cultura*. Vol. 3. Ed. Ana Pizarro. São Paulo: Fundação Memorial da América Latina, 1995. 603-620.

Hutcheon, Linda. *A Poetics of Postmodernism: History, Theory, Fiction*. London: Routledge, 1988.

Ibsen, Kristine. "Entrevistas: Bárbara Jacobs/Carmen Boullosa." *Chasqui* 24 (1995): 46-63.

López González, Aralia. "Dos tendencias en la evolución de la narrativa contemporánea de escritoras mexicanas." *Mujer y literatura mexicana y chicana: Culturas en contacto*. Vol. 2. Eds. Aralia López González, et al. Mexico: Colegio de México, 1990. 21-24.

———. "Narradoras mexicanas: utopía creativa y acción." *Literatura Mexicana* 2.1(1991): 89-107.

———. "Nuevas formas de ser mujer en la narrativa contemporánea de escritoras mexicanas." *Casa de las Américas* 31.183 (1991): 3-8.

Masiello, Francine. "Discurso de mujeres, lenguaje del poder: reflexiones sobre la crítica feminista a mediados de la década del 80." *Hispamérica* 15.45 (1986): 53-60.

Miller, Beth. "A Random Survey of the Ratio of Female Poets to Male in Anthologies." *Latin American Women Writers: Yesterday and Today*. Eds. Yvette Miller and Charles M. Tatum. Pittsburgh: Latin American Literary Review, 1977. 11-17.

Pasternac, Nora, and Ana Rosa Domatella, eds. *Las voces olvidadas: Antología crítica de narradoras mexicanas nacidas en el siglo XIX*. Mexico: Colegio de México,

1991.

Pratt, Mary Louise. "'Don't Interrupt Me': The Gender Essay as Conversation and Countercanon." *Reinterpreting the Spanish American Essay: Women Writers of the 19th and 20th Centuries*. Ed. Doris Meyer. Austin: U of Texas P, 1995. 10–26.

Reisz, Susana. "Hipótesis sobre el tema 'escritura feminina e hispanidad.'" *Tropelías* 1 (1990): 199–213.

Robles, Marta. *La sombra fugitiva: Escritoras en la cultura nacional.* 2 vols. Mexico: U.N.A.M., 1985; rev. ed. Diana, 1989.

Sefchovich, Sara. *Mujeres en espejo: Narradoras latinoamericanas, siglo XX.* 2 vols. Mexico: Folios Ediciones, 1983.

Shea, Maureen. "A Growing Awareness of Sexual Oppression in the Novels of Contemporary Latin American Women Writers." *Confluencia* 4.1 (1988): 53–59.

Smith, Sidonie. *A Poetics of Women's Autobiography: Marginality and the Fictions of Self-Representation*. Bloomington: Indiana UP, 1987.

Zimbalist Rosaldo, Michelle. "Woman, Culture, and Society: A Theoretical Overview." *Woman, Culture and Society*. Eds. Michelle Zimbalist Rosaldo and Louise Lamphere. Stanford, CA.: Stanford UP, 1974. 17–42.

2

DISPLACEMENT: STRATEGIES
OF TRANSFORMATION
IN *ARRÁNCAME LA VIDA*

Danny J. Anderson

Among the Mexican novelists who began to publish their works after 1967, nostalgia stands out as a characteristic tactic for confronting the past. Hand in hand with the trend towards nostalgia, recent years have witnessed a rising number of historical novels.[1] Ángeles Mastretta's critically and commercially successful first novel, *Arráncame la vida* (1985; translated as *Mexican Bolero*, 1989), participates in these tendencies as it turns to Mexican history and popular culture of the 1930s and 1940s as the basis for its novelized world. In its ironic and humorous treatment of these decades, *Arráncame la vida* considers the machinations of power in society in terms of both the upstart, postrevolutionary elite *vis-à-vis* the subordinate classes and the social scripts for men and women within this dominant group. Humor makes the text no less serious in its critical revision of this seldom novelized period of Mexican history.[2] Indeed, as this study will demonstrate, displacement, as a strategy for transformation, and humor combine in *Arráncame la vida* to produce an "effective history" of these decades that have been crucial to the formation of the contemporary Mexican state.[3]

There are principally two strategic levels of displacement in *Arráncame la vida*: (1) at the level of the transformation from the referent (or extratextual reality) to the *histoire* of the novel, and (2) at the level of the transformation between the *histoire* and the *récit*.[4] First, the novel takes as its referent the period of Mexican history extending from about 1927 to 1943. From the history of these years, Mastretta has conceptualized an *histoire* that focuses on the provincial politics of Puebla and particularly the events and popular stories associated with the governorship of Maximino Ávila Camacho. In an interview, Mastretta states:

In *Arráncame la vida* I wanted to talk about the men who were most important to the development of modern Puebla. I wanted to chronicle the daily life of the rich, of the powerful, of figures who were considered great men in the 1940s: Guillermo Jenkins, Espinosa Iglesias, Maximino Ávila Camacho: men who were criticized, hated and feared, but, in the end, the model for success to be followed.[5] (Peralta 25)

Whereas the selection of such a corpus of narratable material in itself constitutes a transformation, a selection from the unprocessed historical record, Mastretta goes one step further and displaces the historical record.[6] Although anyone familiar with Mexican history will recognize the events, conflicts, and power struggles associated with Maximino Ávila Camacho, the *sexenio* of Lázaro Cárdenas (1934–1940), and the early years of the administration of Manuel Ávila Camacho (1940–1946), Mastretta has transformed these events into the story of the political ambitions of Andrés Ascencio, governor of Puebla, and his marriage to Catalina Guzmán.[7] In the words of Mastretta, "The names of the powerful do not appear in my novel; instead, there are other names that form part of the novelist's fiction and we no longer know if what I tell in *Arráncame la vida* is true or false" (Peralta 25). Such a displacement, from the historical record to an "invented" population of politicians, their wives, henchman, and the society they control, gives Mastretta greater freedom in exploring the dynamics of both public and private power relations in these years. Although many characters and events of the novel tend to correspond closely to the historical reality, the creation of the character Catalina Guzmán and her private life radically determines the kind of *récit* that can later be narrated. All of the political contradictions of the period, the class conflicts, and the social roles traditionally assigned to women in this historical and cultural context come to intersect in the figure of the governor's wife.

The second level of displacement, the transformation from *histoire* to *récit*, extends the decisions made in the prior displacement of the historical record. Among the narrative techniques necessary to transform the *histoire* into *récit* is the choice of a narrator whose perspective determines the version of events represented in the text. The choice of Catalina Guzmán de Ascencio, or Cati, as her friends affectionately call her, as the narrator effects two forms of displacement in the transformation of *histoire* into *récit*: (1) she recounts her life as a displacement of the traditional "script" for a conventional marriage, and, (2) she communicates with a "displaced" linguistic register, a humorously and scandalously natural use of vulgarities and profanities not expected from a woman who came of age in such a restricted environment.[8]

In the perspective of the matrimonial script, Cati's first-person, retrospective account of her life with Andrés Ascencio constantly rejects the values associated with a "proper" or traditional marriage and instead produces a displaced *bildungsroman*.[9] In broadest terms, Cati's *récit* begins with the days of her courtship and marriage to Andrés, a manipulating opportunist who struggled to power in the aftermath of the 1910 revolution, and concludes with his funeral. The episode of her affair with the "true love" of her life, Carlos Vives, articulates her education into two distinct moments. In the first thirteen chapters of the novel Cati begins her sentimental and political education. Indeed, the first chapter abounds with words that refer to learning (*aprender, enseñar, saber*), and learn she does: everything from the pleasure of orgasm to jealousy, "long-suffering" discretion, and underhanded political manipulation. She sums up her initial attitude toward Andrés with the remark: "I'd listen to his instructions as though he were God. He'd always be surprising me with something, and he found my ignorance funny" (16/20). By chapter six, however, she recognizes her role as "official accomplice" (55/60) and sets out to learn about Andrés's business and politics. Although Cati often becomes indignant upon confronting isolated instances of Andrés's injustice and abuse, when she reduces her situation to its minimal terms, she unconditionally supports Andrés in his struggle for power: "Besides, I'm on your team and you know it" (99/84).

In the last thirteen chapters of the novel Cati has to depend on her ever-evolving political and sentimental savvy in order to negotiate the triangle among herself, Andrés, and her lover. Carlos Vives, Cati's lover, is the director of the national orchestra; additionally, he is a foreign-educated intellectual and a behind-the-scenes ally with the political radicals who oppose Andrés. In sum, he represents everything that Andrés is not. Moreover, he personalizes for Cati all the dangers she had previously overlooked in her unconditional support of Andrés, both in the private terms of their affair and in the public issue of Carlos's politics. Although Cati at first fears Andrés's revenge and tires of being the wife of a political boss, she learns the extent of Andrés's capabilities when he orchestrates Carlos's kidnapping and murder. By this point, however, Cati has so entwined herself in the power structure that she has no recourse to avenge her loss and the injustice of Carlos's murder. After the murder, she comes to understand Andrés in a different way. No longer afraid of him, she recalls: "I learned to look at him objectively. . . . He slowly stopped seeming so unpredictable and arbitrary" (237/201). From this point to the end of the novel, Cati takes control of the situation. She knowingly watches Andrés slowly poison himself with an herbal tea and at his graveside, after working through her contradictory mass of emotions of love and hate for Andrés, she feels liberated:

I wanted to remember Andrés's face. I couldn't. I wanted to feel the grief of never seeing him again. I couldn't. I felt free. I was afraid. . . . I thought of Carlos, whose funeral I went to forcibly holding back my tears. I could remember him. I remembered his exact smile and hands, taken away so suddenly. At that point, as was fitting for a widow, I began to cry more than my children. (267/226)

When she realizes that she will never again have to return to Andrés's hometown of Zacatlán, where he is being buried, she ceases to cry: "I stopped crying. . . . There were so many things I would never have to do again. I was myself, nobody could order me about. So many things I could do, I thought laughing to myself in the pouring rain. Sitting on the ground, playing with the wet earth around Andrés's grave. Delighted with my future, almost happy" (268–269/226).

In general terms, the particular *bildungsroman* effected by Cati's narration displaces the traditional script for the education of a woman into her socially expected roles as wife, mother, and lady of state, the social codes of all that is "correct," to use the narrator's word. Multiple references to social expectations underscore the education that Cati resists: Society expected her to be "part of the furniture, someone you paid as much attention to as you would a chair that sat at the table and smiled. . . . What counts is being pretty, sweet, impeccable" (62/56). Indeed, throughout the novel Cati refers to the propriety of other women and their acceptance of traditional social roles. For example, she describes the wife of one politician in the following terms:

She was a small squat woman, with big eyes and very black lashes, well rounded tits and a waist [that] . . . was always squeezed with sashes or belts. She liked her husband. Heaven knows why, because he was ghastly, but she was always stroking him and whenever he expressed an opinion she listened as if he were a genius, nodding her head up and down. Perhaps this was why the deputy finished his most eloquent contributions by asking, "Isn't that right, Susy?" to which she replied, "Absolutely, my love," and moved her head one last time. They were a team. I could never have formed a team like that. I didn't have the dedication. (187/160–61)

In reality, Cati does not lack dedication; rather, she consciously resists the traditional social scripts that would be assigned to her in this cultural and historical context.

Such behavior, however, does not go without notice. Almost immediately after this satirical description of the obedient Susy, Cati cites Andres's intervention in the *sobremesa*, which underscores Cati's displacement from her expected social role:

Women are a disaster. We spend our lives educating them, explaining things to them, then one little parrot comes along and they believe everything it says. . . . Anything to contradict her husband. Because that's her new style. You should have met her when she was sixteen—such a sweet, pretty thing, a sponge soaking up everything I said, incapable of seeing anything bad in her husband or of not being in his bed at three in the morning. Ah, women! There's no doubt they're not the same nowadays. Something's ruffled them. Let's hope your's stays as she is, Deputy, there aren't many of them left. Even the most docile ones kick their heels. You should see mine. (188–189/161–62)

Although in conventional terms Cati "turned out to be scandalous" (103), by the end of the novel Andrés recognizes Cati's individuality in her resistance: "'I was right about you, there's no one sharper than you, you're like a man.

. . . I sure fucked up with you: you're fucking remarkable. You're my best old lady and my best old man, damn it'" (211, translation revised). On his deathbed, Andrés again invokes the language of the sex-gender system ("my best old lady"/"my best old man") when he expresses his appreciation for Cati in terms of the *topos* of the "feminine enigma": "'I fucked your life up, didn't I?' he said. . . . 'But what do you want? I've never figured out what you want. Not that I gave it much thought, but I'm not a total fool, I know there are many women inside you and I only knew a few of them" (252/214). In short, *Arráncame la vida* represents the education and transformation of Catalina Guzmán, not into the woman that the dominant social scripts would have her be, but rather into the intelligent and independent widow who is "delighted with my future, almost happy" (260/268).

In this perspective, the choice of such a resolution for the *récit* is quite significant for the *bildungsroman* as a displacement of the traditional marriage tale. As Rachel Blau DuPlessis points out:

One of the great moments of ideological negotiation in any work occurs in the choice of a resolution for the various services it provides. Narrative outcome is the place where transindividual assumptions and values are most clearly visible, and where the word "convention" is found resonating between its literary and its social meanings. Any artistic resolution (especially of a linear form that must unroll in time) can, with greater of lesser success, attempt an ideological solution to the fundamental contradictions that animate the work. (3)

In general terms, romance and marriage plots are a "trope for the sex-gender system as a whole" (5). And it is in the ending, which is the beginning of Cati's life as a widow, that the multiple social contradictions that define her existence in the sex-gender system are displaced yet again. Throughout her life, Cati has negotiated between the contradictions of her private desires and the social conventions of marriage as a public institution; Cati's actions and reactions incessantly invoke her rejection of the oppressive social script for her training into a "proper" or "correct" wife in the dominant sex-gender system. As a widow, however, Cati occupies a unique social position: She enjoys her personal independence from husband and family, the social privilege conceded by her image of having been a "good" wife, and the material benefits of her elite-class social status. As one widow tells her at Andrés's wake:

"I'm happy for you," she said. "Widowhood is the ideal state for women. You bury your dead husband, you honour his memory whenever necessary, and then get on with the things you couldn't do when he was alive. Let me tell you from experience, there's nothing better than being a widow. Especially at your age. As long as you don't make the mistake of getting another man too soon, your life will change for the better. Don't let anyone hear me, but it's true. I hope the poor corpse forgives me for saying so." (260/221)

Arráncame la vida thus manifests the strategy that DuPlessis calls "writing beyond the ending," that is, "the transgressive invention of narrative strategies, strategies that express critical dissent from dominant narrative" (5). Whereas Cati has learned to dissimulate, hide, and to satisfy her desires only in secret, as a widow she has a new future in which many of the social conventions that previously constrained her will no longer have a hold over her life.

The same resistance to dominant social scripts is also observed in the second form of displacement ingredient in the transformation of *histoire* into *récit*: the use of a displaced linguistic register, abundant in humorous and scandalous verbal improprieties. Language use constitutes one of the most rigidly codified forms of social behavior, and the concept of "women's culture" will allow for a consideration of Cati's linguistic comportment *qua* narrator and a characterization of the narrative voice. As Elaine Showalter writes with regard to women's culture: "In defining female culture, historians distinguish between the roles, activities, taste and behaviors prescribed and considered appropriate for women and those activities, behaviors and functions actually generated out of women's lives" (260). In this perspective, Showalter also underscores: "Language, too, comes back into the picture, as we consider the social dimensions and determinants of language use, the shaping of linguistic behavior by cultural ideals" (259–260). Several aspects of linguistic behavior as determined by cultural ideals are thematized in *Arráncame la vida*. For example, at a dinner party hosted by Cati, she learns that Andrés has involved her father in some of his shady business dealings. She takes Andrés aside and reprimands him directly: "'I don't want you to mix Papa up in your affairs. Let him live his life his own way. He hasn't died of starvation yet, don't mess him around'" (69/61). When such directness between wife and husband only provokes a satirical remark from Andrés, Cati adds the following narrative evaluation and cites her response: "I hated it when he behaved as if he owned me. But I took no notice and changed my tone for one that would work better. 'Andrés, I'm asking you from the bottom of my heart. I'll let you give Mapache to Heiss, but don't get Papa involved with Amed'" (69/61). In this exchange, Cati clearly understands the rules of the game: She cannot demand things from Andrés as an equal, and in order to achieve her goal, she must shift to a tone of voice "that would work better" and implicitly recognize Andrés's superiority as she "begs" him to help her father.

Immediately following this exchange, which is governed by the cultural ideal of male dominance, the same set of constraints is broadened to the social arena of the dinner party. I cite at length Cati's description:

I went back to the women. I'd rather have listened to the men, but that wasn't done. Dinners always divided up like that, the men on one side and, on the other, us talking about childbirth, servants and hair-dos. The wonderful world of women, that's what Andrés called it. I liked it when we sat down to dinner because the conversation became more interesting. I wrote out the place-cards and sat each person where it suited me.

I put myself next to Sergio Cuenca, who was handsome and a good talker. I invited him even when I didn't need to because he was one of the few of Andrés's friends I liked. He manoeuvred the conversation and if I sat next to him I could say things under my breath that I wanted said out loud without saying them myself. (69/61)

As narrator, Cati uses narrative summary to evaluate and express dissent from the behavior considered "correct" for women: the division of groups according to gender, the thematic predominance among women of the "wonderful world of women," and the preference for the men's discussion. Yet it is to be noted that Cati does not passively conform to such prescriptions for she tacitly controls the seating at the dinner table and creatively gives expression to her muted voice through a male guest who is allowed to participate in the conversation. It is, nevertheless, once again the cultural ideal of male dominance that constrains Cati, and it is through a man that she must maneuver her access to the conversation.

In addition, this quotation and the preceding exchange of dialogue exemplify Cati's behavior as narrator. In the private conversation with Andrés, Cati relegates the evaluative comments about tone to narrative summary that serves as the introduction of her response. Similarly, her critical judgments about that which is "correct" for women at dinner parties appear as narrative summary. Such a separation serves to underscore the representation of proper or functional behavior (i.e., language use) in the social milieu, while it simultaneously provides readers with the other side of the represented world; Cati's linguistic behavior as narrator produces an image of intimacy with readers, it provides a tone of somewhat "gossipy" honesty and sincerity in her expression of dissent from the dominant cultural ideals. In brief, there is a natural ease in Cati's perceptions and ability to communicate with her audience, to "tell it like it is" —or more aptly, Cati *no tiene pelos en la lengua*.

And yet it is this absence of "hair on the tongue" that constitutes one of the most humorous and surprising aspects of Cati's behavior. In addition to her frank and dissenting remarks, often involving "improper" themes,[10] Cati's narration and dialogues are sprinkled with vulgarities and profanities that at times may seem incongruous with her social position. In contrast to the thematization of other aspects of linguistic behavior, however, this audacious "fluency" is recognized only briefly and indirectly in a verbal exchange between Cati and Carlos Vives. After Carlos and Cati have slipped away from a party and have their first sexual liaison, Carlos tells Cati that she must return home.

"What a damned idiot I am," I said, picking up the clothes I'd left sprayed around the floor. I was so furious I jammed the zipper on my dress and pulled at it until it broke. I looked for my shoes anyway. With my coat on no one would see the back open.
"You and Álvaro are both assholes."
"You've got lovely hair for a girl from Puebla," he replied.
"What do you know about people from Puebla" I yelled. (158/136, translation revised)

In response to Cati's ease in the use of words such as *pendeja* and *culeros*, Carlos inverts the standard idiom to mark Cati's language use: "You've got lovely hair for a girl from Puebla" [*"Para ser poblana tienes bonito pelo"*]. First, he categorizes her socially as a girl from Puebla, a comment that underscores her place in the sex-gender system and implicitly "jabs" at the stereotype of conservative, repressed, *poblano* society. And, second, rather than commenting on the absence of "hair on the tongue"—the directness of her diction—, Carlos points out the use of "improper" language as "lovely hair."

Cati's access to and use of such language, however, is not indiscriminate. Once again she implicitly responds to a social code. In reported speech, the use of vulgarities predominates among men, whether the setting be private or public. Cati, in contrast, uses profanities in private settings with Andrés or Carlos and sometimes among more open-minded women of her same social class. Never does Cati report a dialogue where she or another woman uses such language in public nor with women of a lower social class. Concomitantly, as narrator, in the feigned intimacy of the public literary communication act, Cati exerts her access to such language and appropriately usurps this linguistic register that dominant cultural ideals would reserve for male usage.

Although such linguistic performance may at first strike readers as incongruous or inverisimilar for a woman of Cati's historical period and social position, it constitutes a fundamental aspect of the overall meaning effect of *Arráncame la vida*. It is the primary source of much of the humor of the novel as it conveys surprising, witty, and yet quite direct evaluations of elite society in the 1930s and 1940s. Likewise, the incredulity that one may experience regarding verisimilitude serves to make evident the very constraints of the dominant social order, since such disbelief requires that readers judge the narrator according to the strictures of the same cultural ideals that she resists. In short, as narrator, Cati turns the language of received cultural ideals against themselves and lays bare the restrictions, constraints and contradictions that constitute the social script that she is supposed to adopt. Just as Cati's linguistic performance displaces the "roles, activities, tastes and behaviors considered appropriate for women" (Showalter 260), she also resists and displaces the hold that these cultural ideals have over life.

Catalina Guzmán de Ascencio's role as narrator, therefore, controls the transformation from *histoire* into *récit*. Moreover, her centrality in this transformation displays the machination of power in postrevolutionary Mexican society of the 1930s and 1940s. On the one hand, the story of her marriage displaces the prescribed social script for a proper wife and instead produces a *bildungsroman* of political and sentimental growth and cultural resistance. On the other hand, Cati's linguistic behavior underscores the dominant cultural ideals that would codify her access to language. Together, these displacements dissect the idea of the Proper, *lo correcto*, for women, and thus produce an "effective history" of the milieu. As Michel Foucault writes:

"Effective" history . . . deals with events in terms of their most unique characteristics, their most acute manifestations. An event, consequently, is not a decision, a treaty, a reign or a battle, but the reversal of a relationship of forces, the usurpation of power, the appropriation of a vocabulary turned against those who had once used it, a feeble domination that poisons itself as it grows lax, the entry of a masked "other." (154)

Although *Arráncame la vida* weaves into its texture the elements of a more traditional or androcentric history of public and private power relations, the strategies of displacement shift the focus of interest and make tangible the descent of women's social roles and the emergence of a political apparatus that determines the development of Mexico over the next forty years.[11] Indeed, in the perspective of the "acute manifestation," Cati lives an "event" as she struggles to reverse certain relationships of forces and usurp a degree of power. Nevertheless, Cati cannot be read as role model or ideal figure for women. Mastretta has commented in this respect: "Catalina is not a consciously feminist woman: she is relatively free because she is rich" (Peralta 25).

The overall displacement of cultural ideals effected in *Arráncame la vida* depends on the evaluation of Cati's place in the represented reality. Against this backdrop, readers must consider the contradictions that constitute her social position and how they cross lines of gender and class.[12] In response to the difficulty of such an analysis, the feminist historian Gerda Lerner has written:

It is difficult to conceptualize women as a group, since they are dispersed throughout the population. Except for special-interest organizations, they do not combine together. The subject is full of paradoxes which elude precise definitions and defy synthesis. Women at various times and places were a majority of the population, yet their status was that of an oppressed minority, deprived of the rights men enjoyed. Women have for centuries been excluded from positions of power, both political and economic, yet as members of families, as daughters and wives, they often were closer to actual power than many a man. (6)

Lerner has also observed: "Women are more closely allied to men of their own group than they are to women of other classes and races" (170).

Perhaps as a remembrance of her own humble beginnings or in recognition of women's plight in society, Cati may at first seem to rise above the limitation of class ideology: for example, when she aids a working-class widow at the scene of her husband's murder (67–68/78) or when she gives employment and support to the unwed, pregnant maid Lucina, who soon thereafter miscarries the child (64–65/73). Such acts of altruism, however, only momentarily transcend class boundaries, since the working-class widow goes her own way and Lucina immediately assumes the subordinate role of domestic help. The contrast between Cati and her cook provides another example of Cati's alignment with Andrés's class interests: "She was a little in love with Andrés. She was my age, with a son who lived with her mother in San Pedro. She looked old. She had teeth missing, never dieted, nor did exercises, nor bought face creams. She seemed twenty years older than me. She didn't like me and she was right" (178/153). Although Cati may be keenly perspicacious of women's social scripts in Mexican society and she successfully avoids the archetypal "madonna-whore" dichotomy imposed by an ideology of *machismo* (which has also been dominant in the representation of women in the Mexican literary tradition), she nevertheless shares the class ideology of the political and economic elite.[13] Moreover, she reproduces the same values in her children.[14] In sum, wealth and social status alone provide Cati a means of resisting women's traditional social scripts within her own social class. Even the freedom and privilege of widowhood are determined by and within the values of class and the sex-gender system.[15]

From this perspective, the strategies of displacement are fundamental for the signifying process of the novel. Displacement does not destroy, rather it dislodges, even if only momentarily.[16] In *Arráncame la vida*, the transformational displacement of the historical record, of the story of a traditional marriage, and of the dominant social codes for proper language use disturbs the represented field of values and produces for readers the interstices where the lines of power relations become palpable. This is not to say that *Arráncame la vida* is ultimately a "feminist novel." As Mastretta has pointed out: "There are two possible readings for *Arráncame la vida*: One can read it as a humorous story or one can try to understand the relation between Catalina Guzmán and Andrés Ascencio and the world that surrounds them" (Peralta 25). Perhaps this duality of readings explains the immediate commercial and critical success of the novel: It is equally accessible to consumption in the market for mass-culture because of its humorous love story and simultaneously available for interpretation as cultural criticism. Nevertheless, the main point is that *Arráncame la vida* deals with women near power, and by means of the various strategies of displacement—the transformation of the historical record, the plot that traces a rise from peasant farm girl to widow in the social elite, and the usurpation of language more "properly" reserved for men according to the dominant cultural ideals—makes patent the class, political, and gender contradictions at work in two decades fundamental to the development of the contemporary Mexican state and society.[17]

In conclusion, from the vantage point of the 1990s, widespread disillusionment with the "Mexican miracle" makes quite pertinent Mastretta's interest in the watershed decades of the 1930s and 1940s, the transition from the postrevolutionary military order to the advent of incipient technocracy.[18] *Arráncame la vida* does not offer a counterversion of the emergent history of these decades that would establish a new continuity of events. Rather, the novel maintains events in dispersion, or to use Foucault's phrase, it makes "visible all of those contradictions that cross us" (162). In the final analysis, *Arráncame la vida* does not do away with the past, but displaces the hold that certain versions of the past have upon the present. Cati's new life as a widow still operates within the dominant system of social values, but her sentimental and political education has prepared her to occupy and exploit that position in a conscious, resisting matter; that is, she defends and reproduces her class values while she simultaneously resists the constraints of the gender script assigned to her within that class. Similarly, *Arráncame la vida* does not escape history; rather, within the displacement and disturbance the novel produces a space where readers can perceive the genealogy of the power relations that continue to affect Mexico in the late 1980s and into the 1990s, and thus imaginatively understand the agenda for the future.[19]

NOTES

1. See John S. Brushwood *La novela mexicana (1967-1982)* 59-109 and Alice Reckley.

2. In an interview/review of the novel, Braulio Peralta comments: "The novel of the Mexican Revolution had failed to address the 1940s starting from a love story about the powerful, about those who govern us, those whom the people imitate, for better or for worse. Love and sex seem to take center stage in this kind of novel, although there is more, much more. The theme of the revolution and postrevolution having been forgotten with the 'fashion' of the urban novel, Mastretta's book adds something new and refreshing to the literary panorama" (25).

3. Michel Foucault develops the notion of "effective history" (139-164). More on this idea follows.

4. John S. Brushwood, "Sobre el referente y la transformación narrativa," considers the critical implications of a narratological theory of transformations. Briefly, the term *histoire* refers to the potentially narratable material in chronological order, an abstraction that is never directly available to readers but reconstructed during and after the act of reading the text. *Récit*, in contrast, consists of the discourse of the text, that is, the novel as it is presented for reading. Although this distinction is maintained in many structuralist and narratological studies, Gérard Genette presents the seminal discussion of these terms and their use in narrative analysis.

5. Unless otherwise noted, English citations of Mastretta's novel are from the published version (1989). All other translations have been rendered by the editor in collaboration with the author. The first set of page numbers in parenthesis corresponds to this translation; the second, to the original Spanish text.

6. With reference to the "unprocessed historical record," see Hayden White, *Metahistory: The Historical Imagination in Nineteenth-Century Europe*. On pages 5 through 7 he discusses the explanatory effect of narrative in historical discourse as a mediation among the "*historical field*, the unprocessed *historical record*, other *historical accounts* and an audience" (5, emphasis in the original). Although White underscores the transformation implicit in all historical discourse, from whence derives its explanatory effect, in the case of a novel such transformation is equally ingredient, if not more so. See also Hayden White "The Value of Narrativity in the Representation of Reality."

7. In the interview with Braulio Peralta, Mastretta underscores the extratextual referent of the novel. Indeed the referent is so recognizable that it has caused consternation among some of the descendants of the historical personages novelized in the text. For example, in a popular publication, one of the sons states: "The reality of

my father was overwhelming, whereas this fantasy has been taken out of the gossip columns. I feel embarrassed for Roberto Blanco Moheno and Ángeles Mastretta is atrociously piteous. It is better to live experiences than to tell about them, and my father lived them" ("Manuel Ávila Camacho: Una visión muy particular" 79).

8. With regard to the centrality of Catalina Guzmán as narrator of *Arráncame la vida*, Mastretta's comments to Braulio Peralta are revealing: "As I was writing the novel I learned a lot about the history of that period. The woman who served as my point of departure was the wife of Maximino Ávila Camacho. But everything that I write about her is fiction. History became increasingly complicated, increasingly perceived through the eyes of the protagonist: an intelligent woman, nothing more" (25). Indeed, as the "point of departure," it is the viewpoint of Catalina Guzmán that informs, in every respect, the transformation of *histoire* into *récit*.

9. Anamari Gómez and Fidel de León both point out the changes in Catalina and the characteristics of the *bildungsroman* in *Arráncame la vida*.

10. To cite an example, in the first chapter, Cati goes to see a gypsy in order to discover the mystery of an orgasm. Although the gypsy at first refuses, Cati convinces her, learns about the "little thing" and how to "feel" and surprises her sister that night as she masturbates in bed (13–14/8–9). The lack of information, the secrecy, and even the difficulty in naming the female anatomy point toward the controlled nature of the theme and its social impropriety.

11. Foucault makes explicit the import of "descent" and "emergence" in genealogical investigation and "effective" history (139–164).

12. For a detailed consideration of parameters relevant to an analysis of the social and historical status of woman, see Gayle Greene and Coppélia Kahn.

13. In recent years, several important collections of feminist criticism have considered the representation of women and the Hispanic literary tradition. Gabriela Mora and Karen S. Van Hooft offer particular emphasis both to the status of women's discourse and to the representation of women in Hispanic literature through a variety of critical approaches. Beth Miller includes essays that treat different aspects of women's roles in Hispanic culture and their literary representation. See particularly the essay by Luis Leal, which traces the representation of women in the Mexican literary tradition, and the study by Marcia L. Welles, which deals with a series of novels by Hispanic women whose protagonists confront dilemmas similar to Catalina Guzmán's. Sharon Magnarelli reconsiders the trajectory of the representation of women as hierarchically dependent on men and points out how some contemporary Spanish American novels strategically attempt to "debunk these mythic antitheses and begin to recognize other possibilities" (192).

14. The narrator frequently deals with the theme of maternity and maternal love. At one point, when commenting on the behavior of men, Cati remarks to another woman: "I don't know how we dare reproduce them" (111/95). With more direct reference to her own children, readers may consider Cati's decision to abandon them to a socialization process that consciously accepts Andrés's injustice, or the repetition of muted female nonconformity and resistance when her daughter Lilia is married.

15. Compare, for example, Cati's widowhood with that of the woman she aided in Atencingo (68/78). The same working-class widow, Carmela, reappears later in the novel, tells Cati her life story, and provides the herbal tea that eventually kills Andrés. At issue here, however, is the contrast in the lives of two widows on the basis of social class. Whereas Cati will live a materially comfortable *viudez*, Carmela has continued

to work and to raise her family alone. Carmela reappears as a temporary cook hired to help with the preparations for Lilia's wedding.

16. Mark Krupnick provides an excellent discussion of "displacement." In general terms, I have in mind Jacques Derrida's general strategy of deconstruction, which involves the inversion of a violent hierarchy and a subsequent movement of "displacing" the hierarchy before its inevitable reinscription. See also Jacques Derrida, *Positions* 41–42.

17. Indeed, one might add to this list of contradictions—class, political, and gender—the issue of race, as evidenced in the paternalism and irony of an episode in Coetzalan (46–47/48–50). Andrés is campaigning for his election and yet none of the indigenous community appears for the rally. Meanwhile, Cati and the family don the apparel of "little Indians." When they return to the site of the rally, the political farce begins as Andrés harangues about the unity of family, since all of the indigenous community can see that his family is just like theirs. Throughout the novel, the use of such "images" constantly serves to maneuver across borders of class, political allegiance, gender, and race, while simultaneously protecting the interests of the dominant order.

18. For example, see James D. Cockcroft (115–185). Notably, *machismo* is one of the ideological mechanisms that Cockcroft underscores as particularly crucial to the formation of the contemporary Mexican state (148–150). Moreover, other recent Mexican novels have turned to these decades with similar intents, for example: José Emilio Pacheco, *Las batallas en el desierto* (1981), deals with the *sexenio* of Miguel Alemán; Sergio Pitol, *El desfile del amor* (1984), seeks to understand the enigma of the 1940s in Mexico with respect to the social milieu of German refugees and the context of World War II; and Francisco Martín Moreno, *México negro* (1986), seeks to recount the untold story of the Mexican Revolution—a drama of manipulation by foreign investment and petroleum interests—and covers a period of time from the end of the Porfiriato to the *sexenio* of Lázaro Cárdenas.

19. This chapter was originally published as an essay in 1988 in the *Journal of the Midwest Modern Language Association*. Since that date, *Arráncame la vida* has received frequent critical attention. There is an implicit debate over the nature of the feminist stance in the novel. Sara Sefchovich describes the novel as an example of middle-class nostalgia without literary or social insight; similarly, Aralia López González criticizes Catalina for failing to achieve an autonomous female subjectivity. In contrast to these unfavorable readings, many critics emphasize the positive nature of Catalina's resistance and the feminine strategies she deploys, often strategies related to language: see Janet N. Gold, Jorge Fornet, Kay E. Bailey, and Judit Gerendas. Recent studies valorize Catalina's resistance in the context of postmodernism and postboom writing, such as that by Alicia Llarena and, in the context of popular culture as the hinge between public life and the private affective of popular culture, Claudia Schaefer. In contrast to this ongoing critical attention in the academy, in Mexico's cultural press, *Arráncame la vida*, along with Laura Esquivel's *Como agua para chocolate* (1989) and Sara Sefchovich's *Demasiado amor* (1990) and *La señora de los sueños* (1993), has most frequently been discussed in debates over "literatura *light*" a debate that questions the literary "value" or "quality" in these texts.

REFERENCES

Bailey, Kay E. "El uso de silencios en *Arráncame la vida* por Angeles Mastretta" *Confluencia* 7.1 (1991): 135–142.

Brushwood, John. *La novela mexicana (1967-1982)*. Mexico: Grijalbo, 1985.

_____. "Sobre el referente y la transformación narrativa." *Semiosis* 6 (1981): 39–55.

Cockcroft, James D. *Mexico: Class Formation, Capital Accumulation, and the State*. New York: Monthly Review Press, 1983.

Derrida, Jacques. *Positions*. Trans. Alan Bass. Chicago: U of Chicago P, 1981.

DuPlessis, Rachel Blau. *Writing Beyond the Ending: Narrative Strategies of Twentieth-Century Women Writers*. Bloomington: Indiana UP, 1985.

Fornet, Jorge. "*Arráncame la vida* en la encrucijada." *Casa de las Américas* 178 (1990): 119–124.

Foucault, Michel. "Nietzsche, Genealogy, History." *Language, Counter-Memory, Practice*. Ed. and trans. Donald Bouchard. Ithaca, NY: Cornell UP, 1977. 139–164.

Genette, Gérard. *Narrative Discourse: An Essay in Method*. Trans. Jane E. Lewin. Ithaca, NY: Cornell UP, 1980.

Gerendas, Judit. "Hacia una problematización de la escritura femenina" *Escritura* 31–32 (1991): 91–101.

Gold, Janet N. "*Arráncame la vida*: Textual Complicity and the Boundaries of Rebellion." *Chasqui* 17.2 (1988): 35–40.

Gómez, Anamari. "Ella encarnaba boleros." *Nexos* 91 (July 1985): 51–52.

Greene, Gayle, and Coppélia Kahn. "Feminist Scholarship and the Social Construction of Women," *Making a Difference: Feminist Criticism*. Eds. Gayle Greene and Coppélia Kahn. London: Methuen, 1985. 1–36.

Krupnick, Mark. "Introduction." *Displacement: Derrida and After*. Ed. Mark Krupnick. Bloomington: Indiana UP, 1983. 1–17.

León, Fidel de. "*Arráncame la vida* [review]." *Chasqui* 15.2–3 (1986): 96–97.

Lerner, Gerda. *The Majority Finds Its Past: Placing Women in History*. New York: Oxford UP, 1979.

López González, Aralia. "Nuevas formas de ser mujer en la narrativa contemporánea de escritoras mexicanas." *Casa de las Américas* 183 (1991): 3–8.

Llarena, Alicia. "*Arráncame la vida*, de Ángeles Mastretta: El universo de la intimidad" *Revista Iberoamericana* 159 (1992): 465–75

Magnarelli, Sharon. *The Lost Rib: Female Characters in the Spanish American Novel*. London: Associated UP and Bucknell UP, 1985.

"Manuel Ávila Camacho: Una visión muy particular." *Tele-Guía* (14–20 June 1986): 78–80.

Mastretta, Ángeles. *Arráncame la vida*. Mexico: Oceáno, 1985.

_____. *Mexican Bolero*. Trans. Ann Wright. London: Viking, 1989.

Miller, Beth, ed., *Icons and Fallen Idols: Women in Hispanic Literature*. Berkeley: U of California P, 1983.

Mora, Gabriela and Karen S. Van Hooft, eds., *Theory and Practice of Feminist Literary Criticism*. Ypsilanti, MI: Bilingual P, 1982.

Peralta, Braulio. "Mi novela es una historia, no un ensayo feminista: Ángeles Mastretta." *La Jornada* (11 June 1985): 25.

Reckley, Alice. *Looking Ahead Through the Past: Nostalgia in the Recent*

Mexican Novel. Diss., University of Kansas, 1985 (Ann Arbor: UMI, 1986).

Schaefer, Claudia. "Popular Music as the Nexus of History, Memory, and Desire in Ángeles Mastretta's *Arráncame la vida.*" *Textured Lives: Women, Art and Representation in Modern Mexico*. Tucson: U of Arizona P, 1992. 88–110.

Sefchovich, Sara. *México: País de ideas, país de novelas*. Mexico: Grijalbo, 1987.

Showalter, Elaine. "Feminist Criticism in the Wilderness." *New Feminist Criticism: Essays on Women, Literature, and Theory*. Ed. Elaine Showalter. New York: Pantheon, 1985.

White, Hayden. *Metahistory: The Historical Imagination in Nineteenth-Century Europe*. Baltimore, MD.: Johns Hopkins UP, 1973.

———. "The Value of Narrativity in the Representation of Reality." *On Narrative*. Ed. W.J.T. Mitchell. Chicago: U of Chicago P, 1980. 1–23.

3

TRANSGRESSION IN THE COMIC MODE: ÁNGELES MASTRETTA AND HER CAST OF LIBERATED AUNTS

Dianna Niebylski

In turn-of-the-century Mexico, Clemencia Ortega, one of the big-eyed aunts in Ángeles Mastretta's collection *Mujeres de ojos grandes* [*Big-Eyed Women*] (1990), sees no reason why her eagerness to initiate sexual relations with her lover should constrain her to marry him. When, after a year of sharing a "clandestine bed," she refuses his marriage proposal, her explanation is simply that "it wasn't in my plans to marry . . . not even you" (79).[1] Her suitor, liberal enough to have proposed marriage after deflowering his fiancée but not nearly liberated enough to be able to weather her refusal, turns on her with an insult he hopes will wound her in the most tender spot he knows possible: her reputation. Self-righteously, he asks Clemencia if she plans to be a whore all her life. Infuriated by her lover's words but without missing a beat, Clemencia counterattacks by turning his melodramatic accusation into an invitation to do business. Threatening to behave like the prostitute he has just accused her of being, she tells him he had better leave before she starts charging him for past favors: "Go—she said—go before I charge you for everything you owe me" (77). The swiftness with which Clemencia turns what was to be a lethal blow into a collection notice has the immediate effect of dispelling the specter of the honor myth that the lover has conjured; furthermore, the tone of her rebuttal—angry but witty, and decidedly not tragic—disarms him even more effectively than her unconventional behavior. Not knowing how to respond to a woman who will turn what was to be high drama—or at least operatic melodrama—into something resembling wry farce, the lover leaves despondent but too confused to attempt to ruin Clemencia's reputation in public.

Along with Clemencia Ortega, a large cast of light-hearted and sexually adventurous aunts—seemingly well adapted to the expectations of their traditional social milieu but in fact subversive to the core—populate *Mujeres de ojos grandes*. Following a recipe that brought her almost instant fame with her bestselling novel *Arráncame la vida* [*Mexican Bolero*] (1985), the young Mexican journalist-turned-author places her characters loosely in the historical context of prerevolutionary or revolutionary Mexico and proceeds to tell, in a subtle but unmistakeably comic mode, the stories of their indiscretions. In the best of these stories, the indiscretions are sexual. Although only one of the stories refers openly to revolutionary activity, that act of placing the aunts some three generations removed from her contemporary audience has the effect of highlighting these women's daring, unorthodox behavior. One might even argue that, by setting the action of her stories in the first decades of this century, Mastretta sets out to imagine ways in which not only her fictional aunts but our mothers, grandmothers, and great aunts might have affirmed their identity and satisfied their most forbidden desires without having to pay with their lives—or their sanity, or their happiness—for having done so.[2]

As with Catalina in *Arráncame la vida*, the aunts' routine activities take place within the confines of domesticity. It is partly for this reason that at least one critic has accused Mastretta of turning the heroine of *Arráncame la vida* into a mere caricature of a liberated woman. This reading of Mastretta's novel argues that Catalina's sexual transgression, as well as her allegedly failed attempt at murdering her husband, are ineffective and inauthentic ways of freeing the woman from the patriarchal order that oppresses her.[3] If subversion, transgression, or something resembling liberation is to be achieved only by escaping, denouncing, or renouncing both matrimony and family in its traditional forms, then the aunts of *Mujeres* decidedly do not qualify for these labels. It is as daughters, mothers, and wives that they define themselves; as daughters, mothers, and wives that they find room, time, and energy to perpetrate the transgressions that should earn them, at least from us, the label of rebellious, unorthodox, or subversive. To deny the liberating force of these women's violations of the strict behavioral codes that society expects them to uphold is to deny the need to legitimize transgression in whatever form is available to oppressed women; women who have little freedom to choose how they will affirm their identities or their desires. Mastretta's aunts live and move in a society where there are no formal outlets for expressing militant forms of liberation: In this context, the possibilities of flouting convention or breaking taboos, however secretively or surreptitiously, can be not only gratifying but empowering.

Gratifying is perhaps too mild an adjective to describe the sense of renewed vitality and sheer vigor that Aunt Leonor feels when she discovers that her prepubescent passion for her cousin Sergio is still intact and that, moreover, he is still interested in her perfect navel after so many years. The first of the aunts in the book, Leonor has had to give up her favorite cousin and childhood love years ago because her grandmother—fearing for the health of the family line—condemned their games on the medlar [*níspero*] tree with the warning that cousins who marry each other have idiot children. Seemingly unaffected by this early loss, Leonor soon marries the notary public who handles the family's will when her father dies. A dozen or more years and three pregnancies later, she boasts an adoring husband, three lovely and well-behaved children, and a still perfect navel. Fulfilled she should be, as she has become that most envied of cultural clichés, the happy young wife and mother. Not altogether ironically, both the narrator and Leonor admit that "no one would have dared to ask for more" (10). No one, that is, except the *"desaforada"* Aunt Leonor.

The adjective *"desaforada,"* which needs to be translated as both "boundless" and "outrageous" and appears in several of the stories, merits attention. Like many of the aunts, Leonor is *"desaforada"* because, although she is genuinely happy with her husband and thrilled with her motherhood, she cannot—or will not—let herself be bound by the self-fulfilling prophecies of the stereotype she has come to represent. She's also *"desaforada"* because, as she is the first to recognize, her behavior is outrageous. Having no socially acceptable reason to want anything else (she is neither frustrated nor disillusioned as a wife and mother), her affair with her cousin is loudly and fully transgressive. As an excess of passion, her nostalgic desire for her cousin Sergio is outside the bounds of necessity just as it is outside the bounds of decency, and any fulfillment of it will necessarily involve breaking the rules.

The comic element in this story resides in the unexpected juxtaposition of Leonor's admitted happiness as a wife and mother with the brash and direct encouragement of her cousin's new attempt at seduction. Both Mastretta and Leonor know that the latter is breaking every conceivable rule of manners and morals (in one fell swoop she becomes an adulterous and incestuous woman), yet the light, playful tone of the story is one of complicit, even delighted, affirmation. Furthermore, because the comic perspective coincides with Mastretta's subversive intent, the narrator makes absolutely no attempt to either justify or condemn the aunts' actions by moralizing about them. By the end of the story, as the cousins frolic again in their grandmother's garden, the forbidden passion is affirmed without guilt or regret of any sort. In fact, now that she does not have to worry about the health of the family's genes, even the old matron seems to approve of the cousins's rekindled passion.[4]

From antiquity on, literature and history teem with examples of women who break the rules in order to indulge in forbidden passions, but we all know what a catastrophic price these women generally pay for their transgressions. Often the product (and obsessive fantasy) of male authors who are themselves haunted by the extraordinary, unorthodox heroines they create, in the more canonical texts these "boundless," "outrageous" law-breakers are made to pay for their moral failures before their stories can come to good endings. In other words, the same authors who create these rebellious, erotically charged temptresses seem to enjoy devising appropriately cruel and unusual punishments for them, as if by devising harsh punishments for their heroines's transgressions they could exonerate themselves for the desire to create such lusty rebels in the first place. Nor is it enough to punish them: In traditional texts, women who break the rules must be made to recognize that the punishment that society or fate deals them is eminently just. Without this act of self-condemnation there can be no final catharsis for the good, moral reader. Thus, while female transgression has held and continues to hold great fascination for a patriarchal order that thrives on these excesses for its creative impulses, the promoters of this same order insist that guilt and confession must accompany the transgression and thus warrant a return to normalcy.

By stark contrast and in a welcome turnabout, the aunts of Mastretta's stories not only defy the boundaries of convention—and certainly of respectability—practically without a trace of guilt or regret, but their socially reprehensible and morally dangerous behavior is treated as comic rather than tragic by the author. Hence, it is Mastretta's tone (a tone established from the beginning in Aunt Leonor's story) that foregrounds the subversiveness of her book. Particularly noteworthy is Mastretta's comic-parodic treatment of the figure of the *solterona* [the spinster or, more in keeping with the derogatory nature of the term, the "old maid"]. Traditionally a staple of the realist novel and the melodrama in Spain and Latin America, the *solterona*—who may still be in her mid or late twenties and thus clearly not old—is a woman who pays for her inability to catch a husband, or worse, to hold on to one, by having to care for her aging parents and for her siblings's children. Condemned to live a colorless life and die in the "odor of sanctity," (in other words, a virgin) hers is a particularly sad fate in traditional Hispanic literature.[5] The ways in which Mastretta deftly subverts the image of this much maligned stock character is therefore not only cause for laughter but cause for celebration. In the refreshingly unorthodox world of *Mujeres*, the *solteronas* lead full—sometimes intricate— amorous lives; not one of them fits the stereotype of the lonely, bitter spinster, and none regrets the absence of a husband.

Recent studies of women's humor have argued convincingly that women's use of humor, particularly in contemporary texts, is a frequently used strategy for protesting traditional codes of behavior and for demythifying taboos. One of the first to point this out was another extraordinary Mexican humorist and social critic, Rosario Castellanos. In one of the essays published under the comic yet pointed title *Mujer que sabe latín* (1973),[6] Castellanos proposes to wage a campaign in which women would expose and ridicule the absurd expectations of the patriarchal order that oppressed them by wielding sarcastic laughter as a strategy for both criticism and liberation:

I would recommend a campaign: to charge against social conventions not with the sword of indignation, nor with the sorrowful *tremolo* of tears but to expose their ridiculousness, their staleness, their vulgarity and their imbecility. I assure you, we have endless material for laughter here. And we desperately need to laugh, because laughter is the most immediate way of freeing ourselves from that which oppresses us, and of distancing us from that which imprisons us! (39, my translation)

For comic and parodic effect, but also in order to highlight the stereotypes that her characters will demythify, dissolve, or ridicule, Mastretta, with great mastery, frequently resorts to the hackneyed clichés that make a romantic heroine recognizable as such. Many of the aunts in *Mujeres* have perfect navels, round breasts [*"chichis"*], or porcelain napes, and even the ones who are not conventionally beautiful are described in terms so reminiscent of the *novela rosa* that we cannot help but laugh at the parodic touch. The description of Aunt Cristina Martínez—"she was not pretty . . . but there was something in her skinny legs and her flustered voice that made her interesting" (23)—is a dead ringer for many of Corín Tellado's less than perfect yet nevertheless irresistible heroines.[7] Having moulded her characters into shapes that reflect the masculine myth of the ideal female form, Mastretta then proceeds to endow these women with some glaring nonconventional traits. For example, these big-eyed women are dangerously smart and also dangerously curious.[8] Coupled with their general lustiness, their curiosity and quick wit make the aunts too idiosyncratic to remain typical romantic heroines for long. Although many of the aunts are clever enough to fake a comfortable fit with the stereotypical mold of the modest, subdued, and decent woman, the stereotype crumbles under the weight of so many exceptional traits and of the parodic irony to which it is subjected.

Furthermore, while it is true that despite their superior and slightly mocking wisdom most of the aunts marry, they tend to marry men who, adoring though they are, appear to be noticeably inferior to their wives and unable to match the passion, energy, or sheer resourcefulness of the women they were lucky enough to "snare." Just as she explodes the stereotypical myth of the *solterona*, Mastretta also undermines the cliché of the submissive wife and mother by attacking it on two fronts: by endowing the women with precisely those attributes that put this very myth in peril, and by parodying and redressing the conventional imbalance between the sexes in "normal" marriages.

Because few things are more taboo than women's affirmation of sexuality outside of the prescribed boundaries of matrimony, Mastretta's comic treatment of the married aunts' often explosive and blatantly unorthodox sexual behavior has the effect of questioning, puncturing, or ridiculing the oppressiveness of the social conventions and injunctions that circumscribe the sphere of women's sexual activities and establish punitive measures for those who stray outside of the prescribed boundaries.[9] Among the hyperinflated traditional values that these stories target, repeatedly and with great brio, is that of sexual exclusivity (or fidelity) for women. To appreciate Mastretta's attempt at subversion, it is useful to recall the stubborn insistence with which Western culture in general and Latin cultures in particular have plotted to reduce the number of lovers, husbands, and sexual partners a good woman might have to just one. Virginity or monogamy: The economy of a woman's range of sexual and romantic activities is reductive simplicity itself, while for men the proverbial myth of Don Juan continues to be held as an ideal fantasy of male sexual power and freedom as well as an excellent source of material for male bonding.[10] In *Mujeres de ojos grandes*, Mastretta's aunts—adventurous, libidinous, or simply playful and curious—are intent on redressing the imbalance that, for so long, gave one gender so little room for experimentation while giving the other almost unlimited range of motion. Ignoring or simply breaking the traditional social and moral imperative that would confine their loving to the space of their marital bed, a large number of these big-eyed aunts are happily and unapologetically promiscuous.

One of these happily unfaithful aunts is Fernanda, who grows so pleased with the joyful consequences of infidelity that she comes to credit it (and her discovery that love is "boundless") for the renewed vigour and beauty that she seems to be enjoying, quite unexpectedly, just as she is entering menopause.[11] Accepting the complications as well as the blessings of her situation, Aunt Fernanda comes to the belated realization that "one can't wear out love" (35), not even by expending it outside the bonds of matrimony. It is comically ironic that, as Fernanda proceeds to lavish her new passion on her lover just as generously as she continues to dote on her husband, the latter complains to Fernanda that Mexico's problems started when the country became a liberal republic. Fernanda's motto-like explanation for her ability to manage her two loves while cheating neither out of her affection ("one can't wear out love") belies a *laissez-faire* economy of love, one which flies in the face of the patriarchal sexual code of enforced monogamy for women. It is worth noting that the sexually adventurous aunts of Mastretta's stories rarely consider rejecting one mate in favor of the other, a choice which would reaffirm exclusivity, if not monogamy. Instead, like Fernanda, they insist on their capacity for plural loves.

Not surprisingly, few men in the stories can cope with such a liberal philosophy (or is it a liberal economy?) of love. Aunt Magdalena's insistence that she can love both her husband and her lover with equal ardor and good will drives the latter to break up their affair. One of the most comical and perfectly timed of the stories, this one begins when Magdalena's loving husband is handed a telegram addressed to his wife (Magdalena is not home when the telegram is delivered), in which the lover testily admits that he cannot handle the madness that drives her to affirm that her passion is evenly divided between the two men in her life: "Since every time we talk you confuse yourself with the mad notion that you love me and your husband with the same intensity . . . I have decided not to see you again" (89). The lover's reaction is humorous and disturbing at the same time, and it confirms our worst fears about some men's inability to transcend the expected—and naturally stereotypical—behavior of women, even of women who have themselves obviously stepped outside of their expected role. Since the ability for enjoying multiple and equally intense loves has been, historically, a male prerogative, it was always the male (whether as lover or husband) who expected his wife (or lover) to understand that his erotic excesses did not lessen his love for her. When, as in Magdalena's story, it is the woman who insists on her right to have it both ways, the lover calls her "mad" and leaves her.

In a delightfully unexpected role reversal, the reaction of Magdalena's husband is comic because it is both blatantly gender-transgressive and because it refuses to pay heed to the macho honor code to which his culture would bind him. The man's initial fury upon discovering Magdalena's infidelity is not directed at his wife, nor, in fact, at the infidelity itself, but at the stupidity of the lover who, having been fortunate enough to have enjoyed his wife's love, is foolish enough to make her suffer now: "How could anyone dare to write to her in that tone? Magdalena was a queen, a treasure, a goddess . . . and if at some point she had said to someone, 'I love you,' that someone should have prostrated himself at her feet. How was it possible that someone should want to make her cry?" (90). The humor provoked by such a surprising—and surprisingly unorthodox—reaction does nothing to obscure our knowledge that, had the story been told in a serious (not to mention tragic) tone, the ending would certainly have been much darker.

Just as unexpected as her husband's reaction to the telegram and its contents is Magdalena's counterreaction, first to the news that her lover is leaving her, and then to her husband's subtle way of letting her know that he knows. She mourns the loss of her lover deeply and desperately for one whole morning and part of an afternoon, but by evening, she decides she has shed enough tears, so that her husband is surprised to find her playing jump rope with her daughters when he returns home Monday evening. The humor of the story's denouement allows for a happy ending but, as noted above, at no time does the celebratory conclusion obscure the subversive nature of the story. When Magdalena boisterously brags about having won the jump rope competition against her daughters, her husband brings up the subject of the infidelity in a most genteel manner by telling her that she is "lucky in games, unlucky in love" (93). Undaunted, she replies, "lucky at both . . . or are you also going to give me the news that you don't love me anymore?" (93). Far from proffering apologies or explanations, Magdalena instead chides her husband for being "a clumsy prying sneak" (94). For his part, her husband needs only the mildest form of reassurance for the situation to return to normalcy: He merely wants to be told that if he left her she would be too sad to jump rope. Her mildly encouraging answer, "I don't think so" (94), is all he needs to live again: "Then I'm staying—answered her husband—recovering his soul. And he stayed" (94).

Unlike Magdalena, who had not planned to confess her clandestine love affair but who, once found out, could trust her husband to respond appropriately to the news, most of the aunts would not dream of sharing their illicit relations with their husbands. Suspecting—and rightly so—that few husbands would be as understanding as Magdalena's of their indiscretions, they proceed instead to lead their double lives (sometimes for years) carefully, cautiously, and slyly. In fact, their skill at discreetly hiding their indiscretions is partly what makes these indiscretions possible. It would be easy to accuse these women of being deceitful, and Mastretta of falling victim to another common cliché (this time without parodying or humoring it). Rosario Castellanos, however, would warn us against this facile condemnation. In the collection of essays mentioned earlier, Castellanos compels us to look at women's practice of hypocrisy in a different light: "Women have been accused of being hypocritical and the accusation is not unfounded. But hypocrisy is the answer that the oppressed gives to her oppressor, that the weak give to the strong, that the vanquished turn upon their masters" (25, my translation). For most of the aunts, the end of secrecy would inevitably mean the end of transgression and, therefore, the end of excess, an excess which they feel is wholly compatible with their "boundless" capacity for passion and their "outrageous" natures. The aunts' "deceitful" silence, furthermore, protects not only their transgressive passion but their stable and happy family life. For centuries enforced on women as a necessary part of feminine decorum, silence is appropriated by Mastretta's aunts as a tactic for survival as well as self-fulfillment: turn-about fair play, one is tempted to say. It is imperative to note that the silence these women practice nowhere comes in contact with the guilt normally associated with unconfessed sinners.

There is yet another reason for practicing this "deceitful" silence. For at least some of these adventurous, unorthodox women, the appeal of the other love is precisely the appeal of the forbidden. In one of the micro-stories of the collection, Aunt Amalia explains to her sister that she left her lover ("a forbidden man" [173]) because he came to her one evening eager to share his office troubles with her instead of forgetting them in their illicit embraces. This confusion or carelessness on the part of the lover, who failed to respect the dividing line between quotidian and transgressive space, proved fatal to their love affair. Though the aunt considers this married lover to be "the love of her life" (173), she lets him go because she fears that becoming a party to his everyday routine would mean that she would become, sooner or later, part of that routine. Being of the opinion that the line between her lover's ordinary—and acceptable— activities and their transgressive relation cannot be crossed without risking the inevitable contamination of the latter by the former, Amalia prefers to sacrifice her illicit passion to premature loss rather than see its luster gradually fade under the merciless pressure of habit.

In a revealing and somewhat polemical study of sexuality, pornography, and eroticism subtitled *A Poetics of Obscenity*, Peter Michelson states that the comic approach to sex and pornography is in part a response to the "cultural need to have some fun with sex and relieve the oppressiveness of our preoccupations with it" (188). Mastretta's stories certainly accomplish this task and do so with flair. But there is no question that they do more. By capitalizing on, parodying, exaggerating, exposing, and inverting a number of deeply entrenched clichés, the stories work to exorcise the repressive force of the taboos on which the transgression rests. They do so by making us laugh, not at the aunts, but at the deliciously charming lightness with which these women proceed to break some of their culture's most petrified and petrifying laws.

Speaking with much insight on the subject, Eileen Gillooly notes that women's humor is "unauthorized discourse: not a necessary antithetical principle enforcing the law by negation, but in fact outside the law and therefore danger-ously subversive of its hegemony" (481). By refusing to dramatize the situations in which her passionate protagonists find themselves, Mastretta demythifies the power of the taboos that would turn these women's transgressions into tragedy (or melodrama). Hence, though there is no militant discourse in the book—the aunts' pronouncements tend to be home-grown and not intended for the pulpit or the podium—the comic approach has a persistently subversive intent, for it makes us question and reject the over-blown importance normally assigned to the values associated with the ideal of womanhood.[12]

If Mastretta's approach is light, the way in which the humor underscores and calls into question the clichés that so deplorably circumscribe a woman's range of feeling, action, and expression is deadly serious. Her stories thus exemplify the mode of combat that Castellanos urged her readers to adopt in *Mujer que sabe latín* (39). Under Mastretta's sure comic-transgressive guidance, the aunts target the social conventions and moral injunctions that, under normal circumstances, would constrain them and limit their avenues for action. Moreover, in the transgressive world of Mastretta's stories, there are no un-happy endings for those who break the rules (not every story ends happily, but transgression is never the cause of tragedy). As I indicated earlier, those who benefit most from these comic-parodic reversals are the wives, mothers, and unmarried aunts (the *solteronas*) who have had to wait so long for a literary vindication of their rights, especially their right to romantic and sexual fulfill-ment.

Perhaps no one profits more (or more wildly) from Mastretta's subversive treatment of her behavior than the same quick-witted and free-thinking Clemen-cia Ortega mentioned at the beginning of this chapter. When, almost two de-cades after her initial rejection of her lover's marriage proposal, we meet the aunt and her suitor again, we discover that the jilted suitor has married someone else, has had six children, has become an obsessive smoker of cigars, a res-pectable after-work drunk, and a successful business man with thirty bakeries to his name. He speaks little, has but two tavern friends, and is continually haunted by the bittersweet ghost of that first love. The big-eyed aunt, on the other hand, left to her own devices as a *solterona*, has done what perhaps every conventional *solterona* might have wanted to do but would have been afraid even to imagine: She has had twelve more lovers, all twelve of whom appar-ently continue to seek her company.

At the end of Mastretta's story, when the suitor, now a middle-aged man, can no longer cope with his repressed yearning and runs panting back to her house, Clemencia takes him back into her arms. His only response to their perfect love-making is to propose marriage again (forgetting, supposedly, that he is already married), and the proposal is followed by a second rejection. Hurt but not yet defeated, he then is willing to settle for being told that she loves him more than any of the other twelve. His request parallels the request of Magdalena's husband in the other story, but Clemencia, unlike Magdalena, is an unmarried woman, and one so democratically minded that she refuses to make invidious distinctions between her many loves. Having already told him that she has never stopped loving him, she now refuses to hide the fact that her love is as equitable as it is long. To his hopeful "more than any of the others?," she replies, "the same" (81). Flustered and insulted again, his immediate reaction to her ego-shattering answer mirrors his response of almost two decades before, but he is not allowed to finish his sentence. Before he can call her a . . . ["*eres una* . . . "], Clemencia calmly warns him: "be careful with what you say, because this time I will charge you, and your thirty bakeries won't be enough" (81).

As in many of the other stories in the collection, this happily subversive ending, made possible by Mastretta's comic skills, reflects the incurably optimistic attitude that characterizes the comic vision, an attitude that imagines individuals (even Latin males) capable of radical change. Yet, as it affirms none of the traditional values normally espoused by traditional romances, this is not our usual happy ending. As a celebration of a woman's power to win the day on her own terms, the story's final twist debunks all expectations of a conventionally romantic resolution. When Clemencia opens the mail the morning after this last encounter, she finds the deeds to her lover's thirty bakeries, all thirty now in her name. The repentant lover—who has finally understood that this honest, loving, and promiscuous woman will be bound neither by him nor by convention—has attached a simple note: "You're a stubborn woman" (81).

NOTES

1. All translations are mine.

2. The narrative framework of these stories is loosely reminiscent of Laura Esquivel's *Como agua para chocolate* [*Like Water for Chocolate*]. Although there are no recipes and the kitchen is not a central space in Mastretta's stories, the author, like Esquivel, affirms the tender bond between aunts and nieces, a bond made more interesting for its transgressive possibilities. Whereas in traditional familial relations mothers must be not only nourishers but keepers of their daughters's morals, the aunt-niece rapport has often been characterized by an unusual degree of frankness and freedom. The narrator's loving admiration for her aunts comes through in all of the stories, although it is not until the final story in the collection that the narrative trope is revealed: The stories are a "last resort," a desperate attempt on the part of a young mother to save her gravely ill infant daughter from the almost certain death doctors are predicting for her. We are led to believe that the transgressive power of the aunts' stories have the effect of reviving the child, thus effecting a kind of magic cure. For readers of Mastretta's stories, the aunts' comic transgressions effect a less dramatic, though no less delightful, magic.

3. Aralia López González sees Catalina's illicit affairs and her supposedly failed attempt to murder her husband not as transgressive behavior but as a way of replacing one mode of irrational behavior with another: "Thinking [they] have gained the space of sexuality, they succumb to dependence, frustration and real or imaginary crime. Believing to have gained access to a subjectivity more imagined than real by way of

the body's pleasure and their control of men's bodies, they defy the irrational omnipotence of patriarchy with another kind of irrationality" (23). López González regrets, moreover, the fact that Catalina is unable to break with the traditional role of wife and mother, explaining that as such she remains entrapped in and defined by the discourse of patriarchy. Although this critic is right to point out that Catalina only achieves a significant degree of freedom through the fortunate untimely death of her husband, I think it is of primary importance to recognize that Catalina believes (and takes pleasure in the belief) that she has subverted the patriarchal discourse embodied by her husband and his cronies by breaking some of its most sacred and rigidly upheld rules.

4. When Leonor explains to her grandmother that it took the two of them more than three hours to pick the fruit of the medlar off the tree because they "are out of practice" (12), the grandmother's response is "regain it, regain it, because there is less time than life left" (12). Unless the old matriarch is senile—and there is no indication that she is—she could not possibly fall prey to Leonor's transparent lie, in which case one could safely assume that her advice to "regain it," could only refer to the cousins's ability to engage once again in their forbidden games.

5. Castellanos reminds us that in Spanish the expression "quedarse soltera" (to remain single), an expression which, in this particular form and with this particular verb, applies almost exclusively to women who have remained unmarried, immediately implies that the person addressed by the phrase had no choice in the matter. Says Castellanos: "That one has 'remained single' means that not a single man considered the woman in reference worthy of carrying his name or mending his socks. It means not having been able to graduate from a superfluous and adjectival mode of being to a more necessary and substantive one" (33).

6. Literally, "Latin-knowing woman," Castellano's title is a play on a well-known saying: "*mujer que sabe latín no puede tener buen fin*" [a woman who knows Latin will not fare well (in life)]. Heading a collection of essays by one of the best informed, and wittiest, women of her generation, Castellano's title (half of the saying) wryly mocks the prejudice of cultures that want to keep women, especially women of marriageable age, happily ignorant. (Editor's note: English translations of many of Castellanos's essays may be found in Maureen Ahern's *A Rosario Castellanos Reader*.)

7. Literally translated as "pink-colored" novels, the *novela rosa* is roughly the Hispanic equivalent of the Harlequin romance. The enormously prolific Corín Tellado (who claims to have lost count of how many thousands of romances she has authored) is the popularly revered "queen" of this type of romance.

8. Indeed, their intelligence sometimes has the effect of frightening men away. Such is the case of Aunt Daniela, whose perfect body is not enough to counteract the impression that she is too wise and that in her wisdom she shows disdain for the male gender, so full of weaknesses and inconsistencies. At the same time, intelligence does not prevent these women from falling in love like fools from time to time: "She fell in love as smart women always fall in love: like an idiot" (167).

9. It should be pointed out that a treatment of women's sexuality (from a woman's point of view) which is both comic and celebratory is indeed rare, and for this reason Mastretta's book turns out to be not only subversive but to a large extent ground-breaking as well.

10. A recent Hollywood production on the theme (*Don Juan de Marco*) confirms our cultural fascination with the super-sexed male. The contemporary version of the stereotype is much more sensitive to women's feelings, but no less egotistical (and certainly no less "mad") than the original Don Juan.

11. At first greatly amazed and upset at the "exaggerated benevolence" of a "[d]ivine Providence" that would grant her both the opportunity and the new found ability to love and lust after more than one mate just as she is experiencing her "change of life" (35), Aunt Fernanda soon begins to exult in the new burst of energy and passion that allows her to dote on both her husband and her lover indiscriminately. Her escapades make her so desirable that even her husband of several decades is inflamed by her very presence.

12. Mastretta's book, occasionally flawed by careless lapses and a few unsuccessful stories, is most convincing (and most subversive) when the author is fully in command of this light comic tone.

REFERENCES

Ahern, Maureen, ed. *A Rosario Castellanos Reader: An Anthology of Her Poetry, Short Fiction, Essays and Drama*. Austin: U of Texas P, 1988.

Castellanos, Rosario. *Mujer que sabe latín*. 1973. Rpt. Mexico: SepDiana, 1979.

Gillooly, Eileen. "Women and Humor." *Feminist Studies* 17:3 (1991): 473–492.

López González, Aralia. "Dos tendencias en la evolución de la narrativa contemporánea de escritoras mexicanas." *Mujer y literatura mexicana y chicana: Culturas en contacto, II*. Eds. Aralia López-González, Amelia Malagamba, and Elena Urrutia. Mexico: Colegio de México, 1990. 21–24.

Mastretta, Ángeles. *Arráncame la vida*. 1ra ed. Mexico: Oceáno, 1985.

_____. *Mujeres de ojos grandes*. 1ra ed. Mexico: Cal y Arena, 1990.

Michelson, Peter. *Speaking the Unspeakable: A Poetics of Obscenity*. State U of New York P, 1993.

4

¿EN DÓNDE VAN A FLOREAR?: LA "FLOR DE LIS" AND THE PROBLEMATICS OF IDENTITY

Jeanne Vaughn

"I was a girl madly in love . . . I wanted to deserve her, deep-down, I was waiting for her and the very sight of her crowned my efforts. My dream was to be with her."

—Elena Poniatowska

Elena Poniatowska's semi-autobiographical novel, La "Flor de Lis" (1988), stands out as a singular work in modern Mexican fiction. It is a work that makes manifest—an event rare enough on its own—the female subject's part in the contemporary Oedipal social contract. Further, this is accomplished in such a way that the text creates a space, a starting point, for a nonpatriarchal conception of female subjectivity. "The present task of theoretical feminism and of film practice alike," states Teresa de Lauretis in the context of cinema and feminist theory, "is to articulate the relations of the female subject to representation, meaning, and vision, and in so doing to construct the terms of another frame of reference, *another measure of desire*" (68, emphasis added). This shifting of the field of vision and the creation of "another frame of reference, another measure of desire," is precisely what Poniatowska's text achieves. It brings to the surface the dilemma of the female subject who is psychoanalytically stranded between "look before you leap" and "he who hesitates is lost." Or, in Lacanian terms, between "a desire to desire" or "a desire to be desired," but nowhere with a desire of her own. Within the limits of the standard "contract," a desire of one's own is apparently more difficult to acquire than a room of one's own.

Following the trajectory of *Las genealogías* (1981; translated as *The Family Tree*, 1991) by Margo Glantz, the first in a line of recent women writers to cast a narrative eye at the "other" roots of contemporary Mexican social experience, La "Flor de Lis" can be read as a part of those texts written in the (new) tradition of the female authored immigrant novel.[1] It deals, as do many others, with the problematics of what it means to be a "foreigner" in one's own country and how to balance two (or more) cultures at the same time. While the importance of contesting the idea of national heterogeneity and opening spaces to elaborate experiences previously unarticulated is undeniable, *La "Flor de Lis"* moves far beyond. It is a text that engages, on both a literal and metaphorical level, the questions of female sexuality and desire and the relation between the words *"madre"* and *"patria"* in the term *"madre patria."* Also, and perhaps most importantly, it examines the system that produces or constitutes the various subjectivities that the narrative places under scrutiny.

When considering the corpus of Elena Poniatowska's prolific and highly varied literary, journalistic, documentary, and testimonial writing, *La "Flor de Lis"* has perhaps attracted the least critical attention. Well known for "giving voice" to the voiceless through her chronicles of modern Mexico in *La noche de Tlatelolco* and *Nada, nadie*, or her testimonial novels, *Hasta no verte Jesús mío* and *Gaby Brimmer*, it is perhaps the seemingly "private" and "personal" appearance of *La "Flor de Lis"* that accounts for this critical disinterest: At first glance, it can be read as just another "women's novel" sentimentally dealing with matters of the heart. In a recent article by Jean Franco, "Going Public: Reinhabiting the Private" (1992), the slight mention the text did receive was negative. Franco comes very close to making an outright comparison between the "good" testimonial novels of Poniatowska, and the implicitly "bad" or "self-indulgent" novel *La "Flor de Lis."* Not separating the protagonist, Mariana, from the author, Franco makes the claim that Poniatowska "powerfully affirms her identity with her snobbish and aristocratic mother from whom she cannot separate herself, except by transposing her desire onto the heterogeneous 'mother country,' Mexico, which her biological mother had always rejected" (70). There is, of course, more than one way to interpret both the novel and its protagonist's relation to mother and country, and distancing the text from the personal life of its well-known author is helpful in providing another perspective. Contrary to other interpretations, Poniatowska's text can be read as a strong critique of both class and sexual politics.

The narrative time of the novel covers the childhood and adolescence of the protagonist, Mariana, and her sister, Sofía. *La "Flor de Lis"* is first and foremost the story of a young girl in love with her mother; the story of a woman who years later looking back in analysis is still unable to give up her "obsession": "I talk to her all the time, I talk to her in the language of dreams, her drifting hair, the sad expression in the deep wells of her eyes are always with me. I await her answers within myself and I keep telling her everything until it is time to rest my head on the pillow. And I still talk to her, *waiting for her to answer me in the language of dreams*" (95, emphasis added).[2] Born in Europe, the two sisters form part of the old aristocracy and grow up, until the advent of the second world war, in the presence of their peers: other little dukes and duchesses. When the war begins and Casimiro, their father, enters military service during the French occupation, mother and daughters flee to Mexico via Cuba. Arriving in Havana, the protagonist is surprised to find out that her mother, Luz, is Mexican (a heretofore unmentioned fact, and somewhat of a disgrace according to her paternal grandmother).[3] Luz has always been an enchanted being in the eyes of her daughters, one who floats in and out of their bedroom in elegant gowns on her way to balls and other social obligations, lingering long enough to tuck the children in or to deliver instructions to the nanny. Young, beautiful, rich, and aristocratic, she continues to lead a charmed life in Mexico, and the girls, free from paternal influence, live in an almost entirely female world; the world of their grandmother, their mother, and their aunt Frances: "strong women, frail in intimacy. The house is my universe" (81).

This female intimacy is shattered upon the father's return from the war, and the household is never the same again. "It's the quality of the air that has changed" (88), laments the protagonist, and Luz—the light of their lives in all of its possible meanings—changes with the return of her husband. She acquiesces to his will and is no longer as carefree and daring as before: "Her caramel-colored eyes have clouded over" (88). The children, too, feel the effects in their own behavior: "Papa holds the three of us back. Sofia and I wait. For his word. For his desire. For his being" (88). As one of the servants accurately comments, "Now the mistress is under the hand of a master"(88), although it is not just the mother who comes under the hand (or the Law) of the father. For the girls as well, the return of the father, however anticipated, marks the end of an era: "We also have a master, the master of the house. Before we lived in play time, the whole day was enchanted, always up trees, now we have climbed down to the sidewalk and the sidewalks are serious, grey and monochord, *they lead somewhere, they have a purpose*" (88, emphasis added). The road or course of their lives, then, the place where the sidewalk leads, would seem to be predetermined by the return of Casimiro.

The first and nostalgically beautiful pages of the text are the antithesis of this finality. Mother, sister, governesses, grandmother, and aunt live, at least in the eyes of the child protagonist, in a golden, almost mythical prepaternal era.[4] With the return of their father and the birth of their little brother Fabián,[5] the girls, Sofía and Mariana, are shipped off to a convent school in the United States for two and a half years, prolonging temporarily their female world. Upon their return, Sofía, having taken her place in the world of social/sexual positioning, knows exactly what she wants out of life: a husband, children, and a career in dance. Mariana, on the other hand, remains lost and in love with her mother.

During the latter half of the novel, the mentally ill French priest Jacques Teufel is introduced. This other and more "symbolic" father creates the second and most important conflict in the text: Mariana's desire and identification with both the mother and the "father." If Casimiro's return marks the end of the female world of the past, the appearance of Father Teufel marks the awakening of Mariana's "feminine" sexuality, and this "symbolic" father engenders the struggle between two competing desires: the desire for both the mother and for the father, and a struggle for place within a national context. There are, in effect, two sets of triangulated relations at work in the text. One is the traditional female Oedipal drama, and the other is what Emma Pérez has humorously called the "Oedipal-Conquest-Complex."

In her recent work, *At Face Value: Autobiographical Writing in Spanish America* (1991), Sylvia Molloy discusses the nature of self-figuration in the autobiography, that is, the tropes one uses to represent oneself, as well as the importance of foundational images; those first recollections that give structure and meaning to an autobiographical text whether those memories or images occur at the beginning, the middle, or the end of a piece of writing. While not wishing to make the error cited earlier, of not distinguishing between the protagonist and the author, I believe that Molloy's comments are pertinent to the text at hand. I would, however, like to maintain the distinction between author and text, and do not address the following discussion to the former, but rather to the latter: a novel which, for narrative purposes, assumes the form or guise of the autobiography regardless of the relation, real or imaginary, that the "content" might have to an actual living author. The foundational image, Molloy tells us, is usually encountered at the beginning of the text and it "serves as a sort of epigraph, a self-quotation that, *if not summarizing the gist of the text that follows, will nudge it in the right direction*" (194, emphasis added). In the case of *La "Flor de Lis,"* the opening lines can be read as the mythical starting point, the ground zero of the text. Molloy further tells us that "in the same way that no memory is innocent, no *use* of memory will be innocent" (194, emphasis added). In other words, the foundational image that is selected carries a weight disproportional to the content of the incident narrated. She compares the function of the first memory to a "charge of energy, a nucleus of intensity," that "sets the text in motion."[6] Giving further weight to the importance of the first memory and its position in the narrative, Bruno Vercier states the following: "If one considers that autobiography is primarily a going back to origins, one understands that the *first* recollection will play a very special role and that, as such, it is endowed with mythical value. The individual, and above all the autobiographer, *is* memory. Assimilation occurs very rapidly between that particular faculty and the whole being, so that the first recollection marks the real birth of the individual" (cited in Molloy 253, original emphasis).

The first "nucleus of intensity" that "sets the text in motion" in *La "Flor de Lis"* is an image of the protagonist's mother, and it is literally the base upon which the entire text rests in terms of the narrative structure, as well as on the level of content. The center of the narrative and the center of the protagonist's life revolve around Mariana's image of her mother, and the opening image in the text is one of nostalgia, abandonment, fascination, desire, and fear. Luz appears dressed for bed in a long white gown and a sleeping cap, as if she were the subject of an old engraving or fairy tale. Walking out of an antique wardrobe, she "inadvertently" closes the door on herself, pinching her nose in the process: "I can see her coming out of an antique wardrobe: she is dressed in a long white gown and on her head she wears one of those sleeping caps that appear in the drawings of the Sentimental Library of the Countess of Segur. On closing the door, my mother slams it against herself and pinches her nose. *That fear of doors will never leave me.* The doorjamb will always be crushing or separating something, leaving me outside" (13, emphasis added). The "real" birth of the fictional protagonist occurs, in this case, in the liminal space of a doorway, a space which, so to speak, is neither here nor there. The "primal scene" of wardrobe leaves the protagonist with a lifelong fear of doorways, a fear of abandonment by her mother, the first love that she is never able to relinquish, and also a fear of the limbo, the no-man's land that women occupy in the social context of the narrative. Rather than opening to possibilities as one usually imagines, in this case, doors are devouring entities: It is possible to lose oneself, or (an important) part of oneself, in doorways.[7] While, as with all texts, *La "Flor de Lis"* is open to interpretation on a number of different levels, in this chapter I would like to follow several interrelated threads that begin in the opening lines and continue throughout the narrative: patriarchal sexual relations, social class, and their relation to each other in the formation of a national identity.

The foundational image that the protagonist uses to make sense of the events that she narrates is closely related to her "inheritance" as a woman, both in terms of gender and social class, and the text circles back around to this problematic at the end of the narrative. Luz is as ephemeral a being as her name implies, and she is perceived as always coming and going in the life of the protagonist who never has the means or power to make her stay. As shifting and uncertain as the property for which she is named, in the end Luz is trapped into the social role she is expected to occupy, an entrapment in which she is to some extent complicit. The act of "inadvertently" closing the door on herself may be read as an act of self-closure, of self-limitation, as well as a metaphor for castration. The mother's body is the starting point from which the text is generated, and it is, metaphorically, the final destination of the protagonist.

Above and beyond the mythical value carried by the position of the memory or foundational image, the mother—perhaps the most mythical figure of all in Western narrative—is further endowed with the aura of myth in terms of her representation; in this case, Luz is also marked by her social class. Her attire signals her as a creature from another time, another era, and her image is that of an engraving or illustration from a book of fairy tales. She is, in other words, as are all those of her social ranking—dukes and duchesses—a remnant of a by-gone "romantic" era, which all but vanishes in the second world war. In these changing times of war and social strife, the aristocratic class is a fragile entity unable to stand the bright light of the "new" American continent. In the context of postrevolutionary Mexico, royal titles become practically meaningless to all but the bearers, titles having gone out of fashion with Iturbide. Ironically, the Mexican bourgeoisie, the very merchants and industrialists who appear so vulgar to the aristocracy, become, in effect, the country's new "royalty."

In rethinking her often quoted and influential paper "Visual Pleasure and Narrative Cinema" (1977), Laura Mulvey elaborates in "Afterthoughts" (1981) a position of doubled identification for the female spectator derived from Freud's theory of femininity. She argues that narrative cinema produces a "masculinization" of the female spectator who "may find herself secretly, unconsciously almost, enjoying the freedom of action and control over the diegetic world that identification with a hero provides" (29). Many of us have fantasized ourselves as the doer of deeds and the slayer of dragons, and as both Mulvey and de Lauretis remind us, fantasy is necessarily an "active" proposition. Mulvey re-examines the genre of the Western, particularly the melodramatic Western where it is a female protagonist who assumes center stage in the narrative. She focuses her analysis on those films in which the female protagonist is "unable to achieve a stable sexual identity, torn between the deep blue sea of passive femininity and the devil of regressive masculinity" (30), a condition we will also find foregrounded in the protagonist of *La "Flor de Lis."* Mulvey points out that this dilemma, an oscillation between a feminine and a masculine identification, is doubled by the female spectator sitting in the darkened theater; a position that, further, finds resonance directly in Freud's theory of femininity.

According to Freud, both the little boy and the little girl start out on a parallel track. Since there is only one libido that serves both active and passive aims, the little girl—in Freud's terms—is a little boy during the phallic phase until the "onset" of femininity occurs, and active striving at that point gives way to the process of repetition. A purely passive identification is, of course, impossible to fully obtain, as Freud points out, and the female subject is always on some level torn between the two poles of femininity and masculinity. To quote a much-cited passage from Freud's "Femininity": "Taking its history as a starting point, I will only emphasize here that the development of femininity remains exposed to disturbances by the residual phenomena of the early masculine period. Regressions to the pre-Oedipus phase very frequently occur; in the course of some women's lives there is a repeated alternation between periods in which femininity and masculinity gain the upper hand" (112). Using Freud's observations on the "nature" of femininity, Mulvey argues in "Afterthoughts" that Hollywood narrative cinema is "structured around masculine pleasure," and the active point of identification that is proffered the female spectator allows her "to rediscover that lost aspect of her sexual identity" (31). This covert and secretly pleasurable identification with a preoedipal "masculinity" is precisely the attraction of such films.

In "Desire and Narrative" (1984), Teresa de Lauretis elaborates in much greater detail a related argument that leads to the construction of a theory of the female spectator based on a doubled desire or identification.[8] The two poles of femininity and masculinity, the author tells us, "do not refer so much to qualities or states of being inherent in a person, as to *positions which she occupies in relation to desire. They are terms of identification.* And the alternation between them, Freud seems to suggest, is a specific character of female subjectivity" (142, emphasis mine). Examining the movement of desire and narrative, de Lauretis asks—after a detour through structuralism, narrative theory, semiology, and psychoanalysis—how is it that the female subject is seduced through narrative into femininity. De Lauretis argues that the movement of all narrative discourse is Oedipal.[9] The journey of the mythical (male) subject or actuant is, she tells us, toward a mythical obstacle or object, and the female position corresponds to that of the narrative topography, the place or the "space in which the movement occurs" (143). While film theory is not, of course, directly applicable to literature and attempts to do so have failed spectacularly, it is precisely the element of narrative that de Lauretis reintroduces to film theory.[10] De Lauretis outlines two sets of identificatory relations, examining the manner in which modern narrative cinema, as well as conventional narrative, grammatically or morphologically construct the "female" position as that of object. The first set of identifying relations follow Mulvey's well-known proposition of masculine active gaze and female passive identification with the image or body. The second set, de Lauretis states, is produced by the film apparatus and is its effect; it is the "condition under which what is visible acquires meaning" (144). This second double figural narrative identification consists of (1) an identification with the narrative movement, with the figure of the mythical subject as *he* moves through the narrative topography or plot-space toward the conclusion, and (2) an identification with that of the figure of narrative closure, the narrative image, where within the Oedipal social contract woman "properly represents the fulfillment of the narrative promise (made, as we know, to the little boy)" (140). The female reader or spectator identifies then with both the movement and the plot-space, with both the subject-actuant and the object-obstacle, "both figures can and in fact must be identified with at once, for *they are inherent in narrativity itself*" (144, emphasis added). Furthering Tania Modeleski's reading of Hitchcock's *Rebecca*, de Lauretis examines the film in terms of a double figural identification, in this case the "double relation of desire for the Father and for the Mother" (151). In the case of *Rebecca*, "This double set of identifying relations is relayed to the spectator via the heroine, who then functions as a prism diffracting the image into the double positionalities of female Oedipal desire and sustaining the oscillation between 'femininity' and 'masculinity'" (151–152). Later, in Poniatowska's text, we will see the same diffraction of desire at work: the same oscillation between feminine and masculine identification, a desire for both the mother and the father. De Lauretis's conclusions in this respect are enlightening in terms of the text I will turn to momentarily. The film, de Lauretis emphasizes, marks not only the object of the male's desire, but "the place and object of *a female active desire*" (152, emphasis added). This marking of a female active desire, a desire not coextensive with or subject to the phallic Law of the Father, is of critical importance in the construction of "other" frames of reference.

The result of the oscillation, of the tension created in the narrative by putting into play the two positionalities of desire is, de Lauretis states, that "if the alternation between them is protracted long enough (as has been said of *Rebecca*) or in enough films (and several have already been made), the viewer may come to suspect that such duplicity, such contradictions cannot and perhaps even need not be resolved" (153). In other words, as Freud suggests, not only is a definitive Oedipal resolution impossible for the female subject, but is not, with due respect to recent feminist theory, necessary. The dilemma of the female subject need not be, as Lacan so blithely puts it, that of coming to terms with being the object of desire for man. The social conventions that demand a "passive femininity" are just that; they are conventions open to change, a change that has already begun in feminist literary, filmic, and cultural production. This work entails, de Lauretis tells us, "a continued and sustained work with and against narrative, in order to represent not just the power of female desire but its duplicity and ambivalence" (155–156).

For the protagonist of *La "Flor de Lis,"* her questioning and rejection of a traditional Oedipal resolution is intimately linked with her questioning and rejection of the mythology of her social class, and both, as mentioned earlier, are conceived of by the protagonist as a kind of inheritance or legacy, an inheritance that the protagonist struggles to shed. Practically from the moment of her arrival in Mexico, Mariana, although fully implicated in her aristocratic upbringing, is at the same time constantly questioning the prevailing social order: Why it is that she takes piano lessons and not Magdalena the maid?; Why is it that she attends school and learns to read while the maid, of roughly the same age, does not? Mariana's preoccupation with the working and middle classes is seen in her family as a kind of reverse snobbism. Her mother tells her: "Don't be a Bolshevik. . . . You suffer from reverse snobbism. You only have to see someone in overalls and shoes bought on installments to fall hopelessly in love" (78). The distinction in the family could not be more clear. Those that have to "work" for a living (a word never uttered in the household) are to be pitied, while "decent people" discretely manage their affairs. The hatred of the petit-bourgeoisie is palpable in the text, and the children are instructed in what they need to do to "have class" and thereby avoid the "vulgarity" of the middle class. "We should not get fat, we should have shiny hair, we should dress well, we should know how to receive, we should take care of the family jewels, we should have good manners and above all, have good taste, elegance" (83).[11]

The family expectations regarding the two girls, however, are always somewhat unclear; there is a change in the social system, both on the father's side in terms of the changing face of Europe and on the mother's side in the context of a postrevolutionary Mexico: "Since their haciendas were taken bad luck has pursued them" (80), explains the maternal grandmother, and nowadays the "well-to-do" are reduced to living off their rents. As a result of shifting social and material conditions, the future of the younger generation is not as predetermined as in the past, and little duchesses can no longer be so sure of marrying little dukes. This change manifests itself as a kind of tension in the family; the children must know all that was expected of their foremothers, but they cannot be certain of what good it will do them in the future.

The useless, decorative status of the female world among the aristocracy is perhaps best demonstrated in one of the most beautiful and moving passages in the text, one which occurs shortly before the return of the father. In an inherited rite of femininity, women are compared to flowers, and each woman appropriately has her own correspondingly individual scent. Every morning, the mother and the aunt, like the grandmother and the great-grandmother before them, engage in the activity of arranging flowers. Mariana is instructed in this art by the three of them while the servants wash the flowers, change the water, sweep up the dead leaves, throw out the refuse, and move the crystal vases that are passed on from mother to daughter:

These women who gradually are revealed as they change the water in the jars are my ancestors. . . . It is my turn to gather containers full of water and to place the green stems in them one by one, the water escapes between my fingers, my words turn to liquid and slide away to form puddles. I am on the verge of dropping the vase as it is slipping. They say that Chinese paper flowers bloom. Unlike my great-grandmothers's flowers, my grandmothers's, my mother's, my aunts's, mine will be made of paper. But where will they bloom? (86)

Caught between two worlds on a variety of levels—social class, nationality, traditional femininity, Mariana's adolescent consciousness of her uncertain situation makes the question all more poignant. Where *will* she find her place, and where are her flowers to bloom?

While the ladies of the house arrange, the servants are busy cleaning up the flowery mess. The smell of the refuse, "an intense, melancholy, disturbing smell" (86), the protagonist pointedly tells us, is more suggestive than the scent of the flowers in their vases. The odor of the refuse underscores the dark side of the elegant beauty of the cut crystal and floral arrangements. The labor of the maids is the foundation that makes possible the life of leisure and the useless, if beautiful, inheritance of her female relatives "who pass them on from mother to daughter" (86). It is this foundation that Mariana constantly questions and, in the end, finally rejects. As we shall see later on, there is a direct connection in the text between Mariana's "inheritance" and her identity as a sexed, classed, national subject. It is precisely the relationship between the two which makes the force of the writing so palpable.

Returning from convent school, Sofía, at age seventeen, has fallen into the slot preordained for her, even if there is some token resistance. Mariana, in contrast, is lost: "I don't know anything. . . . Inside me there is a huge confusion and to escape it, I spend time telling myself stories" (107). She lives in adolescent fantasy: One day she is Ingrid Bergman in *Saratoga Trunk*, and the next she is Joan Fontaine in *Rebecca*. While the reference to the protagonist in *Rebecca* is purely incidental in *La "Flor de Lis,"* the position that the two occupy in regard to desire is not, and Mariana, too, will find herself caught in a desire for both her mother and a "father." The purely female world that Mariana knew as a child has disappeared with the return of her father and the birth of her brother Fabián, and yet, Mariana, unlike her mother who acquiesces, refuses to "grow up" and be properly "oedipalized." She refuses to fall into the role expected of her as do her sister and mother. After Mariana returns from the United States, the textual marker in the narrative shifts, and her parents become a single linguistic unit, Luz-Casimiro (108), and her mother is no longer the same: "Mama has changed; she runs from Fabián to Papa, from Papa to Fabián, and she never knows whose hand she is under, like those games where a ring is passed from hand to hand along a cord" (107). Luz sits passively at the dinner table with her European husband, while businessmen discuss the industrialization of "paradise," a linguistic and social process wherein Mexicans become the bane of the country, obstacles in the path of modernization: "Mexico is an immense garden yet to be cultivated. The only problem is the people" (107). She sits folding her napkin "as if unfolding, fold by fold, her future." Mariana wishes in vain to shake her out of her passivity, but for Luz, "passivity" is her only weapon (254):

Mama, I wish I could tell her, Mama, I have the secret movements that you need, Mama don't unfold anything, don't pay attention to the banker, no one is forcing you to look at the bureaucrat's tie, no one, listen to me Mama, no one is forcing you to respond to the whining voice of his wife when she says that papaya disgusts her. At the head of the table, I look into her eyes, deep as a well, and I know that for her, the meat is as hard as a rock. My mother is hard on herself, very hard, if I were to approach her, if halfway through supper I were to get up from my chair and hug her, I know she would protest: "Oh, don't touch me now." (107–108)

Luz has lost her light, so to speak, and adopts a dark mask, a defensive position of apparent absence that Mariana will struggle against years later.

Upon her return to Mexico, Mariana internalizes her father's anxiety. Casimiro, a pianist, comes back from the war unable to finish the pieces he begins to play and moves feverishly from one to another. Late at night he anguishes alone in his room brooding over the family's accounts. Similarly, Mariana is unable to finish what she starts, and she moves from one piece of music to another over the protestations of her piano teacher. Finally she drops the classes: "It's Papa inside me. It's his anxiety. It's his hands, stuck in the shit of toilets at Jaca when he was punished ten days for shouting 'Long live good health' instead of Franco. His hands, bitten by dogs while crossing the Pyrenees. His hands, going over his shaven convict's skull. Papa, I am your daughter. I love you, Papa" (112). If the women of her family leave her an inheritance of one sort, her father leaves her another: "Somewhere along the line someone made a mistake, Papa. Will you also leave me your numbers in the night? Will I fall into a bottomless pit with a sharp pencil in my hand?" (112).

While Mariana agonizes over her identity, on the surface, however, everything appears normal. During this period, her parents congratulate her on her good grades, and her grandmother, collector of stray dogs, wants Mariana to come live with her. After the death of her grandmother's gentleman companion, Mariana muses: "I serve as her husband and go back to the dogs she had when I was eight" (113). The identification with Casimiro and the assumption of the role of husband to the grandmother changes in the second half, when Mariana falls in love with (or under the spell of) a mentally ill priest.

The change between the first and second halves of the text is signaled typographically. The drop letters that introduce each section or chapter of the text change from Roman to Gothic and are accompanied by a series of quotations in Latin. The change is also marked by the end of one stage in the life of the protagonist and the beginning of another. The return from the convent school is an important milestone marking the end of childhood in a certain sense. It is the beginning of her desire for both mother and father, a shift that the text, rather like a concrete poem, graphically suggests.

The event that initiates the second half of the text is Mariana's participation in an all-girl's Easter retreat where she meets the French priest, Father Jacques Teufel. Teufel, as his name would indicate—Teufel means "demon" in German—, proves to be a demonic character. From the beginning, he is described as a manic depressive who chain smokes, gives eight sermons a day, attends confessions, grants audiences, and never sleeps (118). His gaze feels like "burning coal," and his tone of voice is "mocking, almost wounding" (126). Like most madmen, Teuful has a plan. Communist in his beliefs and astute in his observations on class relations in Mexico, his desire is to form "an army of women" (153) from which he will rise as leader of a "new society" in New York. His mission for women is grandiose: "The only ones capable of abolishing social classes are women, women who can have children *with whomever and wherever they please*" (146, emphasis added). This does not imply a new status for women, however, and like many leftist agendas that deal with the "woman question," women are expected to be hard working, long suffering, and above all never show the effort that it costs them: "People should not have to realize what hard work it is being a woman, everything a woman does should appear to be a special gift" (139). Perhaps the most important and revealing part of Teufel's plan is the underlying sexual aspect. A character somewhere between Rasputin and Saint Augustine, Teufel ecstatically extols the virtues of sin: "You have to live and if you do not sin, if you do not humble yourself, if you do not get close to danger, you are not living. Sinning is penance, sin is the only true purifier, if you do not sin, how can you save yourself? What are you saving yourself from? Not to sin is not to live, don't you understand? Live, live for God's sake, live for God" (251).

Teufel's questionable sexual conduct with his charges is made explicit in the text. With the exception of Casilda, Mariana's best friend, all have fallen under his spell and want to obtain a private audience with the priest in his quarters: "To enter there . . . is a transgression, he only summons the privileged girls, however, they emerge with red cheeks, tousled hair, untidy skirts, and the smell and look of someone who has just learned something definitive for their lives" (134). In spite, or perhaps because of this repressed knowledge, Mariana, not one of the "privileged," waits outside of his chambers, longing for an appointment: "The wizard's castle. or the monster's lair, or the ogre's cave. I don't care, whatever it is, I choose it" (136). Mariana is torn at this point between her desire for for mother, "Luz, Luz, and Luz, she is the one I am in love with" (132), and her passion for the priest.With the exception of Sofía and Casilda, Mariana's female relatives and family circle of friends are swept up under the influence of this demonically charismatic figure who comes, in an unpriestly fashion, to live in the household. Toward the end of the text when Teufel makes outright sexual advances toward Mariana's aunt Francisca, the spell is broken. Love letters from Teufel's previous lover are discovered in his quarters, and Luz, who has recently been waging a spiritual battle against the "devil" in her own house, refuses him entry. Eventually, after a scandalous camping trip where the priest disrobes, he is hospitalized.

In terms of this particular text, the choice of priest or "symbolic Father" (in all of the possible meanings of that term), could not be more appropriate. Teufel represents a contradiction and a desire. He is both a priest and not a priest; he has "known" women in the Biblical sense. He represents God, the ultimate representation of Man, as well as the fiction of that representation (in other words, the paucity of the Oedipal social contract for women). The symbolic order that currently organizes social relations is seen for what it is, a sham. The priest is unveiled to show the man, the divine is revealed as the demonic, and if I may stretch the analogy a bit, the Phallus is revealed as merely the penis in disguise. Defrocking himself, on both a literal and metaphorical level, to show himself for what he is, is Teufel's ultimate sin in the text, the origin of his insanity. Surely, according to the logic of the symbolic, it is insane to expose the basis on which the order is founded. Mariana's first object of desire, as for all of us, is her mother, and some of the most lyrical passages of the text articulate that desire. One of the most lucid occurs after her disillusion with Teufel, occasioned by a newly found sexual understanding of her own body:

I get into her bed, to be inside her again like she is inside her bed; her bed is her belly, all that milky whiteness comes from her breasts . . . her bed floats on water lilies, water lilies in between your legs, it's an ocean, your bed . . . and I lose myself in it but I don't manage to sink or disappear. I'm horribly alone here, I'll never emerge singing, I'll never be able to leave you, Mama, I'll never find my way, I'm tied to you, wallowing in your lymph, your tissue, your saliva, the whiteness that dwells inside you, trapped between your glands, your membranes, your cells, your chromosomes, your muscular contractions, the molecular cycle of your living matter. I am a parasite on you, mother, stored forever, Mama, filtering through to you, the synthesis of all your plans. (236)

This active female desire for her mother is contrasted by the position she assumes with regard to the priest. Her desire, here, is to be desired and her identity comes only through him. He is the source of her strength, her courage, and she wants only to live up to his image of her: "I am his guiding stick, his support and his solace. A cripple will cross my way and I will make his limb grow like the branch of a tree: 'No, don't thank me, it has nothing to do with me, I am only the means by which Father Teufel reveals himself'" (172). The sexual connotations of this passage need not be commented on.

When the charade is finally seen for what it is and the priest's "true" identity is discovered, Mariana confronts her patriarchal inheritance as a woman and questions the complicity of her female relatives in the performance (in the legal sense) of that contract. In addition to the vases and the ritual of flower arranging, Mariana is left a sexual inheritance as well, and she examines heterosexual sexual relations within her social sphere. At the end of the text, Mariana, the narrator, sees *herself* seeing herself: "I only have to close my eyes to find Mariana in the depths of my memory, young, unconscious, innocent" (258). She sees the seed in herself which will later germinate, the same one that sprouted in Luz and Francis, in those always foreign women who leave barely perceptible traces (259). The seed or the thread, in other words, that which "ties them to a real man of flesh and blood" (259): "How did they manage to catch them if even they have been diluted? Glglglglglg; the pyramids of Teotihuacán; so dry in the sun, glglglglgl, with a single drop. A man who eats meat and chews and snores, a man who yawns and asks distrustfully: 'What are you thinking?' and who, over the years, has taken to add spitefully: 'if you think at all,' because there is nothing more suspicious and treacherous than this distance, this absence" (259). The absence or distance that Luz wears like a mantle of protection and her only defense is one of the many inheritances, or coping strategies, left to Mariana by her female relatives; an inheritance that she struggles against.

In the double remove of watching herself watching, which constitutes the final section of the text, Mariana sees herself as a gray form ascending a stairway in her mind counting her steps, and she wonders if the person counting is really her; if another woman a hundred years ago in some other part of the world "counted her steps on another stairway *from the living room to the bedroom*" (259–260, emphasis added). The sound of sterile footsteps falling on the stairs hammers away at her "exactly in the place where thoughts hurt a lot" (260). They end precisely "in a soup of sky-brains, brains-sky, a filthy gray mass where not a single answer can be found" (260). And, indeed, there is not an answer for women within the terms of the social contract as written. The answers, if they are to be found, reside in the body through which the unconscious somatically speaks:

The same guts that we have under our waists get tangled in the circumvolutions of our cranial vault . . . but the ones below creak, they scream like words, I hear them go iiiiii,

uuuuuuuu, they are vocal chords, while the ones above only filter anxiety, they drop
lead, swords ready to jerk the day, one's intentions, one's will. They fall into one's eyes
like a soft filthy mass, a thick soup that clogs one's understanding. Is this the inheritance, grandmother, great-grandmother, great-great grandmother, is this the gift you
left me along with your reflections in the mirror, your incomplete gestures? (260)

This blindness that comes from the conscious mind, from years of training,
from acquiescence to a role that one has not created but that yet constitutes one,
is what Mariana recognizes and struggles against. It is this recognition that
motivates the text and provides the critical distance for the narrator.

I can't handle your failed gestures, your idleness, your frustration. Go to hell, go back
to the depths of the mirror and freeze yourselves, you with your icy heads! Go away,
wretched sisters, go away with your diamond combs and your hair brushed a hundred
times, I don't want my ideas to be tamed by your ivory brushes encrusted with herald-
ries. No one will ever know who you were, just like you yourselves never did. No one.
Only I will invoke your name, only I who one day will also forget myself—what a
relief—, only I will know what you never were. (260)

Finally, Mariana negotiates both her position as foreigner and her desire for
her mother as a remarkable merging of "*madre*" and "*patria,*" coupled with
a knowledge of her position as a sexed, gendered, classed subject in a patriarchal, racist, class-based society. In the end, the protagonist goes on to what
one would assume to be a "normal" heterosexual identity; but with a difference.
She refuses the either/or dictum of compulsory heterosexuality and does not
sacrifice her desire for her mother, as evidenced by the advice, years later, of
an analyst: "Later in life an Argentine psychoanalyst would tell me: 'It's time
to leave your mother alone, she doesn't love you the way you do her, forget
that obsession, it's not worth your time'" (95). Luz, and through Luz, Mexico,
will remain the center of her existence: "My country is this stone bench from
which I stare at the sun at midday, my country is this slowness in the sun, my
country is the alarm at the hour of rising, the little frog fountain in front of the
Girls School, my country is violent emotion, my country is the smothered cry
I let out when I say Luz, my country is Luz, love for Luz" (261). Mariana's
mother is both her "mother" and her "mother country." At the same time, the
protagonist joyfully celebrates her desire for mother and country; contrary to
the dictum of her European father, she is also able to recognize and give voice
to the contradictions inherent in her desire for both. Her distancing as other
creates, we might say, the space for another kind of spectator or subject on the
national scene of sex and politics. Adding yet another twist to the "Oedipal-
Conquest-Complex," Poniatowska's text plays out these dynamics in full.
    De Lauretis has claimed that the most important and exciting work in
contemporary feminism is neither antinarrative nor anti-Oedipal, but rather the
opposite. "It is narrative and Oedipal with a vengeance, for it seeks to stress
the duplicity of that scenario and the specific contradiction of the female subject

in it, the contradiction by which historical women must work with and against Oedipus" (157). *La "Flor de Lis"* can be read as a feminist response to traditional constructions of femininity as those constructions are implicated in class, race, and other social relations. It is a narrative that points to the duplicity and the contradictions inherent in "femininity," in the text's attempt to position the female, and in this case, immigrant subject within the context of Mexico in the fifties. *La "Flor de Lis"* stubbornly refuses to choose between the two positions of doubled or divided desire which constitute "femininity" as well as "nationality," and instead represents them in a way that is "Oedipal with a vengeance."

NOTES

1. Works that immediately spring to mind are *Las hojas muertas* by Bárbara Jacobs, Sabina Berman's *La bobe*, Margo Su's *Alta frivalidad*, or Sara Levi Calderón's *Dos mujeres*, among others.

2. Translations by Chlöe Catán.

3. Beth, the American grandmother, shows the girls pictures in *National Geographic* of "savages" with bones in their hair and tells them this is where they are going to live. At one point in the text, Mariana ponders the lack of corresponding coiffure in Mexico.

4. Rather than using the term "pre-Oedipal" with its connotations of immaturity and mergedness, I prefer to simply label it, for the time being, "pre-paternal."

5. Interesting enough, Mariana, at age thirteen, represses all knowledge or memory of her mother's pregnancy. "I don't have a single memory of Mama pregnant, maybe because I don't want to remember" (93).

6. According to Molloy, "A look at first recollections in Spanish American autobiographies will indeed confirm the emotional intensity that seems to characterize them. Most of them speak of violence: Eduardo Wilde and Victoria Ocampo recall misunderstanding and injustice; Darío and Chocano, abandonment; López Albújar, shame; María Rosa Oliver, shock at the birth of a sibling; Subercaseaux, violent sickness; Torres Bodet, death; González Martínez, a memory so troublesome that, years later, it still cannot be named— 'A tragic and penetrating mystery that even now pierces my heart'" (194).

7. Luz's inadvertent action can also be read as a sign under which the women in Mariana's family operate—their complicity in their own social or symbolic castration.

8. For a use of this theory in another context see Rey Chow, who elaborates a position for the ethnic spectator based on De Lauretis's doubled identification. As Chow states regarding de Lauretis's work, "The political question of female subjectivity is now posed in different terms: not simply that 'woman is reduced to the image' but 'woman' is a locus of double identification. It is through a careful discussion of what this 'doubleness' signifies that the 'female spectator' offers the potential of a new means of sociocultural inquiry" (20).

9. "[T]o say that narrative is the production of Oedipus is to say that each reader—male or female—is constrained and defined within the two positions of a sexual difference thus conceived: male-hero-human, on the side of the subject; and female-obstacle-boundary-space, on the other" (121).

10. "Narrative and narrativity (by 'narrativity' I mean both the making and the working of narrative, its construction and its effects of meaning) are fundamental issues in semiotics and cinema. And if film studies cannot do without narrative theory, *any theory of narrative should be informed by the critical discourse on narrative that has been elaborated within film theory*" (de Lauretis 10, emphasis added).

11. Fisherman and farmers, the mother comments, "don't spoil the view," but the middle class does: "What's awful is this lower middle class that is pushing and shoving its way through the world, in Europe as well, believe it or not. Those who dribble spaghetti down their chins, those who bring their babies to the beach instead of leaving them with the nanny, those who smell like—have you noticed what they smell like?— . . . How vulgar humanity is becoming! This so-called democracy is making everything common and coarse" (79–80). The bourgeoisie or upper middle class are not spared either, and at one point in the text the mother explains the difference between those who have real antiques (meaning things that have been in the family hundreds of years) and those who have reproductions.

REFERENCES

Chow, Rey. *Chinese Women and Modernity: The Politics of Reading Between East and West*. Minneapolis: U of Minnesota P, 1991.

De Lauretis, Teresa. *Alice Doesn't: Feminism, Semiotics, Cinema*. Bloomington: Indiana UP, 1984.

Franco, Jean. "Going Public: Reinhabiting the Private." *On Edge: The Crisis of Contemporary Latin American Culture*. Ed. George Yúdice, et al. Minneapolis: U of Minnesota P, 1992.

Freud, Sigmund. "Femininity (1933)." *Standard Edition*, vol. XXII. London: Hogarth, 1964.

Modleski, Tania. "'Never to be Thirty-Six Years Old': *Rebecca* as Female Oedipal Drama." *Wide Angle* 5.1 (1982): 34–41.

Molloy, Sylvia. *At Face Value: Autobiographical Writing in Spanish America*. New York: Cambridge UP, 1991.

Mulvey, Laura. *Visual and Other Pleasures*. Bloomington: Indiana UP, 1989.

Pérez, Emma. "Oedipal-Conquest-Complex." *Chicana Lesbians*. Ed. Carla Trujillo. Berkeley, CA.: Third Woman Press, 1991. 159–184.

Poniatowska, Elena. *La "Flor de Lis."* Mexico: Era, 1988.

5

LIGHT-WRITING: BIOGRAPHY
AND PHOTOGRAPHY IN *TINÍSIMA*

Beth E. Jörgensen

> "*What a Life She Red*: Tina Modotti's pictures have a hard time living up
> to her lovers, politics and death."
>
> —*Newsweek*

It was serendipity to come across the headline quoted above in the October 2, 1995 issue of *Newsweek* magazine just as I was completing this chapter on Elena Poniatowska's novel *Tinísima* (1992; English translation, 1996). The Philadelphia Museum of Art's Fall 1995 exhibition of Tina Modotti's work, made possible by a "generous donation by Madonna" (88), occurred just a few months short of the centennial of Modotti's birth in August 1896, a propitious moment for a new look at her still relatively little-known photographs from the 1920s and for an assessment of the growing number of accounts of her life written in recent years. The *Newsweek* headline with its lame pun condenses the popular mythology surrounding Modotti into three terms: lovers, (communist) politics, death. The major biographical works that have been published since 1975, on the contrary, aim to demythologize Tina Modotti by countering the scandalous image first created by the Mexican press in 1929 and now casually exploited by *Newsweek*. The financing of the museum exhibition throws together the long overlooked Modotti and one of our time's most visible pop icons in an ironic embrace. These contradictions provide a fitting frame for an analysis of Elena Poniatowska's splendid and puzzling biographical novel about Tina Modotti because they epitomize the many tensions inherent in biographical writing in general and in Modotti's life story in particular.

Tinísima was published as a novel, but like many of the Mexican writer's works, it is a hybrid text that moves across the fluid boundaries between fictional and factual discourses. Specifically, it invites a reading as both biography and novel, as Elena Poniatowska's own commentary suggests: "[*Tinísima*] is going to be a novel but as faithful as possible to Tina's reality. There is a lot of information on Tina in Mexico. We have Edward Weston's *Daybooks*, which are very nice. . . . But there is almost nothing on Tina in Germany or Russia and very little on her in Spain. The boundaries between fiction and history are going to be very confused. For example, all of the spy missions are pure invention because it is known that she did that work, but it is not documented" (unpublished interview with the author, July 1991).[1] This study of *Tinísima* will examine the text as a biographical novel using recent feminist approaches to biography in order to analyze the construction of its historical and fictive subject. I will conclude with a discussion of the relationship between the photographic record left by Tina Modotti, including both the photos that she took and those for which she modeled, and the verbal image of her created by Poniatowska. That is, I want to address how Elena Poniatowska used photographs as a "source" for her vision of Modotti and how photographic reproductions are an integral part of the published book.

Studies of biography as a literary genre have flourished in recent decades, as has the publication of biographies and particularly an increasing number of biographies of women. Leon Edel, an early theorist of biography, wrote in 1957 that all biographical writing has in common "that it is concerned with the truth of life and the truth of experience." A biographer answers the questions: "What is the essence of a life? Which are the true witnesses of this or that life and which the false?" (2) Edel's ideal biography assumes the existence of a unified and stable historical self whose true story is recoverable through the careful, measured work of the biographer. Contemporary theories of language and subjectivity, on the contrary, posit the constructed, contingent nature of human identity and encourage us therefore to look closely in a biography or a novel at how a multifaceted, unstable, internally contradictory subject is constituted in language. Further, the tension between research and story telling is a constant in all biography. Practitioners and readers alike acknowledge the genre's employment of documentary and novelistic techniques, biographical and autobiographical material to present a kaleidoscopic version of an ever-elusive subject.[2]

The historical Tina Modotti turns out to be an extraordinarily elusive subject for biographical research and writing. The existing written records are incomplete, and her story juxtaposes periods of high visibility with others of complete anonymity and invisibility. The picture is both densely detailed and full of gaps, and a further complication for anyone wishing to recover the "authentic" Tina Modotti is the fact that she left few written materials. The records of her own voice are sparse in comparison with the testimonies of others about her. Modotti, it seems, was always susceptible to becoming a creature of others's invention. Born in Udine, Italy, in 1896 to a working-class family, Modotti's childhood was marked by poverty and a heavy burden of responsibility in the family after her father's departure for America in 1906. The Modotti family eventually joined him there, and Tina worked as a seamstress and a semiprofessional stage actress in San Francisco's Little Italy district. After her marriage to Roubaix de l'Abrie Richey, an American of wealthy background, she moved to Los Angeles, where she and her husband adopted a bohemian lifestyle. He was an aspiring poet and artist who created outstanding batiks, and she sewed and made dolls while pursuing an acting career. She appeared in a few Hollywood B films, invariably cast as the exotic "other woman." Tina and her husband's circle of friends included other artists and intellectuals with a shared interest in Eastern mysticism and a disdain for middle-class American mores. The photographer Edward Weston became their close friend. Tina modeled for him, and they were lovers even before Richey's death in 1922. Weston and Modotti went to Mexico together in 1923. She started out as his apprentice and photographer's assistant, and they enjoyed an active social life with a wide group of prominent Mexicans and foreigners. Diego Rivera and Lupe Marín, David Alfaro Siqueiros, Anita Brenner, Carleton Beals, Pablo O'Higgins, Xavier Guerrero, and Manuel Hernández Galván figured among their closest acquaintances. Modotti posed often for Weston and also for Diego Rivera, most notably as the nude model for "Virgin Earth" and "Germination" in the famous Chapingo murals. She established a reputation as a respected and successful professional photographer in her own right, and she remained in Mexico City when Weston returned to the United States in 1926. In 1927, she joined the Mexican Communist Party and began to direct her photography toward social and political ends while maintaining her portrait business. In 1930, Tina Modotti, by now a recognized Communist Party activist, was expelled from Mexico, falsely accused of involvement in the assassination attempt on newly inaugurated President Pascual Ortiz Rubio.

In contrast to her highly visible and often controversial identity in Mexico (foreigner; professional woman; nude model; companion "without benefit of marriage" to Weston, Guerrero, and Julio Antonio Mella; public speaker; Communist), after 1930 Tina Modotti "disappeared" into a decade of virtually invisible work for the International Red Aid. Going first to Germany and then to Moscow, she abandoned photography and lived as the companion of fellow Italian and Party member Vittorio Vidali. Unquestioning supporters of Stalin, they worked for the party in a number of capacities. Modotti's knowledge of foreign languages made her useful as a translator and interpreter for the Red Aid office in Moscow. Together and separately, Modotti and Vidali took part in numerous espionage and humanitarian missions throughout Europe. From 1936 to 1939, they were stationed in Spain where Modotti worked in a hospital, and Vidali trained volunteers for the renowned Fifth Regiment and was a prominent representative for Moscow in support of the Republican cause. During this period, Modotti lived under various aliases, traveling with false documents and working in disguise so that even close associates often did not know who she was. In Spain, Tina Modotti, photographer, completely vanished behind the assumed identity of María Sánchez, physicians's assistant and refuge relief worker. The distinctions between "core identity" and "role," between the true face and the mask/alias are, of course, false dichotomies in anyone's case, but the biographer's investigation into the existing versions and memories of Tina/María in Spain is greatly complicated because of the deliberate taking on of a different name and background.

With the defeat of the Spanish Republic in 1939, Modotti and Vidali left Spain for refuge in France and then traveled back to the Americas where they settled again in Mexico. Tina entered Mexico illegally with a Spanish passport due to her prior expulsion. At first she tried to pass unnoticed by her former friends and associates. Little by little she re-emerged, but her friends found her much changed by the difficult years in Europe and particularly by the long agony of the Spanish Civil War. Eventually her immigration status was cleared, and she was able to live openly in Mexico as Tina Modotti, but she died soon after, on January 6, 1942.

Tina Modotti was a woman who constantly reinvented herself throughout her adult life, as the above synopsis shows. Her capacity for change and her abrupt moves between an almost overexposed visibility and an anonymous invisibility make her a challenging and yet worthy subject of writing. The principal written records of her life story consist of contemporary material, which tends to be fragmentary and partial, and retrospective attempts to provide a more complete and internally coherent representation. Among the former, which could be considered "primary" source documents, are Tina Modotti's letters to Edward Weston; Weston's *Daybooks*; newspaper accounts of Modotti and Weston's exhibitions and, later, of Modotti's alleged complicity in Julio Antonio Mella's assassination and her eventual expulsion from Mexico; diaries and letters written by her friends and family; and legal documents such as baptismal and death certificates. None of this is simply "raw material," but rather all written accounts are already versions that create and do not merely record the meaning of events and individual identities. What is striking in Modotti's case is how little she wrote, a fact that forces her biographers to rely heavily on the writings of others and on their memories as elicited in oral interviews. As a consequence, any life story of Tina Modotti necessarily foregrounds the construction of identity in the words and the silences of its competing versions.

In 1975 Mildred Constantine published *Tina Modotti: A Fragile Life*, a groundbreaking volume that combines a biography of Modotti with numerous photographic reproductions. This was the first book to appear, meaning that it took more than thirty years after Modotti's death for her life to receive serious, sustained attention. Since 1975, other publications have followed. Vittorio Vidali wrote his version, *Storia di donna*, which was translated into Spanish and published in Mexico in 1984 as *Retrato de mujer: Una vida con Tina Modotti*. Cristiane Barckhausen-Canale published her lengthy biography, *Verdad y leyenda de Tina Modotti*, in Cuba in 1988, and *Tina Modotti: Photographer and Revolutionary* by Margaret Hooks came out in 1993. Tina Modotti's letters to Edward Weston were edited and published by Amy Conger in 1986 and translated into Spanish in 1992. Elena Poniatowska's *Tinísima*, therefore, is one of a number of significant projects of research and recreation of Tina Modotti's life, politics, and artistic production carried out from diverse ideological perspectives. I do not propose to undertake a comparative analysis of these versions of Tina Modotti, except to note that by conceiving of her book as a novel, albeit a biographical one, Poniatowska has given herself the greatest freedom to fill in the many gaps in the historical record. In particular, she envisions the shadowy years in Berlin, Moscow, and Spain with singular force of detail.

As with all of Elena Poniatowska's books, there is a story behind the writing of *Tinísima*. In 1980, Poniatowska was approached to write a script for a movie on the photographer. Under the pressure of a deadline, she sketched out a script based on the Constantine biography and a few interviews with people who had known Modotti in Mexico. When the funding for the movie fell through, Poniatowska's growing interest in Modotti and the scarcity of reliable published accounts of her life prompted the Mexican writer to undertake a long journey of investigation and creation. Each new interview that she conducted and each document or photograph that she examined led to another contact and another archive, until her life and her living space were literally taken over: "Tina Modotti became part of my daily life for the last ten years. Always with Tina accompanying me I traveled, I read, I studied, I ate, I inflicted myself on others" (June 1991 interview with the author).

Three densely packed pages of acknowledgments at the end of the novel attest to the unique complexity of the research process leading to the writing of *Tinísima*. Poniatowska carried out dozens of interviews in Mexico and abroad with those who knew Modotti: her sister, Yolanda Magrini; the Mexican photographer Manuel Alvarez Bravo; Lola Alvarez Bravo; Guadalupe Marín; and Pablo O'Higgins, to name just a few. Perhaps her most significant original contribution to research on Modotti is the lengthy interview with Vittorio Vidali that she recorded during a ten-day period in Trieste, Italy, a few years before his death. Poniatowska studied Weston's *Daybooks*, Pablo Neruda's autobiography, and writings by Anita Brenner and Bertram Wolfe. She also dug into the archives for *El Machete* and reviewed the mainstream press accounts of Modotti's trial in 1929 for the murder of Julio Antonio Mella and her expulsion from Mexico in 1930, the principal sources of the "black legend" of Modotti as a Mata Hari of the Comintern. Finally, she read extensively, even exhaustively, on the social, political, and historical context of Mexico in the 1920s, Russia in the 1930s, and the Spanish Civil War. The story that had begun as a modest movie script took on a life of its own, claiming ten years of work, filling a room, and spilling over into 663 pages of text.

Feminist perspectives on the writing of biographies by women about women raise issues and provide explanatory schema that are useful in elucidating both the achievements and the limitations of *Tinísima*'s version(s) of Tina Modotti. Sharon O'Brien confirms that biography remains a powerful way of reinscribing women in history and of narrating women's lives, in spite of objections raised by some feminist scholars to the perpetuation of the "exceptional woman" model of history. While she rejects traditional, and still popular, assumptions that biography can recover its subject's "true self," O'Brien defends the value of individual life stories, especially those written in an experimental mode. She encourages explicitly dialogic and open-ended forms to break up the biographer's tendency for monologue. For example, she proposes options such as the insertion without interpretation of letters, diaries and photos, more work on living women whose lives are still incomplete, and the extension of biography well beyond the date of death of its subject. Elizabeth Kamarck Minnich characterizes biography as a gesture of friendship across time between women and a struggle for a sense of self, which involves both the biographer and the biographical subject. She notes, as do other critics, that feminist research should not be conceived as a search for ideal role models measured according to present-day expectations. Finally, Bell Gale Chevigny describes the writing of biography as an act of mutual mothering and mutual reparation in which biographer and subject give and take life and autonomy one from the other. Almost all recent biographical theory, feminist or not, further acknowledges the auto-biographical dimension of writing another's life. I should clarify that it is not my intent to verify or validate one version of Modotti's life story, *Tinísima*, as opposed to any other, nor is it to prove that Elena Poniatowska has either found in Tina Modotti a feminist foremother or written an example of a successful feminist biographical novel, whatever that might be. Rather, I want to offer an informed reading of the text's construction of its subject and weave in a discussion of the factors at play in the process of writing *Tinísima*.

Tinísima's Tina Modotti is, to put it simply, a puzzle. On the one hand, the novel portrays in positive terms a woman of immense energy and artistic talent, constant activity, strong loyalties and personal dignity, generosity, beauty, and uninhibited sexuality. Surely here is a life that demands recognition for the productive links between creative work, political and social activism, and personal life and relationships. On the other hand, as a reader I was struck by Modotti's frequent absences from lengthy sections of "her" novel and by the detailed attention given to the men in her life, who literally take over the narrative as they also seem to dominate Modotti. The tension between the independent, professional Modotti and the almost frighteningly dependent and obedient one is a pervasive and perplexing aspect of the novel, and it is the aspect that I will focus on in the following analysis.

The overall structure of the text establishes the contradiction for us early on. The first chapter is dated January 10, 1929, the day on which Tina Modotti's companion, Julio Antonio Mella, was shot and killed at her side while walking home. The moment is dramatic and its consequences are haunting, but to foreground it means opening with an image of Tina Modotti as a victim, as a lover mourning her loss, and as a very public and specifically female object of scandal and attack who has little control over the events that threaten her. Modotti is cast in a predominantly defensive role and as an object of the male gaze in the first one hundred pages of the text and repeatedly at other crucial moments. An early chapter goes so far as to move out of Mexico and out of Tina's life entirely to recreate Mella's final years in Cuba before his expulsion by the Machado government. Julio Antonio Mella was a Cuban student activist who advocated the overthrow of the Machado regime and a socialist revolution for Cuba. In Mexico, where he met Tina, he quickly established himself as a rising star in the Communist Party. His murder and the Mexican government's failure to prosecute his attacker were political events of some importance. They also spelled the beginning of the end of Tina Modotti's first residence in Mexico because she was initially accused of complicity in the murder, and during her trial, the press seized upon letters, diaries, and photographs (nudes by Weston of Modotti and her own nudes of Mella) to sensationalize the case and to defame her character. A year later, the government could, with impunity, expel her from the country on different, but equally trumped up charges.

Anyone researching Modotti's life has to confront the 1929–1930 newspaper record, the counter-arguments published by such influential friends as Diego Rivera, and the very real impact of the scandal on Modotti's future. This highly visible moment in her story is a double-edged sword, however, because it distorts and obscures Modotti's achievements and relationships in Mexico by the very way in which it calls attention to them. In *Tinísima*, Poniatowska reproduces the language of the attacks, but she also imagines Modotti's inner turmoil during the crisis and presents it as a counter-discourse to the prevailing anti-communism, xenophobia, and misogyny of the press. Her desire to know the truth and to remain in control of her emotions throughout the trial period, which included house arrest and constant surveillance, are two constants of this version of a resisting, self-possessed Modotti. But a third compelling element, which contrasts sharply to the public demeanor, is the description of nightmares suffered by the protagonist after Mella's death. If we take dreams to have a privileged relationship to a person's psychological state, then it is clear that the novel is sympathetically exploring the breakdown of self-identity and self-determination in the face of intense pressures from outside. The breathless pace of the narration of the trial, the incorporation of language taken from the newspapers, and the constant mention of men staring at Modotti successfully evoke the hostile atmosphere to which she was subjected both mentally and physically. Her nightmares dwell on the dangerous but pleasurable power of the sea and the fear of drowning, and also a scenario in which she is stripped of her skin and stands before two men as if in judgment: her father, Giuseppe Modotti, and a headless Julio Antonio Mella. Giuseppe and Julio condemn her to freedom and to responsibility for her own actions, a sentence that seems to provoke her complete disintegration: "Without her skin, she is no longer Tina. She tries to step down, her heart and head filled with foam don't respond; she spits out foam from her mouth" (111). The sea that tempts and frightens, the desire for death and its attendant oblivion, and the loss of skin and flesh are motifs that recur throughout the novel. They suggest a fragile, vulnerable subjectivity, which sought completion by giving itself over to others and yet also understood that such a gesture invites annihilation.

After the opening sequence, *Tinísima* narrates Modotti's life in roughly chronological order, with the exception of her childhood and adolescence, which are remembered many years later in Moscow. A key issue is Modotti's constant struggle to define herself within changing sentimental, social, and historical contexts. The novel's presentation of this struggle foregrounds Modotti's tendency to alleviate her anxiety and seek self-affirmation through her lovers and her eager taking up of their work and their causes to justify her existence. Following Mella's death, the second major grouping of chapters covers her life from 1917–1921 with her husband, Roubaix de l'Abrie Richey, or Robo, her affair with Weston, and their years together in Mexico (August 1923 to November 1926). The figure of Weston dominates these chapters, beginning with their friendship in Los Angeles where, "Delighted, Tina looked for the savior, the one with the answers. The smallest occurrence could give her a clue. Her guests's pronouncements contained signs, she would figure them out" (120–121). The nightmare of freedom and self-determination is kept at bay by relationships with powerful men. With Weston, the answers are photography and the creation of beauty as an absolute ideal. Tina "sees" herself for the first time in Weston's nude photographs of her, although her own photographic work takes on a distinctive, socially conscious dimension that is not her master's invention.

As they grow apart emotionally, Modotti moves toward a commitment to social change through revolutionary activity that is diametrically opposed to the philosophy that she had adopted with Weston. Again she follows the lead of a man, an artist who is also a Communist Party member. The novel signals this change with a description of how Xavier Guerrero's books, papers, and obsessions soon invade and fill up Tina's apartment. The image of his cap hanging on a framed Weston print signifies the defeat of the artistic project by the utilitarian exigencies of the revolutionary struggle. Under his influence, Tina spends the better part of her day tied to a typewriter at Party headquarters and equally subject to Party discipline and ideology. Her later love affair with Julio Antonio Mella, cut short by his murder, strengthens her dedication to the cause. His death provides a further incentive: Now her life will be an homage to his struggle and her absorption in it will dull the sense of loss.

Modotti continues to write to Weston from Mexico and later from Europe until her last letter in 1931. Those letters, fragments of which are reproduced in the novel, poignantly express the difficult transition from one world and one mode of being to another quite different one. Still torn between the demands of art and the demands of politics, in 1927, she produces some fine quality photographs to send to Weston, while at the Party office she chafes at seeing everything "*desde la sombra,*" from under a shadow. She questions whether the political work of the party is as useful as a more practical, direct activism would be, and she longs to go out into the community and serve the people's immediate needs. Nevertheless, for the most part, she is portrayed as a loyal and hard-working member, with the letters to Weston providing the principal evidence of her initial doubts and her progressively more hard-line position. At the time that Diego Rivera is expelled from the party, for example, Tina writes to Weston that she absolutely accepts the wisdom of this decision against their old friend. The novel explains her willingness to leave behind friends and a certain concept of art to enter wholeheartedly into the work of the party in part as a return to her childhood: "the reencounter with her essence, becoming again the child riding on Giuseppe's shoulders at the demonstrations, Demetrio Canale's godchild, fist raised in the air" (237). Again it is significant that her self-identity is consistently given in terms of her attachment to the important men in her life.

The second half of the novel treats the years from 1930 to 1942 and traverses the geography of her exile and her nomadic existence as an agent for the International Red Aid: Berlin, Moscow, Paris, Yugoslavia, Romania, Spain, and finally back to Mexico. Vittorio Vidali now steps in as Modotti's companion and emotional anchor. One dilemma faced by all of her biographers is to explain why Modotti, who chose to go to Berlin because she had professional contacts there, gave up photography after taking just a very few photographs in Germany. In Mexico, she seemed to have successfully combined the demands of politically oriented work for *El Machete* with her preoccupation for superior technique and composition, and she produced some of her best work in the period from 1927–1929. But in Germany, she tried and abandoned photography, and later in Russia and Spain, she rejected invitations to work with the camera again. Poniatowska's novel emphasizes how difficult it would have been for Modotti to adapt to new equipment and a new way of working (rapid-fire journalistic picture taking), completely unlike her training with Weston. She takes this cue from a letter that Tina wrote to Weston from Berlin in which she characterizes herself and women in general as ill-suited for such an aggressive mode of photography. *Tinísima* also develops the idea that Modotti felt real conflicts and shame over her former lifestyle and her lack of preparation in socialist ideology, suggesting that it gave a kind of relief to submerge herself in a new identity within the communist experiment in Russia. Later in Spain, "María Sánchez" thinks, "What a relief not to be Tina anymore!" (434). Here the reader is constantly pulled between admiration for Modotti's courage, physical endurance, intelligence, and capacity for self-sacrifice, and an equally strong sense of disappointment or irritation over the image of blind obedience to an authoritarianism whose cruel excesses may now seem all too obvious.

The re-creation of Modotti's final years in Mexico is interesting for a number of reasons. To some extent, she remains the party loyalist, faithful to the extreme to "papá Stalin" and angrily resentful, therefore, of Trotsky's presence in Mexico under Cárdenas's protection. Logically enough, she dedicates herself to helping Spanish Republican exiles settle into a new country, and she continues to live as Vittorio Vidali's companion. But several events challenge the fixity of her world view. Stalin's pact with Hitler is completely incomprehensible to Modotti, who cannot tolerate any concession to fascism. Second, in ill health and prematurely aging, she finds that the loss of physical beauty is a liberating experience. She is described as almost transparent, slender to the point of "losing" her breasts and hips. Modotti thinks back to 1929, when her body was the object of desire and hatred, and thanks "*bendita vejez*," blessed old age, for freeing her. Finally there is mention of a book titled *Dos antagonismos*, which a woman friend gives Modotti to read. It treats the subordination of women in patriarchy, and it makes Tina think critically about the inferior place of women in the Communist Party, especially in Mexico where an acquaintance once said that the women in the party "had confused the word *camarada* [comrade] with the word *cama* [bed]" (618). The final chapters of *Tinísima* seem to be pointing toward a new stage in Modotti's life, perhaps one in which her obedience to the "father" might turn into a more self-assertive and critical posture. But her death cuts short any potential change, and the massive novel leaves us with a sympathetic but ambiguous portrait, indeed.

The construction of a biography or a biographical novel begins with a search for materials closely connected to the subject's life and times. I have already described the research that Elena Poniatowska carried out over the course of ten years to compile the enormous body of information that she incorporates into her novel. That dedication of time and energy is in itself a "gesture of friendship" and a tribute to an individual life whose complexity had been obscured by the myth making and mystifying power of the press. All of the books published since 1975 claim to denounce and correct or repair the "black legend" of Tina Modotti. It is important now to elaborate on the factors that influenced Elena Poniatowska's particular corrective version of the Modotti story. I believe that there are three crucial factors to consider: (1) the nature of her sources, (2) Poniatowska's relationship to those sources, and (3) the conjunction of the biographical (Tina Modotti) and the autobiographical (Elena Poniatowska) in *Tinísima*.

I have already mentioned that written documentation in Modotti's own hand consists primarily of the letters that Edward Weston preserved from their correspondence between 1922 and 1931. Poniatowska incorporates these traces of Modotti's voice into *Tinísima* by quoting directly from the letters and by expanding on the ideas, moods, and language found there. However, the letters from Mexico after Weston's departure often focus on Tina's reactions to and praise for Weston's work, which contributes to the image of a self-effacing subject. The reader of *Tinísima* who is familiar with the *Daybooks* immediately perceives the tremendous impact of Weston's own voice on Poniatowska's text. The *Daybooks* provide information on their mutual friends, details of their daily life together, observations on Mexican society, and some record of Modotti's role in Weston's professional success there. However, what is striking about the *Daybooks* is precisely how little Weston writes about Modotti. Considering her central place in his life from 1923 to 1926, it is astonishing to find relatively few extended passages about her. Compared to the lengthy meditations on his work and the descriptions of friends like Rivera and Galván—even compared to the attention given to the servants with whom he had casual sexual relations—Modotti occupies little space in the *Daybooks*. I found her exclusion by Weston to be a telling and surprising revelation that helps explain why he is frequently the focus of attention in certain chapters of *Tinísima*. It also suggests that although Poniatowska followed his account quite closely, she also had to have made a great effort of investigation and imagination to create a more complete image of Modotti during those years. The debt to Weston is undeniable, but it is an influence that is partially contested by Poniatowska's investigative and creative labor.

The other verbal source that shapes *Tinísima* in visible and significant ways is Vittorio Vidali. He shared twelve years of life with Modotti, twelve years during which she was living in disguise and under cover. Like Weston and Mella earlier in the novel, at times Vidali replaces Modotti as the protagonist of the most interesting actions narrated. This is especially the case in the chapters on the Spanish Civil War, when "Comandante Carlos" is a compelling figure and "María Sánchez" seems to disappear into the deadening routine of constant work and life-threatening exhaustion. The interviews that Poniatowska conducted with Vidali almost forty years after Modotti's death, and his two books, *Retrato de mujer* and *Comandante Carlos*, are perhaps the single most important source for *Tinísima*. Poniatowska's characterization of her subject largely conforms to Vidali's vision of his companion and her life: a gentle, capable, humane and determined woman (7); full of loyalty and goodness (8); nerves of steel, never sick (35). He also cites the central importance of Mella's death in her political radicalization and her unquestioning acceptance of Party decisions, and he offers a view of Tina's sexuality that contradicts the press's attempts to label her as a licentious, dangerously seductive, and immoral woman. *Tinísima* recreates scenes of sexual pleasure along the lines of Vidali's testimony to a "natural," generous, and happy intimacy free of prudishness.

Elena Poniatowska has been a professional interviewer for four decades, and she has based many of her books on oral testimonies. It is worth noting how she views the interview process and the knowledge gained in conversations with another person. Once when prodded to judge the value of information gleaned from various types of sources, she responded that the sources she trusts most are her own interviews. She claims to trust absolutely in the veracity of what she hears and in her own intentions in shaping her questions and in attending carefully to the responses.[3] Further, she considers another person's words and name, offered as testimony to an interviewer, to be precious, fragile materials deserving of the highest esteem. Given this attitude and her expressions of friendship and sympathy toward Vittorio Vidali, it is not surprising that *Tinísima*, while going far beyond the scope of his writings and even of his memory, respects in large measure his version of Tina Modotti.

A different kind of source studied by Elena Poniatowska and incorporated into *Tinísima* is photography, and the record left by Tina Modotti's work on both sides of the camera offers another way of seeing the subject. As a favorite model for one of the pre-eminent American photographers of this century, Modotti's face and body are captured in dozens of black and white prints shot by Edward Weston. Here is the woman seen by a specifically male gaze. Alternatively, the photographs taken by Modotti, all but a very few done in Mexico between 1923 and early 1930, give insights into how she viewed the world around her. As Susan Sontag puts it, the early idea that the camera provides an objective image "soon yielded to the fact that photographs are evidence not only of what's there but of what an individual saw, not just a record but an evaluation of the world" (88). This is a common enough understanding of the subjective nature of photography, but it suggests that careful and sustained viewing of Modotti's work may give a kind of access to her seeing I/eye. Elena Poniatowska, who values photography as an art form and as an integral part of modern journalism, has contributed texts to a number of collaboratively conceived photographic essays. Her eye has had long practice in viewing the photographic image. In the course of researching Tina Modotti, she visited museum archives in Mexico and the United States, and she has viewed most of the approximately 160 photographs attributed to Modotti. Their impact can be detected in the verbal image that Poniatowska constructs in her novel. The fact that Tina Modotti selected her subjects and composed her photographs with great care and deliberation further justifies such a reading. I believe that the photographs partially compensated Poniatowska for the lack of an ample written record of Modotti's voice and also helped offset the reliance on masculine versions of her and its attendant limitations. Finally, they are the best proof of Modotti's creative genius and of her place as an influential figure in the Mexican photographic tradition.

On its cover, the published book reproduces an early Weston print of Modotti's face with her eyes closed and her hands touching her cheeks. Each chapter begins with a small photograph, many of them either of or by Tina Modotti. While the quality of these images is not high, they serve as a visual reminder of the centrality of photography in the life story being told. The textual presence of the Tina seen and photographed by Weston is strongest in the first one-third of the novel. *Tinísima* is narrated throughout by an external omniscient narrator, but Poniatowska makes effective use of interior monologue, dialogue, and direct quotations from her sources to communicate multiple perspectives. The most prominent single voice and point of view shaping the chapters on California and Mexico belong to Weston. Tina filtered through his eyes and emotions appears as the object of the male gaze and desire, a woman whose body attracted constant attention. The *Daybooks* provide the key terms: jealousy, bemusement, admiration, and estrangement, and the photos are the basis for the verbal descriptions of Modotti in the narrative.

When we "see" her sunbathing nude on the rooftop, relaxing in a silk kimono, wringing out her wet hair with her arms raised and her breasts lifted, stretching out her legs or reciting poetry, we are seeing Weston's Tina. Many of his photographs picture a vulnerable, passive beauty, and a sexuality in waiting, as well as a remarkable dignity and calm. Weston's nudes of Modotti include both head and sex, a marked innovation in his framing of the female nude, but her eyes are usually closed or her head is turned away, conveying the impression of a subject spied upon and caught unawares. We look at Modotti, but she does not often look back from Weston's photographs. Likewise, in the novel at times we see Modotti but are left wondering how she sees herself and others.

An alternative perspective figures into Poniatowska's novel to fill in that gap, as I have suggested. The majority of Modotti's own photographs fall into a number of broad thematic categories: portraits of friends and clients, the work of the Mexican muralists, flowers and cacti, architectural details, revolutionary symbols arranged in still lifes, images of modernization, and the Mexican working and lower classes (poor children, workers, peasants, indigenous women). Increasingly during her life there, the Mexico that Modotti saw and photographed was a society torn by gross inequalities and human suffering but also a society in a process of change. Her photographs of workers's hands dignify hard labor and the struggle for survival. A blurred shot from above a crowd of men marching in a demonstration shows the dynamic energy of people mobilized on their own behalf. Her indigenous women stand erect, eyes wide open, or unself-consciously nurture their children and pursue their daily tasks. This is an idealized picture, to be sure, but it idealizes the collective struggle and the demands of justice in a socially conscious way. There is a clear correspondence of purpose and sympathy between Modotti's photography and Elena Poniatowska's chronicles of contemporary Mexican society that must have drawn the one to the other. An investment in the documentary value of photographic images and of factual modes of writing further links the creative work of the two women. *Tinísima* affords a panoramic view of the tumultuous social and historical milieu in which Modotti lived, as well as focusing on the individual life. Poniatowska portrays her subject's photography and her revolutionary militancy as equally serious manifestations of her struggle for self-definition (in art, in the other) and for social change. The carefully researched and vividly depicted social context of Mexico, Russia, and Spain in the novel is a tribute to Modotti's engagement in her own historical circumstances. Her photography, by leaving a visible trace of her eye contact with the world, helps make possible Poniatowska's version of that world as Modotti experienced it.

Up to this point, I have been primarily concerned to show what Elizabeth Stanley calls "the cup of plenty that a person's life and their contemporaries's views of it represents" (21). *Tinísima* is a kaleidoscope made up of shifting bits and pieces of multiple versions of Tina Modotti's life and mixing what we might consider relatively more factual material with clearly fictionalized episodes. Stanley and other critics also try to account for the interaction between the writer's subjectivity and that of her biographical subject. Writing a biography is not just an other-oriented process, but rather, to one degree or another, the biographer recognizes, re-examines, and re-creates herself in the other. Identification with the other is a corollary to engagement with her, an endeavour that Chevigny calls "mutual mothering." Whoever the subjects are, "the act of daughters writing about them is likely to be, on some level, an act of retrieval which is experienced as rescue" and indirectly as rescue of ourselves (97–98). It is not difficult to discern the presence of autobiographical elements in *Tinísima*, elements that make visible the "fantasy of reciprocity" (95) that is part of the biographical project.

It is, of course, only coincidence that Tina Modotti died in 1942, the very year that the French-born Elena Poniatowska, her mother, and sister arrived in Mexico from war-torn France. It is coincidence, too, that the young socialite, Paula Amor, sat for a portrait by Edward Weston in his Mexico City studio two decades earlier. But it is not coincidence that Poniatowska dedicated this novel, among her many books, to her mother, Paula Amor. The dedication is a deliberate choice that offers the daughter's creation as a gift to the mother. The gift is the story of a woman of her mother's generation, and it is, in part, the story of the daughter as well. Elena Poniatowska found a great deal of common ground across time with Tina Modotti, and she inscribed her version of Modotti with language and motifs that she has often used to describe herself. Writing the other appears to have embraced a process of self-discovery and self-affirmation.

Poniatowska has testified eloquently to her desire, upon arriving in Mexico at the age of ten, to learn the Spanish language and to belong to her new homeland as fully as possible. With linguistic competence came a window onto other cultures and other social classes. Spanish was her entry to *mexicanidad*. The feelings that she attributes to Tina Modotti, whom she describes as particularly "at home" linguistically and culturally in Mexico in the 1920s and as capable of establishing an easy communication and rapport with people of all walks of life, thus recall Elena Poniatowska's own strong attachments.

Other characteristics assigned to Tina Modotti reiterate statements made in Elena Poniatowska's explicitly autobiographical writings and in interviews. The lack of a clear self-definition and an eagerness to look to others for answers are obvious examples. Consider this passage from the autobiographical essay "A Question Mark Engraved on My Eyelids": "I have always wanted to lose myself in others, to belong to other people, to be the same as them. It is always others who are right, who hold the key to the enigma. Since then, my capacity for entering the lives of other people has been unlimited, to the point that I could no longer hold myself back, define my limits, much less define myself" (85). We have already seen these themes in Poniatowska's portrayal of Modotti in Los Angeles and in the nightmares that she suffered after Julio Antonio Mella's death.

The notion of work as a kind of lifeline and the struggle to reconcile the demands of artistic creation with the demands of everyday life are other constants in Elena Poniatowska's self-portraits and also of Tina Modotti's life story. A quote from one of Modotti's letters to Edward Weston could be Poniatowska's own words, and it shows the reciprocal nature of the interaction in biography: "[I]n my case life is always struggling to predominate and art naturally suffers. . . . I put too much art in my life—too much energy—and consequently I have not much left to give to art" (Stark 39–40). Surely Elena Poniatowska recognized her own struggle for autonomy as a woman and a writer in Modotti's life and work, and the two women nurtured each other in a complex auto/biographical process.

I will conclude with a final, poignant example. In *Tinísima*, Tina Modotti meets the French philosopher, Simone Weil, on the border between France and Spain. Weil has come to join in the defense of the Republic, and Modotti screens her as part of the entrance process. The encounter is brief, and it may be historically accurate or it may be a product of Poniatowska's creative liberty. That does not really matter. What makes it significant is to remember the importance of Simone Weil's writings and example for Elena Poniatowska's social thought.[4] Her appearance in *Tinísima* brings together two women of the previous generation, two "foremothers" whose accomplishments have inspired Poniatowska and to whom she in turn gives life in memory and in words.

Tinísima celebrates Tina Modotti the artist, the social revolutionary, and the woman of extraordinary beauty, integrity, and courage. Modotti claimed an identity as an artist in the 1920s, and she expected others to take her seriously as one. Clearly she also sought a different way to live as a woman in a world that was fundamentally hostile to a woman's self-determination and militancy. At the same time, the novel details many symptoms of a specifically feminine lack of autonomy and obedience to authority. I have tried to show that these tensions are present throughout the novel and that they may be attributed to a complex interplay of factors: the nature of the written and oral sources employed by Elena Poniatowska, her respect for those sources, the photographs, and the intersection of the biographical and the autobiographical. *Tinísima* is a valuable and original contribution to the repertoire of stories that now constitute Tina Modotti in history and that honor the splendid puzzle of human subjectivity.

NOTES

1. All translations from Spanish are mine. (Editor's note: an English translation of *Tinísima* was published in late 1996.)

2. Gail Porter Mandell's introduction to her book *Life Into Art* provides a concise and useful overview of predominant issues in contemporary theories of biography.

3. I base this on my interview with her in 1991 when I asked her the question about her opinion of the truthfulness of sources.

4. I treat this topic in the second chapter of my book, *The Writing of Elena Poniatowska*, 55–57.

REFERENCES

Chevigny, Bell Gale. "Daughters Writing: Toward a Theory of Women's Biography." *Feminist Studies* 9.1 (1983): 79–102.

Edel, Leon. *Literary Biography*. Toronto: U of Toronto P, 1957.

Jörgensen, Beth E. *The Writing of Elena Poniatowska: Engaging Dialogues*. Austin: U of Texas P, 1994.

Mandell, Gail Porter. *Life Into Art: Conversations with Seven Contemporary Biographers*. Fayetteville: U of Arkansas P, 1991.

Minnich, Elizabeth Kamarck. "Friendship Between Women: The Art of Feminist Biography." *Feminist Studies* 11.2 (1985): 287–305.

O'Brien, Sharon. "Feminist Theory and Literary Biography." *Contesting the Subject*. Ed. William H. Epstein. West Lafayette, IN: Purdue UP, 1991. 123–133.

Plagens, Peter. "What a Life She Red." *Newsweek* (October 2, 1995): 88.

Poniatowska, Elena. "A Question Mark Engraved on My Eyelids." *The Writer and Her Work*. Ed. Janet Sternberg. New York: Norton, 1991. 82–96.

———. *Tinísima*. Mexico: Era, 1992.

———. *Tinísima*. Trans. Katherine Silver. New York: Farrar, Straus, Giroux, 1996.

Sontag, Susan. *On Photography*. New York: Farrar, Straus and Giroux, 1977.

Stanley, Elizabeth. "Biography as Microscope or Kaleidoscope? The Case of 'Power' in Hannah Cullwick's Relationship with Arthur Munby." *Women's Studies International Forum* 10.1 (1987): 19–31.

Stark, Amy, ed. *The Letters of Tina Modotti to Edward Weston*. Special issue of *The Archive* 22 (January 1986).

Vidali, Vittorio. *Retrato de mujer: Una vida con Tina Modotti*. Trans. Antonella Fagetti. Puebla: Universidad Autónoma de Puebla, 1984.

Weston, Edward. *The Daybooks of Edward Weston*. Rochester, NY: The George Eastman House, n.d.

6

TINÍSIMA: THE CONSTRUCTION OF THE SELF THROUGH THE STRUCTURES OF NARRATIVE DISCOURSE

Charlotte Ekland

Elena Poniatowska's *Tinísima* (1992; English translation, 1996) appeared at a moment in literary history when authors seeking to explore female identity found themselves in a paradoxical situation. On the one hand, there existed a demand to right the omissions of past literary production by creating myths of female identity to counterbalance the prevalent masculine prototypes. At the same time, contemporary notions of subjectivity and of consciousness invalidated claims of a unitary, coherent self, making such representations suspect. Poniatowska takes a rather unique approach to solving this dilemma. Instead of opting for one definition of identity over the other, she incorporates both into the narrative, transforming the vision of the self in varying contexts. A fictionalized biography, *Tinísima* narrates the life of Italian-born photographer and model Tina Modotti (1896–1942). The novel creates a protagonist whose story mirrors the transformations of the real-life Modotti. To the diverse contexts of Modotti's life story—from Los Angeles to post-revolutionary Mexico, from the early Soviet Union to the Spanish Civil War—Poniatowska adds a multiplicity of divergent literary practices. This fiction incorporates conflicting narrative approaches to discourse within the confines of a single novel.

The novel starts well past the midpoint of Modotti's life, with the traumatic assassination of Julio Antonio Mella, a fellow communist and Tina's greatest love. Because she was walking at his side at the time of the murder, she becomes a suspect in the case. In this first part of the novel, the narration reflects a contemporary conception of the self as provisional and changing (9–117). The narrator gives the reader a glimpse into the complex, confusing, and sometimes contradictory workings within the protagonist. Discontinuity, disruptions, and shifting perspectives typify this part of the novel. Framed by a notion of subjectivity as unstable, the second part of the book, which retrogresses to the period of Tina's relationship with photographer Edward Weston, reconstructs a meaningful (i.e., coherent and consistent) identity. The protagonist ponders her past, shaping it into an autobiographical sketch, the "legend of Edward and Tina."

In this chapter I will limit my analysis to the vision of the self as it is presented in the first part of the book. Here Tina appears not as a defined being, but rather as one that is evolving and changing. A confrontation of opposing impulses and constraints, she embodies a process, a becoming. Tina is continually transformed by her interaction with other people, by the changing social-political context, by the environment that surrounds her, by what she reads, by her own body. Not ultimately constructed at some particular point in the novel, she evolves through her decisions and indecisions.[1] The novel becomes a vehicle for the unfolding of the process of self-consciousness. It provides the changing historical, political, and social conditions in which the protagonist forges her identity.

THE AMBIGUITY OF THE SELF AS EXPRESSED THROUGH THE VOICE OF THE NARRATOR

In *Tinísima*, the voice of the narrator plays a central role in the revelation of the self. While the novel is narrated almost entirely in the third person, the narrator's voice does not signify an unchanging, detached viewpoint. The "no-person" fluctuates between objective reporting and a projection of the narrator into the subjectivity of the characters, especially into that of the protagonist. Our first view of Tina is actually the photograph of her taken by Edward Weston and used on the front cover of the book. A photograph she took of her lover, Julio Antonio Mella, heads the first page of the novel, introducing him to us before her words. In the opening lines of the novel, we see Tina not from the outside, but through her own eyes as she apprehensively watches the approach of her lover: "A smile hidden under the brim of his hat draws near. In four long steps he crosses the telegraph office. Tina's sense of oppression diminishes. Two arms which soon will enfold her approach" (9).[2] The focus of the lines is physical: a cinematographic image of the smile, the hat, the arms, the anticipation of the embrace. The narrative voice, though undefined, seems to emanate from the protagonist's body. The narrator draws the reader into Tina to watch and await Julio. The photograph of Julio Antonio directly above the lines invites us to imagine his arms enfolding her. This intimacy creates an identification with the protagonist, the reader feels her anxiety, her need to be held. The reassurance of a mere verbal explanation will not satisfy her.

In these opening chapters there is almost no description of Tina's appearance: no allusion to the color of her eyes, the texture of her skin, the length of her hair. Rather, the narrator builds Tina's physical being partially from within as we learn how the protagonist experiences her body, partially from the photographs included in the text and finally through the eyes of the other characters. The narrator, instead of commenting on the disparity of the height between Tina and Julio in an external description, lets the reader feel this difference as Tina does: "Tina takes four steps for every two of his. . . . Julio slips his arm under her black jacket around her waist. Tina would like to merge herself into his side, for the two of them to become a single aroma in the night. If only she had longer legs, they would walk entwined" (10). The visual image of the two of them walking together assumes secondary importance to the way the protagonist feels as Mella leads her toward the apartment. The longing for Tina's body to fuse with his indicates a desire to immerse her individual being into that of her lover. His death a few lines later ends with violent abruptness the possibility of relying on him for her self-definition.

From the first page of the novel, the narrator stresses the pre-eminence of the corporeal in Tina. Tina's voice, articulated through the narrator, expresses the body as an integral part of the self. When the narration shifts to the subjectivity of other characters, we gain a vision of Tina from the outside that confirms the prominence of the physical in the perception others have of her. After Julio Antonio's assassination, Tina spends days in the courtroom as police, lawyers, judges, journalists, and witnesses ogle her. Luz Ardizana, a friend and fellow Communist, puzzles over the magnetic attraction Tina exercises over the men who cannot take their eyes off her:

[The men in the courtroom] looked her up and down, seeking out her thighs. Tina moved continuously, her body reacted to every question. . . . Her body was more convincing than her testimony; her hands, which always captured the gesture when her voice didn't find the word, suddenly traced a design on her skirt revealing the curves beneath. Luz concluded that Tina captivated the men because they had never seen a woman who was so attuned to her own body, as if she had just made love and the plenitude of her flesh were contagious. (61)[3]

Luz observes that although Tina makes no effort to draw attention to herself, the spontaneous movement of her body with every word, with every thought, draws men to her. Poniatowska's decision to have the narrator look through the eyes of Luz at this moment is very effective. The reader needs an external vision of Tina to understand what is going on in the courtroom, the view of someone with the insight to comprehend the interplay of male and female, Mexican and Italian. Why are the men so stimulated by Tina's presence? What makes a woman dressed in a dark suit so provocative? As Tina's close friend and admirer, Luz may object to the men's conduct, but as a Mexican woman who has grown up in the shadow of *machismo*, she easily sees how the body language of her Italian comrade provokes such a commotion.

The author also plays with the contrasts obvious in the demeanor of the two characters. While Tina embodies female sexuality, Luz emerges as an asexual figure: "From a distance it was easy to take Luz for an adolescent boy. She wore pants, a masculine black jacket, and the nape of her neck, though perhaps a bit more fragile, had the same haircut, the same large ears as a little boy's" (58). This boyish woman accompanies Tina with steadfast devotion to the courtroom every day, she hides the most vicious newspaper accounts of the trial from Tina, she writes and circulates among their women comrades a petition of solidarity.

Luz clearly adores Tina and agonizes over the position in which her friend finds herself: "I have to do something, oh Tina, how I love you, you are everything, my life, my calling" (67). While there is no implication of a sexual liaison between the two women, Luz does replace Julio Antonio as Tina's protector. In the end, however, embarrassed and confused by wild speculations about Tina's sex life accompanied by nude photographs of Tina and Julio on the front pages of the newspapers, Luz sees herself as inadequate to protect her comrade: "Luz wondered what she really knew about her best friend and she was at a loss. Oh Tina! Now what do we do? No one is going to understand you, Julio would find a way to defend you, but alone, without him, you're nothing, a shameless woman. Luz wrung her hands, What shall I do? What can I do?" (72). Still indignant over the treatment of Tina by the press, Luz wrings her hands in frustrated desperation. She sees herself as no match for the male establishment set on condemning Tina for transgressing their rules.

The narrative viewpoint of the novel shifts continually, often ambiguously, without formal demarcation. Poniatowska sometimes starts an episode with a memory or an impression held by someone involved in the drama. For example, one passage starts with the memory of Luz: "Luz Ardizana remembers the first hearing, when they asked Tina how she was walking with Mella down Abraham González Street 'that fatal night'" (60). As the passage evolves, Tina and Quintana reenact the scene just before the murder. The text contains both dialogue and commentary, but Luz is not mentioned again. Thus, it remains unclear how long (or even if) the vision of Luz mediates the narration. Are we seeing the scene as Luz remembers it or "as it happened"?

At other times, a paragraph starts as if the narration represented an impersonal third person, but it becomes clear as the passage goes on that we are reading the thoughts of one of the characters. In the paragraph below, the narrator weighs the pros and cons of the case against Modotti:

The communists accuse Magriñá, he has a criminal record, the Italian woman doesn't. Tina has loose morals, but that is what women of the old world are like. How dearly she's paying for it. And yet, seeing her, she doesn't give the impression of being frivolous. She's getting grey hair, you can see wrinkles around her eyes, she's thin. There's something wrong. It's not good to be a woman, Pino Cámara thinks . . . "Poor woman, they have really destroyed her." (108)

The first mention of Pino Cámara, the judge who eventually clears Tina of all charges in the murder of Mella, comes in the last lines of the paragraph. Nevertheless, viewing the whole paragraph, all the ideas appear to be the thoughts Cámara mulls over in his head. The paragraph ends with a quotation, but grammatically, it could be argued that the entire paragraph should be in quotes. The deliberate lack of quotation marks at the beginning of the passage reinforces the ambiguity of the narrative voice. Who precisely is telling the story?

Through the continual shift in the narrator, Poniatowska achieves an effect similar to that in *La noche de Tlatelolco* (1971) in which she exploits the voices of others (without misrepresenting them) to create a text filled with unresolved opposing views. As in *Tlatelolco*, the narrative inclines the reader toward an interpretation of the events but provides no ultimate, comfortable resolution. All facts are filtered through *someone's* subjectivity. Unmediated truth remains inaccessible. The narrator leaves questions, confusions, and uncertainties open, unresolved. In the scene in which Julio Antonio is shot, Tina does not know whether she calls out or not: "'Julio, Julio,' does she shout, call out, say nothing?" (10). The next day she cannot recall Julio's last words: "She sees Julio's dried blood, she feels Julio's head in her arms, she hears Julio's voice, 'I'm dying for the revolution.' Or was she the one who imagined these words?" (17). Alleged witnesses to the event confront Tina with completely different versions of the incident, but the narrator does not step outside the vision of the various characters to clarify what "really happened." When illuminating Tina through Luz [Light], which Poniatowska frequently does in this part of the novel, she chooses a viewpoint explicitly sympathetic both to Tina and to her predicament, countering the scathing attack the protagonist suffers at the hands of the court and the press. The narrative undoubtedly leans in Tina's favor; still, the continual change in the narrative voice leaves the opposing viewpoints in play. The narrator resists the opportunity to resolve the contradictions through the use of an authoritative, detached commentary. There is no single, irrefutable version of the facts.

There are isolated moments when no individual character in the novel would have the knowledge necessary to make certain statements. For example, the narrator, returning again to the attraction Tina held for men, posits that Communist comrades came to her apartment with the pretext of visiting Julio, but they really wanted to see her: "Tina would never suspect that, if at first they went to see Julio, later they would go to see her" (39). The narrator who speaks, if not omniscient, must at least know what everyone thinks. Neither Tina nor the visitors would have the authority to make such a statement. Interspersed between dialogues and narration that can be tentatively attributed to one character or another, there are passages written in historical or journalistic prose, which give the appearance of objectivity. These passages, detached from the viewpoint of specific characters elusively flow in and out of the rest of the narration. Much of the material covered in these passages would qualify as background (historical and/or biographical) to the action of the novel. Some of it consists of strictly factual material—dates and places of incidents documented in histories—some could be seen as interpretations of events held by groups in the novel or the public at large.[4] Not infrequently, the novel presents opposing versions of the more important events.

The shifting and ambivalent viewpoint of the narrator contributes to the

conditional vision of the self. Tina modifies and changes in different contexts
and from different perspectives. There is a continual play as we view her from
differing distances. The reader witnesses her inner dialogue as well as her
intercourse with other characters, hearing her commentary not only on what
goes on around her, but also the criticism she levels against herself as she
continually transforms and re-evaluates herself. We see her interact with others
and hear their reflections on her behavior. Conflicts and inconsistencies coexist
in the vision that ultimately comes out of the novel. Though we are flooded
with information on Tina, she remains elusive, undefined.

TINA ON TRIAL: THE SELF IN PROCESS

In moments of crisis, the driving forces of the self, which are sometimes
obscured by the routines of daily life, come to the fore and make themselves
visible. The death of Mella throws Tina's equilibrium completely off balance.
Poniatowska takes a close look at the protagonist under the acute strain of this
situation. She explores the complex interplay of inner and outer tensions that
compel Tina to act as she does as she re-defines herself and her role in the
absence of Mella. We see the pain and suffering that accompany the evolution
of the self. Hesitation and uncertainty take their place along side of strength
and endurance. Tina strikes us as intensely human in this moment of great loss.
Engulfed in total emotional turmoil, Tina makes a supreme effort to appear
stoically in control. She undergoes painful scrutiny, which brings into question
her lifestyle and, indeed, her very being.

Julia Kristeva, in her study of the human subject, offers a number of insights that shed light on the process of self-definition central to *Tinísima*. Following theories of Bakhtin, Kristeva looks at the subject as it is constituted in
language.[5] For her, the subject results from the dialogue between two basic
dimensions, the symbolic and the semiotic.[6] The semiotic comprises the uname-
able drives of the body, the unconscious, the intuitive, the irrational. Heterogeneous to signification, the semiotic threatens the symbolic order (*Desire in
Language* 133). The disruption of the symbolic by the semiotic destabilizes
meaning and, with it, the subject. The resulting subject is what Kristeva refers
to as "*le sujet en procès*": "'Process' in the sense of process but also in the
sense of legal proceeding where the subject is committed to trial, because our
identities in life are constantly called into question, brought to trial, overruled"
("A Question of Subjectivity" 128–129). Thus at the root of the self lies a
problematic division between two opposing forces with which the subject must
constantly contend in an effort to establish a precarious balance. For Kristeva
the joy of living (*jouissance*) ensues from the challenge of this vital struggle.[7]

Kristeva proposes that poetic language embodies the contradictions and
tensions inherent in the divided self: "Art—this semiotization of the symbolic—thus represents the flow of *jouissance* into language. . . . In cracking the
socio-symbolic order, splitting it open, changing vocabulary, syntax, the word

itself, and releasing from beneath them the drives borne by vocalic or kinetic differences, *jouissance* works its way into the social and symbolic" (*Revolution in Poetic Language* 79–80). Literature "becomes the very place where social code is destroyed and renewed" (*Desire* 132), a safe outlet for the rupture of the symbolic by the semiotic. It functions as a forum where author and reader can experience the implications of this division both in the social realm and in the individual subject. Reading *Tinísima*—the first part in particular—alongside this theory could be viewed as an experiment in *jouissance*.

If the "subject in process" contains within it the idea of the subject on trial, then the courtroom where Tina was literally put on trial seems a particularly appropriate place to start exploring the interaction of conflicting forces that constitute her identity. Tina stands judged before the public. Though the death of Mella precipitates incredible emotional upheaval in the protagonist, she refuses to expose her feelings to those who scrutinize her every move: "She makes an effort to keep her emotion from showing, but she lights one cigarette after another. She smokes, devoured by the images of Julio that the testimony evokes" (59). To all outward appearances, Tina remains firmly in control. Many even consider her composure unnatural under the circumstances, condemning her as cold and unfeeling. Yet the cigarette is a telltale sign of inner turmoil which the narrator will use repeatedly as the novel progresses.

In her apartment at Abraham González where she is kept under house arrest during the judicial proceedings, Tina suffers from terrifying nightmares. On awakening she grasps a cigarette battling to save herself from the undertow of the dream world: "She comes back from the depths gasping, her chest in pain and her head ready to explode. Her trembling hands light a cigarette; the water tries to drag her into another nightmare; Tina grasps the cigarette hard between her lips and blows the smoke out her nose so that the sea cannot enter her mouth" (105). Here, as in the courtroom, the cigarette, like a lifesaver thrown to a drowning victim, gives her something to clasp in her struggle to vanquish the forces of the subconscious and re-enter the world of reason.[8]

The text shifts between the waking world and the world of nightmare without transition, obscuring the objective sequence of events. Tina dwells on certain incidents, returning to them over and over. Memory colors the past with foreboding and regret, as her mind repeatedly returns to the scene of Mella's death. Her days are filled with repetitive and contradictory testimony in court; her nights overflow with dreams that symbolically re-enact the murder. The disjunctures in the temporal sequence of the narration reveal the conflict between the conscious imposition of order on the self (the symbolic) and the underlying structures of her being (the semiotic) that resist the objective construct of time.[9]

The protagonist of the novel exists between these two modalities of time. Corresponding to the symbolic, we have the time of history. The clock objectively measures time into segments—hours, minutes, seconds, whose duration is indistinguishable from other hours, minutes, and seconds. The days of the calendar pass from the future to the present to the past in infinite progression along a continually unfolding linear projection. On the other hand, the semiotic coincides with a more intimate perception of time, what Kristeva refers to as "women's time." For Kristeva, women experience time as cyclical (the repetitions of the rhythms of nature) and monumental, a "massive presence . . . without cleavage or escape" ("Women's Time" 472). Time is perceived as both discontinuous and simultaneous; events do not conform to the uniformity of the calendar, but respond to the resurgence of biological rhythms and mythic timelessness. Tina, like the female subject Kristeva describes, experiences time as the moment of the pulse beat, the nights and days of sleep and awakening, the months of the menstrual cycle, the years of aging that eventually lead to her death. Tina perceives time as a continuum punctuated by unique moments, the "monuments" that mark her life, yet, as a member of Western society, she is inevitably circumscribed by historical time as well.

The narration of the novel reproduces the problematic interrelation between these two conceptions of time. Reflecting the subjectivity of the protagonist, the narrative revolves around the vertical axis of the self, sometimes prolonging, sometimes compressing segments of time. The text retrogresses, repeats, and skips around, subverting the objective progression of events in the protagonist's life. At the same time, all entries in the novel are dated, a constant reminder of the objective framework within which the subject operates. The narration alternates between a sequential unfolding of events and the discontinuity of the protagonist's consciousness, which follows an erratic path of associations. The recurrent strands of linear narration do not confine or control the movement of memory, dreams, emotion. This split in the narration corresponds to the condition of the protagonist balanced on a precipice between rational and irrational aspects of the self.

The first paragraph of the January 15th entry (46) illustrates this liquidity between dream and reality, memory and perception, past and present. Tina closes her eyes as the paragraph starts, removing herself (and the reader) from the temporal and spatial framework of the outside reality that surrounds her. It remains unclear in the scene that follows whether Tina sits in the courtroom as her mind wanders off into a nightmare, or if indeed she sleeps and dreams of the courtroom while actually in her apartment. Her inner chronology is ruled not by the conscious, theoretical construct of the calendar, but by involuntary memory transformed by emotion, sensory stimulation, and the surrealistic imagery of dreams. Water immerses Tina and removes her from the tangible space that surrounds her. Caught in the flow of recurrent nightmares that plague her life, Tina returns to January 10th, re-enacting an oneiric version of the murder of Mella. An overwhelming sense of impotence replaces the confusion that reigned in the original murder scene:

She closes her eyes. The water engulfs her, she sinks, drifting out to sea; near the corner of Morelos and Abraham González, the mercenary hidden behind the hedge aims his weapon at Mella; one bullet in his back, the other in his elbow. A current of icy water pulls at Tina, it drags her further in. . . . Tina screams help, help, but only air bubbles come out of her mouth. "No one hears me, no one understands me." Once again she hears, "Pepe Magriñá is behind this." (46)

In the dream ambiance, Tina functions both as participant and witness. She sees herself, yet has no control over her actions. Lost in the current of the swirling water, Tina looks on helplessly as the assassin shoots Julio. She cannot even cry out for help: the water swallows her voice and transforms it into inaudible bubbles. Although she now understands what is happening, the icy waters of the subconscious have stripped her of all power of agency, leaving behind only the cold chill of death and despair.

In mid-sentence, the scene reverts to the inquest, five days later. Tina sees Magriñá enter the courtroom like an enormous, gleaming water snake, ready to attack her. Julio's accusation "Pepe Magriñá is behind this" (46) and the memory of Magriñá's horrible voice on the telephone precede his words in court. Tina calls up Julio's words like an incantation to ward off the evil sea serpent, Magriñá, but to no avail. His protruding eyes pierce her as he condemns her actions the night of the murder. His criticism reinforces the misgivings she already felt: her confusion over what actually transpired, her feelings of guilt for surviving when the one she loved fell at her side.

With Magriñá's accusation, the text drifts out of the nightmare and into Tina's inner dialogue of self-recrimination. Suddenly the scene shifts back to the courtroom, Magriñá transformed from a loathsome water snake to a "pillar of society": "In the courtroom, Magriñá, dressed in a navy blue flannel suit, with his hair slicked back with pomade, makes a good impression. He looks prosperous; he has the attributes of decency, white handkerchief in his breast pocket, polished shoes, a discreet tie. His friends are the ambassador, the businessman, the family man" (46). Magriñá's appearance provides him a mask of respectability that associates him with decency, prosperity, law and order. The irony, of course, is that he will eventually be indicted for his part in Mella's assassination, while Tina is absolved of all guilt. The courtroom, center of the patriarchal establishment, stands in judgment of Tina, a woman who has transgressed the rules of propriety, an artist and "adventuress" who cohabited with the deceased, a married man.

The very language of the court stifles Tina, simplifying the complexities of the situation, masking ambiguities with false clarity, denying the validity of her emotions in the search for the "truth." When initially questioned by the police, she falsified her identity, giving a bogus name, address, and profession. She later asserted she did so out of fear that the adverse publicity over the murder could damage her professional reputation. Though Tina decides to cooperate fully with the murder investigation, there remains an uncomfortable friction between her and court officials. Her way of expressing herself does not conform to the detached, impersonal, rational discourse of the legal system. She recoils upon hearing her own words translated into the official record: "In the courtroom, Tina listens to the deposition she made at the Red Cross . . . and her words sound cruelly impersonal: 'at twenty-one hours Mella arrived and, accompanied by the witness, went by foot toward Balderas.'" (48).

Tina becomes the witness, literally, *la que habla,* "the one who speaks." The translation of her words into indirect discourse puts a further barrier between her and her deposition. Stripped of all personal attributes, the arid language of the discourse divests the crisis of emotion. The dry facts fail to convey the sheer terror of the moment, the horror and confusion that gripped Tina as she realized what was happening. Her identity and that of Mella have been reduced to empty words, witness/suspect and victim at the intersection of Morelos and Abraham González. Again, Tina finds herself caught between the turmoil of her feelings and the dispassionate language of the court that so inadequately expresses her experience.[10]

The courtroom, its languages, and procedures represent the public arena, the social system, the patriarchal power structure, the bright light of reason, the sober dictates of the law. The bedroom filters the outside light, bringing it into an intimate space, a place designed to service the body, a place of emotion, sexuality, the playfulness of nudity, the eruption of the irrational, dark nightmares punctuated with screams. The text makes visible the balancing act of the self as Tina vacillates between these two spaces: She sits in the courtroom confronted by testimony about her sex life, she lies in bed at home dreaming of the inquisition of the courtroom. In order to exist she must bridge the gap between the conflicting realms, not in an act of transcendence, but rather through an uneasy integration of opposing forces that continually threatens to collapse. *Jouissance* for Tina entails living with these unresolved, internal divisions. Her life cannot ultimately reconcile the contradictions of the self, she must instead recognize her own provisional, contingent nature.

Having textually created Tina as a subject in process in the first part of the novel, the narrator changes gears in the ensuing chapters, reverting to a traditional humanistic approach to biography. The narrative fictionalizes the provisional and changing self into a coherent identity, an individual set of realizing her potential. The interplay of contrasting approaches to feminine identity within the confines of the novel adds to the rich texture, complexity, and ambivalence of Poniatowska's *Tinísima.*

NOTES

1. The elusive identity Poniatowska puts forward through her protagonist coincides with many contemporary views of subjectivity. For example, in *Feminist Studies/Critical Studies,* Teresa de Lauretis explores the concept of consciousness not as a fixed identity but as the term of a process: "In this perspective, the very notion of identity undergoes a shift: identity is not the goal but rather the point of departure of the process of self-consciousness, a process by which one begins to know that and how the personal is political, that and how the subject is specifically and materially en-gendered in its social conditions and possibilities of existence" (8–9). Many others, Sidonie Smith and Julia

Kristeva to name just two, put forward similar views of subjectivity.

2. All translations are mine. (Editor's note: an English translation of *Tinísima* was published in late 1996.)

3. Sidonie Smith addresses the abhorrence felt toward female independence in the patriarchal society: "To the extent that woman represses the body, erasing her sexual desire and individual identity while embracing encumbering identities in service to family, community, and country, she positions herself as a proper lady who surmounts her negative identification with the body through selflessness. To the degree that woman contests such roles and postures by pursuing her own desire and independence from men, she becomes a cultural grotesque" (*Subjectivity, Identity, and the Body* 16).

4. The "disembodied" parts of the narrative tend to be the least interesting in the novel. These frequent digressions interrupt the flow of the novel with a plethora of historical details that often add little or nothing to the construction of the protagonist and discourage the reader.

5. David Crownfield, in the introduction to *Body/Text in Julia Kristeva*, discusses Bakhtin's view of the primacy of language in the construction of the subject: "Bakhtin held that the human subject is not an original and autonomous entity, but is constituted socially and above all by language" (x). As Catherine Belsey puts it: "The subject speaks, but only insofar as language permits the production of meaning, including the meaning of the subject's own identity, subjectivity itself. 'Man speaks, then, but it is because the symbol has made him man'" (131).

6. Kristeva discusses these two opposing aspects of language, the one reflecting rhythms, intonations, the other tied to meaning: referential and rational. The semiotic, both logically and chronologically prior to the symbolic, "takes us back to the pre-linguistic states of childhood" ("A Question of Subjectivity" 129). The symbolic is the "inevitable attribute of meaning, sign, and the signified object for the consciousness of Husserl's transcendental ego. Language as social practice necessarily presupposes these two dispositions, though combined in different ways to constitute *types of discourse*, types of signifying practices" (*Desire in Language* 134).

7. In his introduction to *Desire in Language*, Leon S. Roudiez points out that Kristeva uses the term *jouissance* essentially the same way as Lacan. For both, "'*jouissance*' is sexual, spiritual, physical, conceptual at one and the same time" (16). For an excellent discussion of *jouissance*, see Jean Graybeal's article, "Joying in the Truth of Self-Division."

8. Kristeva suggests that to fall out of the balance between the two aspects of language leads to disaster. If we lean too far toward the "symbolic," "the overly constraining and reductive meaning of a language made up of universals causes us to suffer, the call of the unnameable . . . issuing from those borders where signification vanishes, hurls us into the void of a psychosis" (*Desire in Language* x).

9. For Sidonie Smith such disruptions typify the feminine text: "And yet an unspoken presence, that feminine unconscious repressed by the masculine logos, always threatens to disrupt the narrative order and to destabilize the fiction of identity the autobiographer inscribes" (*A Poetics of Women's Autobiography* 40).

10. In her interview with Susan Sellers, Kristeva addresses the alienation many of her female patients sense with respect to language: "On the one hand, many women . . . complain that they experience language as something secondary, cold, foreign to their lives. To their passion. To their suffering. To their desire. As if language were a foreign body. And when they say this we are often given the impression that what

they question is language as a logical exercise" ("A Question of Subjectivity" 131).

REFERENCES

Belsey, Catherine. *Critical Practice*. New York: Methuen, 1980.

Crownfield, David R., ed. *Body/Text in Julia Kristeva*. Albany: State U of New York P, 1992.

De Lauretis, Teresa. "Feminist Studies/Critical Studies: Issues, Terms, Contexts." *Feminist Studies/Critical Studies*. Ed. Teresa De Lauretis. Bloomington: Indiana UP, 1986.

Graybeal, Jean. "Joying in the Truth of Self-Division." *Body/Text in Julia Kristeva*. Ed. David R. Crownfield. Albany: State U of New York P, 1992. 129–138.

Kristeva, Julia. *Desire in Language: A Semiotic Approach to Literature and Art*. Ed. Leon S. Roudiez. Trans. Thomas Gora, Alice Jardine, Leon S. Roudiez. New York: Columbia UP, 1980.

———. "A Question of Subjectivity: an Interview with Susan Sellers." *Modern Literary Theory: A Reader*. Eds. Philip Rice and Patricia Waugh. London: Edward Arnold, 1989. 128–134.

———. *Revolution in Poetic Language*. Trans. Margaret Waller. New York: Columbia UP, 1984.

———. "Women's Time." *Critical Theory Since 1965*. Eds. Hazard Adams and Leroy Searle. Trans. Alice Jardine and Harry Blake. Tallahassee: Florida State UP, 1986. 471–485.

Poniatowska, Elena. *La noche de Tlatelolco: Testimonios de historia oral*. Mexico: Era, 1971.

———. *Tinísima*. Mexico: Era, 1992.

———. *Tinísima*. Trans. Katherine Silver. New York: Farrar, Straus, Giroux, 1996.

Smith, Sidonie. *A Poetics of Women's Autobiography: Marginality and the Fictions of Self-Representation*. Bloomington: Indiana UP, 1987.

———. *Subjectivity, Identity, and the Body: Women's Autobiographical Practices in the Twentieth Century*. Indianapolis: Indiana UP, 1993.

7

HISTORIOGRAPHIC METAFICTION OR THE REWRITING OF HISTORY IN *SON VACAS, SOMOS PUERCOS*

Cynthia M. Tompkins

Alexandre Olivier Exquemelin's (1645–1707) *De Americaensche Zeerovers* was published in Amsterdam in 1678. Prompt translation into Spanish in 1681 and English in 1684 attests to the success of the Dutch text. Yet, as William Swan Stallybras—editor of the modernized English version—notes, the discrepancies between the translations arise from the emphasis given to the respective national heroes (E v).[1] Thus, in addition to the Preface from the Dutch Publisher (v–vii), a Note from the Translator (viii–x) and a verse Description of the Islands of the Atlantic and America by Capitán Don Miguel de Barrios (xi–xxiv), Alonso de Buena-Maison's translation *Piratas de la América: y Luz a la Defensa de las Costas de las Indias Occidentales* includes an account of Captain Morgan's defeat by Don Juan Pérez de Guzmán and a transcription of a letter he received from the Spanish Admiral Don Alonso de Campo y Espinosa (Chapters IV and VII of Part Two, respectively). On the other hand, the 1924 rendition of *The Buccaneers of America*, based on the second edition of the English translation published by William Crooke in 1684, adds three chapters to Part Three, namely Chapter X, on the encounter between the Count of Estres, a French admiral, and the Dutch vice-admiral, Heer Jacob Hinkes, and Chapters XI and XII on the adventures of Captains Cook and Sharp, respectively, in addition to Part Four, consisting of twenty-five chapters based on the diary of English buccaneer Basil Ringrose.

Intertextuality allows us to view Carmen Boullosa's *Son vacas, somos puercos* (*They're Cattle, We're Swine*, 1991) as a paradigmatic case of historiographic metafiction insofar as Boullosa simultaneously inscribes and subverts Exquemelin's text through condensation, aporias, and the continued shifting of "Otherness." Linda Hutcheon argues that simultaneous inscription and subversion is characteristic of postmodern intertextuality: "[It] directly confronts the past of literature—and of historiography, for it too derives from other texts (documents). It uses and abuses those intertextual echoes, inscribing their powerful allusions and then subverting that power through irony" (118). Irony, however, is crucial since "there is always a paradox at the heart of that 'post': irony does indeed mark the difference from the past, but the intertextual echoing simultaneously works to affirm—textually and hermeneutically—the connection with the past" (125). Along these lines, Boullosa's parodic recreation refutes the egalitarian nature of the filibuster's brotherhood, emphasizing its intrinsic racism and sexism by reinscribing the "Other(s)"—African slaves, aborigines, and women—at the center of the narrative.

From a formal standpoint, Boullosa's text reproduces the asymmetry of the original. Exquemelin's tripartite structure: seven chapters in Parts One and Two respectively, and ten in Part Three, is mirrored by Boullosa's six chapters in Part One and fourteen in Part Two. Likewise, Boullosa maintains the focus on a national figure; yet while Exquemelin devotes ten of the twenty-four chapters to Morgan's exploits (Chapters IV–VII of Part Two and I–VI of Part Three), Boullosa sets aside twelve of the twenty chapters (or fourteen in Part Two) to develop the adventures of Nau, L'Olonnais. Boullosa condenses the epic compilation of exploits of the preceding texts into thematic kernels arrived at either through paradigmatic cases or through the deployment of rhetorical devices. Paradigmatic cases, in turn, encompass both experiences common to all buccaneers and figures of excess, which appear to subsume all others of their kind. The former, semantic kernels presented as "rites of passage," include departure in the service of the West India Company of France (E 9–13; B 16–29; B-M 1–3), followed by an intense period of apprenticeship (matelot slavery), which may incorporate repeated sales: The narrator is sold twice (E & B-M Chapter II, Part One; B 34, 45). Attacks on Spanish ships and towns (E & B-M Chapters I–III Part Two; B Chapters IV–IX, Part Two) allow for kidnapping, which may not necessarily end in ransom (E 98; B-M 81; B 101). Pillaging includes raping the enemies's women, who pay dearly for the pirates' (re)assertion of masculinity by being henceforth barred from the marriage circuit (B 106). Dissolute behavior is normative. Carousing (B 69; B-M 57; E 73) and gambling take place in the bordellos of Port Royal: "Such of these Pirates are found who will spend 2 or 3 thousand pieces-of-eight in one night, [*with which they could live like gentlemen for years], not leaving themselves peradventure a good shirt to wear on their backs in the morning" (B 69; E 74–75; [*missing in B-M 59 & E 75]).[2] Dissipation, ironically, propels them into action (B 118). Figures of excess, assumed to subsume all others of their kind, also result in thematic condensation. The gang rape of mother and daughter in the episode of the "Marquesa de la Poza Rica" constitutes a major lesson against bribery. In attempting to trade honor for riches, the women are transformed "from prudes to whores and from whores into mangled flesh" (B 109).[3] Nonetheless, in spite of their state—"flesh either bleeding or exposed, with sores in their privy parts and the surrounding area" (B 109)—one of them challenges: "Enjoy me, pirate!" (B 109). Furthermore, their choosing to burn to death upon the pirates' exit implies a symbolic restoration of honor. Along these lines discussion of the pleasure resulting from murdering the (female) partner during intercourse (B 119) is almost anticlimactic. Other than rape, figures of excess include torturing the body beyond recognition, "What my hands held had been a head and a body, the utterly wounded shapeless mass had been flogged and beaten, cut up and burned. I tried to give it something to drink but there were no lips" (B 127). The horror includes chopping a prisoner up (B 97; E 94; B-M 76), carving a guide's heart out while alive (B 97; E 94; B-M 76) and starving prisoners to death (E 97; B-M 80; B 100–101).[4] In striving for condensation, Boullosa complements thematic kernels and figures of excess with rhetorical devices such as hyperbole, metonymy, intertextuality and self-reflexivity. Rhetorical questions assert omniscience[5] as they lead to hyperbolic recapitulations (B 93; E 85–86; B-M 66–67) and generalizations such as: "Seen it? I have seen it all. Heard it? I have heard it all" (B 13). Hyperbole leads to condensation via magical realism when the galley slaves of a Spanish vessel take advantage of the confusion arising from the pirates' attack, "[T]hough chained, they passed the officer who had mistreated them till recently from one to another, chewing him up bite by bite, till all that was left of him, after that horrendous lament ended, were lifeless bones" (B 123). By its very nature, metonymy stresses condensation: "I was no one but the fist brandishing the blood-stained sword, the aim-taking eye, or the finger depressing the trigger" (B 106). Likewise, "mirroring" falls into this category insofar as the six remaining prisoners "shadow" Negro Miel as if they were one: "the seven of us kneeled down to examine the wound. We seven got closer . . . so that the chain would allow my hands to retrieve some powder from the leather band. . . . Once again, we seven leaned toward the one with the boot . . . so that I could apply the powder. Then we got up, so that the wound would be in the open air" (B 39–40). In spite of the complexity of the intertextual web, self-reflexive assertions purportedly made by historical characters lead to condensation by stressing the implicit similarities: "Henry Morgan obliged us (the editor and me) to add the following paragraph; 'Exquemelin is mistaken concerning the origins of Sir Henry Morgan. . . . He is the son of a gentleman of ancient lineage, from the county of Monmouth, and he has never served anyone but His Majesty, the King of England'" (B 15).[6]

While Boullosa's data on the contractual obligations of the crew echoes Exquemelin (B 77; E 60–61; B-M 48), self-reflexive intratextual allusions stress condensation: "It is not an easy task . . . to fix images and sounds in the order they took place, memory enjoys mocking the tyranny of time. But, even if [the images] jump at us at random . . . I shall try to restrain myself to go back to the beginning of the story" (B 15–16).[7] Even if articulated in magical realist terms, intratextuality necessarily stresses condensation: "During our failed expedition, there was a point in which the memories with which Negro Miel peopled the gloom of his blindness came out of the blue. . . . Even now, grateful for the blindness the passing of centuries granted me, Negro Miel lives where the Earth achieves perfection" (B 132).[8]

By focusing the text on the experiences of the narrator, Boullosa enhances condensation. Initially, generic expectations point at the picaresque, "My first position had been that of a servant, a servant of a servant to be more accurate, but it didn't last because I was lucky enough to run into the priest that. . . " (B 17). The narrator's apparent development allows us to recast the work as a *bildungsroman*, especially considering conventions such as that of geographic distancing paralleling self-discovery, "Smeeks devotes the first stretch of the trip . . . to try to reach into himself: a few afternoons ago, he was a thirteen-year-old boy wandering aimlessly around Flanders" (B 16).[9]

Though the restricted perspective of Boullosa's first-person narrator creates the illusion of a voice immersed in the action, realism is put under erasure[10] by having the narrator fluctuate between a number of subject positions, namely: "Oexmelin," "Esquemelin," "Alejandro Oliverio Esquemelin," "Jean Smeeks," and "El Trepanador" (B 13). Perhaps Boullosa's main accomplishment is the deployment of aporias—unresolvable paradoxes—arising from the creation of a fantasmatic narrator slipping between different subject positions, coupled with an emphasis on the body as the measure of all things, in turn put under erasure by being subjected to unimaginable torment: torture, rape, cannibalization. In terms of the initial paradox, while defined by roles, the narrator's subject positions appear to be interchangeable:

When I began to tell my tale, I stated I had the eyes and ears of Smeeks, The Trepanator or Exquemelin, according to the name I chose for myself or the one others gave me. In keeping with the order of that story, I have already been Smeeks, the ceremony [of initiation into the Brotherhood] has taken place, and I think I have always been Exquemelin, because he is the one who usually tells my story, so as not to call attention on to Smeeks. (B 93)

The fluid transition between subject positions subsumes, thereby undercuts, dichotomies such as victim/victimizer, active/passive: "Even though I was not the one who shot and brandished the sword, I was the bodies they killed . . . for the pleasure of watching them die . . . and I was the bodies I'd healed" (B 106). Boullosa subverts realism by undermining the anchorage provided by time and place, "Let's return to Europe, from where I now tell (if I still have a location) these stories" (B 118), or "Scribbling to preserve the memory of Negro Miel and in spite of the hundreds of years elapsed since I was a filibuster risking my life in defense of the Brotherhood, I'm still moved (in memory) by the dream of the Brotherhood of the Coast" (B 80).[11] In addition, the constant interplay between presence and absence challenges the notion of the unified subject:

Didn't my father figures Negro Miel and Pineau teach me secrets of nobility and grandeur? I was a Brother at last. . . . No, I could not reconstruct myself. But I felt such satisfaction that my body was almost dulled by the taste for adventure, the pleasure of the filibuster. Had I lost myself? In asking myself that question I knew I had lost my body, I had only been a slave, a matelot, and being that no longer, I was a slave who had lost his body. (B 106)

The transition between subject positions is complemented by the paradox resulting from the conjunction of the body as the site of subjectivity and its erasure by being subjected to unimaginably horrendous acts. The tale about L'Olonnais's fate is rendered by a disembodied voice (E 116; B-M 98; B 131):[12]

I was not burned in one piece: I was roasted by parts, first a limb, then another and yet another . . . I was still alive as I watched how the children devoured parts of my body . . . till the loss of blood made me lose consciousness and I gave up the ghost as they stuck a pole up my trunk to roast what remained of it together with my head. I didn't feel the flames. I never found out how the ceremony in which the "Darien" Indians feasted on my body ended. (B 131)[13]

On the other hand, self-reflexive comments on the creative process incorporate direct addresses to the fantasmatic body of the implied reader: "Had it not been for the warm company of your body, I wouldn't have been able to traverse the story . . . because I abandon myself, I let go, as I see your body approaching mine" (B 65). Finally, by arguing, "flesh reveals what neither sight nor reason can glean" (B 65), the body is privileged with a kind of knowledge that cannot be grasped rationally. Ironically, the pendulum then swings back, positing discourse as the site of "reality": "This story is all I have to believe myself true" (B 65). Aporia also arises from breaking the law of noncontradiction by supporting the co-existence of parallel narrative strands. The interpolated story of "Negro Piedra" (B 64), a parodic rendition based on the protagonic figure of Negro Miel, is explained away metaphorically on the basis of divergent hermeneutical approaches. The point is illustrated by noting how different the bordello would look if we replaced the "sumptuous" effect of the horizontal gaze with a vertical sweep, thus highlighting "dead flies, dirt, decay and sadness" (B 64–65).

In addition to condensation and the above aporias, the parodic value of Boullosa's text stems from the fluid construction and displacement of "othering," which culminates in the rewriting of history by placing African slaves, natives, and women at its center. Initially, "othering"[14] is articulated oppositionally by a series of interrelated terms: France vs. Spain; "Buccaneers" vs. The West India Company of France; *Matelots* vs. Owners; Buccaneers vs. Women; Pirates vs. Spanish settlers; Pirates vs. Indigenous Peoples.[15] The mere presence of the buccaneers turns them into insurgents, since navigation in the Caribbean was restricted to Spaniards; if not by birth, then, by having been granted legal consent from the Spanish throne (Mota 97–98). Thus, Spain is the primordial, unnamed "other." On the other hand, as transpires from the physical description, Tortuga itself is "othered":

The nature of Tortuga is so peculiar that the transluscent waters of those seas lose transparency upon approaching her coasts, which . . . leads one to believe that the harshness of the climate of the island is such that it makes them boil, since they do not cool the scorching air, likewise, the exposed roots of the trees refuse to fit into the crevices of the rocks, as if the harshness of the climate prevented them from doing so. . . . Boiled, burned, baked by its climate, Tortuga transformed whomsoever approached her. (B 32)

Geography predetermines cultural production: "The physical appearance of Tortuga was odd, arrhythmic as the songs I would hear during the night: insane, tormented rhythms, rhythms I would have never imagined" (B 31–32). The opposition between "*vacas*" [cattle] and "*puercos*" [swine] is traced back to the primitive hunters's preference for cattle or boars (B-M 33; Mota 98). "Buccaneer" lifestyle was communal; cabins and resources were freely shared (Mota 99), so the rebellion against the monopoly of the West India Company of France was inevitable. In reprisal for the destruction of a budding tobacco plantation, hunters, planters, and pirates—implicitly identified as "*puercos*" [swine]—write a gory ultimatum with the watchman's limbs prior to attacking the armed forces sent in by the company (B 33).[16] In Boullosa's text, the communal spirit of the Brotherhood is undermined by the implicit exploitation of providers of alcohol, women and gambling (B 119).[17] Benazet usurps land and labor to sell tobacco "as if it were gold" (B 115). He also profits from gambling: "As neither gaming is regulated nor are there taxes levied in Tortuga, he pays the governor a fixed rate and amasses a fortune" (B 114). By having the governor purchase a shipload of cacao nuts for a fraction (one-twentieth) of its price, Boullosa suggests both the collusion of the administration and the systematic nature of exploitation (B 117).

Boullosa's treatment of the "Indios Bravos" and "Negro Miel" may be defined as postmodern in that it inscribes and subverts the tradition of Latin American critical discourse. According to Ángel Rama, since the eighteenth century, *criollo* [creole] literary struggle toward independence focused on "two recurrent topics—the helpless Indian, the afflicted African—to deploy them rhetorically in listing the affronts of the colonizers, using [these topics] as a pretense to reclaim their own rights" (12, my translation). By reclaiming these figures, Boullosa reinscribes the Latin American critical tradition; however, she also simultaneously subverts it by having them share it with women, the silenced other of the Dutch text.

Boullosa's departure from the Dutch is particularly noticeable in the creation of Negro Miel, whose only antecedent is the black henchman sent in with the fleet with which the governor of Cuba attempted to put an end to L'Olonnais (E 85; B 94; B-M 66). Negro Miel's origin is utopic:

I was born in a place where the earth achieves perfection. The weather is perfect: neither heat nor cold incite one to cover up because the air wraps up the skin delicately. There are prodigious and abundant fruits, and all plants, without exception, are edible from the root to the flower. . . . Water runs in fresh rivulets. Since childhood, my father, my mother, and her siblings taught me the secrets of nature, which spirits hid in each shape and how to invoke them to heal the sick, to cure wounds, and to make sadness disappear. (B 37)

In keeping with literary conventions, Negro Miel is a blind sage; however, he attributes the condition to exile: "I left my land believing I would return, as all of my people had, never imagining I would be plucked away forever from my beloved valley. That's why Negro Miel . . . prefers to keep his eyesight for his memories, for what his eyes could not see even if they were open" (B 37). In the Western intellectual tradition, silence precludes defining the "other," hence reproducing clichés ascribed to the "dark continent." Negro Miel speaks French to preserve his native language, which is transformed into a protective power (B 37). Negro Miel embodies multiple "otherings." The leather band of herbs sewn onto this chest "others" him from members of the community to which he is apprenticed. When the community is defeated, the sign is over-looked, and the prisoners are sold to the British. When they are overtaken by French pirates, Negro Miel's ability to heal "others" him from the slaves. According to the buccaneers, his literacy "others" him from his race (B 37–40).

As a Frenchman, Pineau is othered by religion (Huguenot). Yet the protagonist's father figures share the following similarities: They devote them-selves to healing; they cherish the communal heritage of the buccaneers; their fatherly roles do not preclude sexuality; they teach the narrator their trade, and they are murdered for opposing the interests of the Company. Their legacy is passed on to the narrator: "If I managed to live with them it was because I knew that they inherited a great dream that allowed men to grab what did not legitimately belong to anyone and because the ripples of this dream, bathed alternately in violence or in alcohol, gave me something no other lifestyle would" (B 138).

It is, perhaps, in Boullosa's treatment of the "noble savage" that *Son vacas* differs the most from the Dutch text, since Exquemelin fully justifies the use of wild dogs to exterminate the natives (E 41; B 48; B-M 30):

Perceiving the dominion of the Spaniards laid a great restriction upon their lazy and brutish customs, they conceived an incredible odium against them, such as never was to be reconciled. But more especially, because they saw them take possession of their kingdoms and dominions. Hereupon they made against them all the resistance they were capable of, opposing everywhere their designs to the utmost of their power, until that the Spaniards, finding themselves to be cruelly hated by those Indians, and nowhere secure from their treacheries, resolved to extirpate and ruin them every one; especially seeing that they could neither tame them by the civilities of their customs, nor conquer them by the sword. (E 41; B-M 30)

Exquemelin's descriptions of indigenous peoples appear to waver between the quasi-ethnographic accounts of the inhabitants of Honduras and Yucatán (E 109–

110; B-M 90–92) and the ethnocentric reports about the natives of the "Pertas" islands:

[They] are properly savages, as not having at any time known or conversed with any civil people. . . . They are tall in stature and very nimble in running, which they perform almost as fast as horses. . . . [T]hey use no other arms than such as are made of wood. . . . They have neither bows nor arrows among them . . . but their common weapon is a sort of lances. . . . Some are of the opinion that these Indians eat human flesh. (E 113–114; B-M 95–96)[18]

In Boullosa's text, as traditional enemies of the Spaniards, the "bravos"[19] considered short-lived strategic alliances with the pirates. They are instrumental in the fall of Maracaibo (B 85). Among the numerous incidents that attest to their bravery (B 86–87), perhaps the most dramatic is the challenging attitude of the "bravo" who spits at L'Olonnais after his heart is torn out (B 100). Furthermore, his people are massacred for contesting L'Olonnais's action: "We finished them all off. And their women. The children wailed at home, and they hurled sticks and stones at us as they saw us go by, not for nothing are they called 'bravos,' and they would have resisted us courageously, had [we not burned their] weapons" (B 104).

In a seminal special issue on representation of the postcolonial female other titled "The Inappropriate/d Other" (1986–1987)—in which the term "other" is under erasure—guest editor Trinh Minh-Ha argues against facile binary polarities: "The Other of the West, the Other of man: one is never installed within marginality, one never dwells outside it" (3), noting that the multiplicity of levels of difference (political, economic, ethnic/racial, gendered, religious) allows for multilayered interconnected configurations that are always already in flux: "Difference in this context undermines opposition as well as separatism. Neither a claim for special treatment, nor a return to an authentic core (the 'unspoiled' Real Other), it acknowledges in each of its moves, the coming together and the drifting apart both within and between identity/ies" (3). The silencing of women in Exquemlin's text suggests they constitute the most subversive level of "otherness." In contradistinction, early on, Boullosa places them at the center of the text. The episode of the cross-dressed female sailor (B 18–22) may be read as an allusion to famous female pirates such as Anne Bonny and Mary Read (B 121).[20] Moreover, by allowing us to tease out the multiplicity of levels in which the term "woman" is deployed, Boullosa's version dramatizes the notion of multiple subject positions. Initially, "woman" connotates routine: "I realized I had been living as a woman since I'd left Europe, repeating the routine of the same sheltered corner to sleep in, and doing so almost at the same time day after day. So many people live like women, locked behind the walls of a convent, barracks, a house, or a workshop" (B 79).[21] Women are banished from Tortuga to prevent rivalries not only because they are considered "non-transferable piece[s] of property," but because "they in turn [would want] their own things and lands and they would infest the island with useless slaves" (B 62).[22] Along these lines, the introduction of fifty marriageable women, who insist on being sold with a cabin, heralds the end of utopia (B 132–133).[23] Homi Bhabha's views on the multiple economic and political interconnections of racial and sexual "othering" in colonial discourse are helpful in focusing in on the political unconscious posited in Boullosa's text:

[t]he construction of the colonial subject in discourse, and the exercise of colonial power through discourse, demands an articulation of forms of difference—racial and sexual. Such an articulation becomes crucial if it is held that the body is always simultaneously inscribed in both the economy of pleasure and desire and the economy of discourse, domination, and power. . . . [T]here is a theoretical space and a political place for such an *articulation*—in the sense in which that word itself denies an 'original' identity or a 'singularity' to objects of difference—sexual or racial. If such a view is taken . . . it follows that the epithets racial or sexual come to be seen as modes of differentiation, realised as multiple, cross-cutting determinations, polymorphous and perverse, always demanding a specific and strategic calculation of their effects. (19)

Since the abhorrence of women is rooted in the perceived link between women and private property, the fluctuations between hetero- and homosexuality may also be attributed to economics. Heterosexual impulses are channeled through women via rape and prostitution: "Isabel took it upon herself to explain the secrets of the female body to me. I shan't say I enjoyed it. I had to do what had been done to me till then. . . . I had an erection, which I had only experienced on my own before, and before realizing it, I found myself in her body. I shook my hips as Negro Miel would do with me. . . . I thought about the priest who taught me how to read, who used my body for the very first time and I remembered the pain" (B 52).[24] As illustrated by the narrator's infatuation with the cross-dressed sailor (B 20) and Captain Morgan's vain attempt at seducing "a woman of exceptional beauty and virtue," falling in love is construed as an "illness" (B 72; B-M 193–195, 198).[25] Though voyeurism leads to a form of courtly love—the narrator's cult of the cross-dressed sailor—it also allows for an assertion of heterosexuality, paradoxically expressed in homosexual terms: "She almost doesn't smell like a woman, which I appreciate" (B 70).[26] Promiscuity is a figure of excess: "There was a time when I could have covered the seas . . . with the skin of the flesh offering itself to us for coins . . . and covered the seas twice with the skin of the women we raped" (B 22). Yet promiscuity precludes progeny. The paradoxical nature of this statement is emphasized by extending its validity both to Negro Miel and Pineau, the narrator's role models. Representation of the body may provide a clue to the conundrum, "if women served to clean men of their seed, the body of another male could serve that function just as well, or even better, and since it was harmless, those who did not share that belief would do well to practice it" (B 62).

According to Mota, white women were forbidden on Tortuga but the interdiction did not apply to black or indigenous women (106–107). Though references to black women are almost nonexistent, the three native women L'Olonnais receives as a token of affection make a vivid impression on the narrator: "perfect had it not been for having had their entire body covered with lively hues for the occasion and for having their hair done in a strange way, as if they had applied mud to set it unnaturally. . . . In the broad daylight the openness of their nakedness was rather grotesque, especially . . . the enormous buttons in which their pointed breasts end [and] . . . the long black hair they wear loose" (B 86–87). While ethnocentrism may prevent an appreciation of the native aesthetics, the unspoken socio-economic code articulates female sexuality as repugnant: "I don't know if he touched them because in front of us he made out he felt repelled by the naked bodies, especially when they were no longer dyed, which was almost immediately, because the natives are used to bathing once or several times a day . . . and the dyes they use for their skin run with water" (B 86).[27]

Thus, we may conclude that Boullosa's *Son vacas* constitutes a paradigmatic case of historiographic metafiction as it simultaneously inscribes and subverts Exquemelin's text through condensation, aporias, and the continued shifting of "otherness." However, by placing Africans, aborigines, and women at the center of the narrative, Boullosa undercuts the egalitarian nature of the filibuster's brotherhood, suggesting that their liberating communal ideology replicated the imperialistic position of the Spaniards given their racist attitudes on the extermination of the natives and their endorsement of African slavery. But it was sexism that finally did them in. Women are barred from Tortuga so as to avoid unleashing the inherent selfishness of private property. Nonetheless, rather than preserving the buccaneer's livelihood, this measure allowed for the relentless enrichment of the "service sector": the providers of women, alcohol and gambling, in collusion with representatives of the French administration.

Defining logocentrism as the belief according to "which signs have an already fixed meaning recognized by the self-consciousness of the rational subject" (25), allows us to argue that in Boullosa's text logocentrism is undermined by the simultaneous displacement of "othering(s)" along axes such as gender, race/ethnicity, religion, and economics. In other words, this fluid set of "otherings" is emblematic of the difference and deferral represented by *différance*. Boullosa's re-creation also undermines the notion of the unified subject by allowing for the narrator's fluctuation among a number of subject positions.

Julia Kristeva describes the state generated by abjection in the following terms:

There looms, within abjection, one of those violent, dark revolts of being, directed against a threat that seems to emanate from an exorbitant outside or inside, ejected beyond the scope of the possible, the tolerable, the thinkable. It lies there, quite close, but it cannot be assimilated. It beseeches, worries, and fascinates desire, which nevertheless, does not let itself be seduced. Apprehensive, desire turns aside; sickened, it rejects. . . . Unflaggingly, like an inescapable boomerang, a vortex of summons and repulsion places the one haunted by it literally beside himself. (1)

Kristeva's description leads us to conclude that abjection, resulting from the gamut of tortures the body is subjected to—including the unspeakable suffering resulting from its complete annihilation while the body is still alive—is pivotal in Boullosa's text. Deployed in paradigmatic cases, such as the episode of the "Marquesa de la Poza Rica," or to reinforce aporias, such as the disembodied voice of L'Olonnais, abjection is instrumental in precluding rationalization. Furthermore, as Gregory Ulmer states, "the effect of the *vomi* is the destruction of representation and the pleasure associated with it, exposing one instead to the experience of *jouissance* (beyond pleasure)" (57). Thus, the intellectual challenge of Boullosa's highly ironic parody is matched by an equally strong visceral reaction. By rewriting the communal utopia placing the silenced others—African slaves, aborigines, women—at the center, Boullosa's text constitutes a veiled critique of Western imperialism as it suggests that racism, sexism, and capitalism ultimately did in the Brotherhood of the Coast.[28]

NOTES

1. Hereinafter quotation sources will be preceded by "B," "E," and/or "B-M" to indicate Boullosa, Exquemelin, and/or Buena-Maison.

2. See Francisco Mota on the process whereby Port Royal—capital of Morgan's Jamaica—became a bordello as of 1660 and for a rationale on the buccaneer's turning to alcohol and gambling and the effects of these practices (107).

3. All translations are mine.

4. Whereas in Boullosa's text, the victim is a native, in Exquemelin's it is a Spaniard (E 103; B-M 87).

5. The temporal perspective of the narrators of *One Hundred Years* and *Son vacas* coincide: "The narrator is positioned in a temporal bracket which encompasses the predicament of the characters both before their demise and thereafter" (Vargas Llosa 546, my translation).

6. Crooke was sued and Morgan won the case. In addition to a 200 pound fine, the printer was obliged to add the aforementioned paragraph (Mota 114).

7. While Boullosa attributes the bitterness to the crabs, Exquemlin and Buena-Maison attribute it to a seed eaten by the birds (E 17; B-M 6). All agree on the giddiness resulting from the consumption of crab meat (E 17; B-M 6).

8. See Mota on freedom and fair distribution of booty as pillars of buccaneer mores. Note freedom of faith, communal ownership of land and vessels, and democratic decision-making processes (106).

9. See B. R. Berg's "To Train Up a Buccaneer" (*Sodomy and the Perception of Evil* 43–68) on the socio-economic factors in seventeenth-century England that led to emigration to America.

10. In her preface to Derrida's *Of Grammatology*, Gayatri Chakravorty Spivak translates "*sous rature*" as "under erasure," noting: "This is to write a word, cross it out, and then print both word and deletion. (Since the word is inaccurate, it is crossed out. Since it is necessary, it remains legible). To take an example from Derrida. . . : 'the sign i̶s̶ that ill-named t̶h̶i̶n̶g̶ . . . which escapes the instituting question of philosophy'. . . . In examining familiar things we come to such unfamiliar conclusions that our very language is twisted and bent even as it guides us. Writing 'under erasure' is the mark of this contortion" (xiv).

11. Though in a different context—the conquest of America—Beatriz Pastor's discussion of Louis Marin's *Utopics: Spatial Play*, is particularly relevant with regard to the communal utopia of the buccaneers. Pastor notes, "according to Marin, a figurative discourse utopia . . . is the ambiguous representation of the equivocal image of a possible synthesis and difference. It points to a reconciliation and reveals a current contradiction between discourse and history" (Marin 8). Thus, Pastor concludes that "utopia represents an equivocal image that articulates symbolically the fundamental and unsoluble ideological conflict inherent in utopic praxis. And that symbolic resolution centers on a totalizing representation of a harmony that simultaneously conceals and reveals the fundamental contradictions of its foundational ideological order" (34, my translation).

12. Mota dates L'Olonnais's shipwreck to 1670 or 1671 (128). On the other hand, Laura Antillano's "Tuna de mar" extends the saga by chronicling the adventures of L'Olonnais' son, "Juan David Nau" and "Ana María" a.k.a "la Tuna," who take to the sea as pirates and share a fate similar to L'Olonnais: "Their heads were displayed at the port . . . and their bodies thrown to the sharks" (19). Subversion marks the cyclical nature of the story. In both instances, the finality of the nature of the fathers's deaths is debunked by the survival of their sons.

13. Exquemelin's version is slightly different: "within a few days after his arrival [the Indians] took him prisoner and tore him in pieces alive, throwing his body limb by limb into the fire, and his ashes into the air, to the intent that no trace or memory might remain of such an infamous, inhuman creature" (E 116; B-M 98).

14. Boullosa's *Llanto* also explores the question of the "other." Prompted by Fray Bernardino de Sahagún's (and the trilingual indigenous peoples who collaborated with him) *Historia General de las cosas de Nueva España* and Tzvetan Todorov's *La conquista de América, la cuestión del otro*, the narrator laments the hermeneutic impossibility of an accurate understanding of "Motecuhzoma's" mindset.

15. Among other cultural critics, Ashis Nandy explores the Western investment in a dichotomous ideology which "believes in the absolute superiority of the human over the nonhuman or subhuman, the masculine over the feminine, the adult over the child, the historical over the ahistorical, and the modern or progressive over the traditional or the savage" (x).

16. The economic monopoly of the West India Company of France was enforced politically by a designated governor (B 21). Dates on incorporation of Tortuga to the company vary: 1662 (B 32), 1664 (E 20; B-M 10).

17. Gambling, in particular, is condemned because it lured men away from the sea (B 137).

18. Assuming, of course, that these translations are faithful, in spirit, to the original.

19. Exquemlin refers to their name, "In some of these islands that belong unto the lake, and in other places hereabouts, do inhabit many savage Indians, whom the Spaniards call 'bravos,' or Wild. These Indians could never agree as yet, nor be reduced to any accord with the Spaniards, by reason of their brutish and untamable nature" (E 90; B-M 72).

20. Mota dwells both on Anne Bonny's pregnancy and on an affair thwarted by the discovery that the "other" was a woman (139).

21. "Domesticity" as "routine" is shunned by the pirates, "we don't eat every day, but when we do, either abundantly or monastically, our fares are always different" (B 79).

22. Stuart Zane Charmé prefaces his statements on Sartre's ideology by noting: "What begins as a microcosmic conflict within every individual—the tension between spirit and flesh, consciousness and body, civilized and vulgar—ends up being projected into a macrocosmic model of humanity. Those groups with the power to define social categories have usually defined themselves with the transcendent qualities of the human, while they equate those groups that they have defined as Other with the immanent qualities of nature. It is, for example, always the Other who threatens to undermine the values of society by his or her uncontrollable sexual instincts, deviant habits, and vulgar behavior" (147). Regarding womanhood, Charmé adds: "As Simone de Beauvoir made clear in *The Second Sex*, culturally accepted polarities like that of 'human' and 'nature,' 'self' and 'other,' 'good,' and 'evil' have produced a corresponding polarity in our conceptions of male and female. Within Christian tradition and elsewhere, men have often defined the realm of the spiritual, the intellectual, the rational, and the civilized as primarily, if not exclusively, male territory: whereas the realm of the physical, natural, and instinctual has been the province of women. The accepted ascendancy of culture over nature has consistently been associated with the suppression of women" (148).

23. Mota (106–107) also dwells on the devastating effects of the introduction of women in Tortuga.

24. A psychological approach to the Other would also stress its interconnection with the Self. However, Lacanian concepts such as "[m]an's desire is the desire of the Other" (235) ought to be contextualized, since, according to Lacan, "[t]he Other is the locus in which is situated the chain of the signifier that governs whatever may be made present of the subject—it is the field of that living being in which the subject has to appear" (203).

25. See Berg for an analysis on the possible psychological impact of the captive women's race and culture on the behavior of pirates (117–120).

26. Both Exquemelin and Buena-Maison record the episode of the strumpet who is offered 500 pieces-of-eight to be seen naked (E 75; B-M 59); however, Boullosa stresses condensation by using the episode (B 69) to signal transference from homosexuality to heterosexuality.

27. Neither Exquemelin nor Buena-Maison record the incident of the indigenous women the "Bravos" gave L'Olonnais as a token of affection.

28. Different stages of this project have been funded by the Scholarship, Research and Creative Activities Grant Program at Arizona State University West (Summer Stipend for 1992–93; 1993–94 & 1994–95). Carmen Boullosa (1954), was awarded the famous Xavier Villaurrutia prize in 1989. Boullosa's other novels include: *Duerme* (1994), *La Milagrosa* (1993; translated as *The Miracle Worker*, 1994), *Llanto: Novelas*

imposibles (1992), *Antes* (1989) and *Mejor desaparece* (1987).

REFERENCES

Antillano, Laura. *Tuna de mar*. Caracas: Fundarte, 1991.

Bhabha, Homi. "The Other Question: The Stereotype and Colonial Discourse." *Screen* 24.6 (1983): 18–36.

Berg, B. R. (Barry Richard). *Sodomy and the Perception of Evil: English Sea Rovers in the Seventeenth-Century Caribbean*. New York: New York UP, 1983.

Boullosa, Carmen. *Llanto: Novelas imposibles*. Mexico: Era, 1992.

————. *Son vacas, somos puercos*. Mexico: Era, 1991.

Charmé, Stuart Zane. *Vulgarity and Authenticity: Dimensions of Otherness in the World of Jean-Paul Sartre*. Amherst: U of Massachusetts P, 1991.

Derrida, Jacques. *Of Grammatology*. Trans. Gayatri Chakravorti Spivak. Baltimore, MD. and London: Johns Hopkins UP, 1974.

Esquemeling, John. *The Buccaneers of America*. Ed. William Swan Stallybrass. London: Routledge, 1924.

Exquemelin, Alexandre Olivier. *Piratas de la America: y Luz a la Defensa de las Costas de Indias Occidentales*. Trans. Alonso de Buena-Maison. Madrid: Ramón Ruiz, 1793.

Hutcheon, Linda. *A Poetics of Postmodernism: History, Theory, Fiction*. New York: Routledge, 1988.

Kristeva, Julia. *Powers of Horror: An Essay on Abjection*. Trans. Leon S. Roudiez. New York: Columbia UP, 1982.

Lacan, Jacques. *The Fundamental Concepts of Psycho-Analysis*. Trans. Alan Sheridan. New York: W. W. Norton & Company, 1978.

Marin, Louis. *Utopics: Spatial Play*. London: Macmillan, 1984.

Minh-Ha, Trinh. "Difference: A Special Third World Women Issue." *Discourse* 8 (1986–87): 11–38.

Mota, Francisco. *Piratas en el caribe*. Cuba: Casa de las Américas, 1984.

Nandy, Ashis. *The Intimate Enemy: Loss and Recovery of Self under Colonialism*. Delhi, Bombay, Calcutta, Madras: Oxford UP, 1983.

Pastor, Beatriz. "Utopía y conquista." *Nuevo Texto Crítico* 5.9–10 (1992): 33–46.

Rama, Angel. *Transculturación narrativa en América Latina*. Mexico: Siglo XXI, 1982.

Todorov, Tzvetan. *La conquista de América: el problema del otro*. Mexico: Siglo XXI, 1987.

Ulmer, Gregory. *Applied Grammatology*. Baltimore, MD.: Johns Hopkins UP, 1985.

Vargas Llosa, Mario. *Historia de un deicidio*. Barcelona: Barral, 1971.

8

CROSS-DRESSING AND THE BIRTH OF A NATION: *DUERME* BY CARMEN BOULLOSA

Salvador Oropesa

"If the penis was the phallus men would have no need of feathers or ties or medals."

—Eugénie Lemoine-Luccioni

Carmen Boullosa is one of the most challenging and important writers in present-day Mexico. Part of the postmodern literary movement that has renovated Mexico's theater, Boullosa is also well known for her poetry and defines herself as first and foremost a poet. Although she is less known as a novelist, *Duerme* (1994) is her seventh novel. *Duerme* tells the story of Claire, a French woman who arrives in New Spain dressed as a man in 1571. This is a key moment in the history of the colony for two reasons: (1), due to the wealth represented by the millions of bullions of silver sent by the colony to the metropolis, which permitted the realization of America as a utopia, and, (2), due to the first major tension between the Spanish crown (Phillip II) and the sons of the conquistadors, the first Creole generation, regarding the administration of the *encomiendas* (Kandell 180–194). The second half of the sixteenth century represented the birth of New Spain/Mexico as an incipient Western nation, once the conquest of the central provinces of the country (the Valley of Mexico, Puebla, Oaxaca, Querétaro, Guadalajara, the mining zone of Zacatecas and the port of Veracruz) was complete.

The novel starts *in medias res*: Claire is semiconscious, and some servants are undressing her; an Indian maid is about to discover that under the man's clothes there is a woman. Boullosa has chosen a motif of the stories of sailors to the colonies, that of the cross-dressed woman, to tell the story of the birth of a nation and the cultural anxieties that this will trigger. The historians Rudolph M. Dekker and Lotte C. van de Pol have documented that during the sixteenth century many women traveled from Europe to the colonies dressed as men: "In the early modern era passing oneself off as a man was a real and viable option for women who had fallen into bad times and were struggling to overcome their difficult circumstances" (1–2). Claire, like the actual cases documented by Dekker and Pol, is a prostitute who does not want to continue her dissolute life:

We therefore conclude that in view of the fact that prostitutes and female cross-dressers were very much alike in age, class, and background, the choice for cross-dressing when confronted with difficult circumstances implied a clear rejection of the alternative of prostitution. Simply and generally stated, those who became prostitutes followed the female, passive, sexual path, while those who "became men" followed the male, active and sexless path, at the same time preserving their sexual honor. (39)

It was commonly believed that even an unmarried woman could have a prosperous and easy life there [in overseas territories]. And there was another advantage; no one demanded an irreprehensible past. Even the lowest white woman was considerably exalted above native women. (34)

To develop this story, Boullosa's *Duerme* takes two elements of Golden Age literature: the topic of honor and the picaresque genre. Golden Age theater—Lope de Vega's *Fuenteovejuna* is one of the best examples—shows a new ideological pattern: that of a new bourgeoisie that is demanding the right to honor. Honor had previously been restricted to the aristocracy; now, people from other classes, based on their money, work, and social aspirations, started to demand the same recognition as those of the aristocracy. It was a double struggle: class and gender. Claire's case is as follows: "I remember Mama. I can see her making me use boy's clothes since I was very little, so that I could go with her from here to there, in her endless pilgrimage as a prostitute, traveling with the armies" (34).[1] Her mother is killed by a soldier and s/he enters the service of a colonel:

The last thing I can distinguish is how he abuses me, when inadvertently he sees my clothes stained with menstrual blood, and he realizes I am a woman, and I see how I abandon him, and that I take the same job as Mama did, with my legs in the same position as hers . . . I can see myself with the last client, getting him drunk, stealing his clothes, boarding the ship at the very last moment where a few days before I had signed on my false brother. (35)

It should be noted that honor was inherited via men. Women could not give it to their sons and daughters; it had to be the men who provided character to the family. Claire, like her sisters in Golden Age theater, is demanding honor for her gender. Spanish honor literature has had for the most part a reactionary reading (Alonso, Dunn), but I see it as the opposite. These women demanded respect for their bodies. Laurencia in *Fuenteovejuna* says that her only love is her honor (234); Claire with her cross-dressing demands honor for herself, something not admitted by sixteenth-century society. Claire tells the viceroy: "My sword is good only to defend Your Excellency. I am ashamed of having used it, as it happened, to defend my honor" (85). According to José Antonio Maravall: "what characterizes the *pícaro* is to be born to infamy; that is, in accord with the times, to be born in those social levels in which 'honor' had no place" (643, my translation). To Maravall, the key ideologeme to understand the picaresque is the desire of *pícaros* to reach the highest social status possible, and the means to do so are through *usurpation* (525–590). My *Webster's* dictionary indicates that "by force" or "without right" are the conditions necessary "to usurp" (499). Claire, in her double state of belonging to the "wrong" gender, female, and to the "wrong" social class, the lower one, thinks there is a possibility to overcome these handicaps: America. In her case, what is known at that moment as New Spain, a place in which, because it is *new,* traditional concepts of gender and class of a society based on rigid states can be challenged; but a place that is at the same time the *old* Europe, Spain. This resulted in the European notion that they could exercise a right in the dominion of the indigenous population. New Spain is an oxymoron whose true meaning is deferred, and it is in the gap of the deferral where Claire tries to put him/herself, himself as a nobleman whose margin and abyss is herself as a prostitute. America should be the utopian place where Claire can become a noble*man*.

I would like to establish a parallelism between the construction of New Spain and the cultural paradigms in conflict to define the new territory and the definition of gender given by Judith Butler:

Gender is a complexity whose totality is permanently deferred, never fully what it is at any given juncture in time. An open coalition, then, will affirm identities that are alternately instituted and relinquished according to the purposes at hand, it will be an open assemblage that permits multiple convergences and divergences without obedience to a normative telos of definitional closure. (16)

It seems that Boullosa and Butler coincide in how they see gender, because the Mexican writer is using the negotiation of Claire's gender to put some order to the idea of what the colony was and how this past is affecting present-day Mexico.

EPISTEMOLOGY OF THE TRANSVESTITE

Marjorie Garber asserts the importance of cross-dressing: "The transvestite makes culture possible . . . there can be no culture without the transvestite because the transvestite marks the entrance into the symbolic" (34). Those of us who understand literature as the production of culture can easily relate to Garber's statement. Claire's clothes allow Boullosa to tell the story of the first modernity of Mexico as a Western nation. The realm of the symbolic is developed through the mutations and changes endured by Claire. According to

Garber:

One of the cultural functions of the transvestite is precisely to mark this kind of displacement, substitution, or slippage: from class to gender, gender to class; or, equally plausi-
bly, from gender to race or religion. The transvestite is both a signifier and that which
signifies the undecidability of signification. It points towards itself—or, rather, toward
the place it is not. The transvestite as object of desire—as, indeed, the embodied construction of mimetic desire—is the manifestation of Freud's concept of the overestimation
of the object, as set forth in his essay on narcissism. For the transvestite is there and
gone at once. (37)

Garber sees transvestism as a *différance* in the Derridean sense of production
of differences (Adamson 534–535). Transvestism is the mechanism used by
Boullosa to explain the birth of Mexico as a nation of the Western world. The
deferral of meaning, paradoxically, is the only possible way to attempt a definition of the new territory ("the undecidability of signification"). For example,
there is a moment in the novel in which the Spanish poet Pedro de Ocejo is
writing a play in Mexico based on the European cultural paradigms of the
Renaissance, but when he wants to describe the winds of Mexico City, he
realizes he cannot use the classical winds—Austro, Zephyr, Boreas, and Eurus—
and he asks himself: "What winds belong to these lands?, because no one can
tell me that here the wind does not blow" (102). Pedro is right, the wind blows
in America, but these are winds, hurricanes, tornados that resist traditional
classifications and, simultaneously, challenge classical, Western culture and its
explanations of the world. Pedro's concern serves as an example of the modern
crisis of Western metaphysics, that at a theoretical level is expressed in the
Derridean concept of history shown in Boullosa's historical novel.

At the beginning of the novel, Claire is described by an indigenous medicine woman as "neither man nor woman, neither Nahuatl nor Spaniard nor
mestizo, neither Count nor laborer, you do not deserve to die" (28). The reader
will notice the logical pairs: man/woman, Nahuatl/Spanish, but the *tú/usted*
pairing that challenges hierarchical society should also be noted. The transvestite
is a crisis of category that blurs boundaries between male and female and undermines the attempt to construct stable binary categories of oppositional difference
(Clark and Sponsler). To use Garber's model, Claire, the transvestite, marks
the displacements and becomes the object of desire (this point will be developed
later). Claire is a signifier, and its void/presence can be filled by the different
meanings necessary to explain the new social construct that is Mexico. Claire
is Mexico's synecdoche. This idea also has a parallel in Butler: "If the body
is synecdochal for the social system *per se* or a site in which open systems
converge, then any kind of unregulated permeability constitutes a site of pollution and endangerment" (132).

To modify the previous statement: Claire's body is Mexico's synecdoche.
But Boullosa's explanation of Mexico through Claires's body is neither naive
nor dogmatic. The author is conscious of the limits of her interpretation and

the rationalization behind the episteme she is displaying. The synecdoche is a powerful tool because it is a well-regulated trope, part for the whole or the other metonymies: producer for product, object used for user, controller for controlled. Because language and its mechanisms have "naturalized" this possibility, it is very effective in subversive discourse: It makes acceptable (or seemingly acceptable) messages that constructed metaphorically would have been easier to detect as not "natural."

In the first page of the novel, Claire is dressed as an ordinary European man; then she is undressed and dressed up as a nobleman with the clothes of the Conde de Enrique de Urquiza y Rivadeneira. She is undressed for a second time and dressed as an Indian woman but with the count's clothes over her. At this moment of the plot, Claire is going to be executed instead of Urquiza, but Claire is not going to die because the medicine woman has put pure water of the Aztec lakes in her veins. When Claire is buried, she takes her man's clothes off and appears as a *mestiza* with indigenous clothes. After several adventures, Claire goes under the protection of the viceroy and is dressed as a European woman. Claire, now Clara Flor, is then put in command of troops and dressed as a male soldier. When she returns, wounded but alive because she cannot bleed (and she cannot menstruate, the mark of womanhood) she is dressed again as a Spanish woman. At the end of the novel, the cycle is complete, and Claire returns to the clothes of an ordinary Spanish man to start a Creole insurrection against the Spanish crown.

It should be understood that during the hierarchical society of the sixteenth century the social being, the class, the state (social status) are more important than the individual. This is why clothes are so important because they literally define identity. When Claire is dressed as an Indian woman, the count rapes her and other Spanish men attempt to rape her because she is considered Indian in spite of the color of her skin. The color does not work as a deterrent; the logic of the European man is that if another European man raped this Indian's mother, he can do the same. In this society, indeed, "the clothes make the man." According to Maravall:

Chombart de Lauwe has made interesting observations about the connection between clothing and what he calls "the aspiration to be recognized," which is the attempt to reach a certain status using symbols of prestige that can elevate someone in the social scale. The expectation of this advancement may be legitimate and within the rules of the established system . . . but it can also be used to try to reach a superior level by fraudulent means, a behavior that presupposes a deviation from the system. This is the expectation of the *pícaro* that from a formal point of view is illegitimate since it deceives everyone else. (552, my translation)

Claire is a *pícara* in the sense that her goal is to usurp a social status that she does not deserve according to the social norms of the second half of the sixteenth century. In all Western nations during the transition from feudalism to the modern era, governments tried unsuccessfully to regulate clothing to avoid challenges to the social system (Maravall 552; Bullough 78). The change of clothes ended up signaling the changes from the old system to the new. But Claire does not want to change the hierarchical society. What she wants is to climb the pyramid and reach the top, but in her attempt to accomplish this goal, she is challenging the patriarchal and hierarchical assumptions of her epoch and denouncing that besides the biological differences between men and women there are other dissimilarities that have been constructed by men. Claire is not the only transvestite in the novel:

The guests are dressed in lavish clothes: those who do not have silk buttoned boots are wearing velvet ones, and their clothes are *overflowing* with embroidery and precious stones, with jewels on their heads, their arms, and their necks, unless they are covered with ruffles and lace. (61)

Pedro de Ocejo says that the people here make him laugh with their pretentious ploys to show off which lead them to *ridiculous excesses,* not just in their carriages: the clothing here is unrivaled in any European country, in part because the materials are extremely fine . . . in part because every Spaniard has several outfits, and also because the cuts of the clothes have become so *grotesquely exaggerated*, the collars are gigantic, the sleeves trail to the ground, and it is common to wear four sleeves in the doublets, and it is not because we are people with four arms. (79, emphasis added)

The Renaissance represented the first moment in Western history when the individual was promised a better future by the society in which s/he lived. It has not been until this century that this promise has been achieved large scale in the rich Western nations, thus, for this reason it has not been until now that we have been able to realize that we have been immersed in a task that has lasted for five centuries and that continues to this day. This is how we can connect the New Spain of the sixteenth century with present-day Mexico, 1994, when the novel was published. Mexico as a Western nation is promising its citizens that they have the right to aim for a better life. Simultaneously, there is a minority like the Spaniards described in the paragraphs above that live in a luxurious environment. And today's Mexican elite, like the Creole cream of 1571, is despised by the "true" European elites. In their attempt to imitate the uses of the metropolis, they only "ape" the defects of those who hold the key to the "true wealth and culture." Or at least this is how Pedro, the Spaniard artist, perceives the rich Creoles. Mexico's schizophrenia is the vision of itself as a Western nation. This is what makes *Duerme* a reflection on this very difficult question: What is Mexico? How do you square the circle of a Western nation that can include at the same time the indigenous component of its idiosyncrasy? The only possible answer is a cluster of paradoxes and/or deferred definitions. This is why postmodernism gives an epistemological break to Mexico because the success of postmodernity has been that it reduces the authority of the importance of the term "contradiction," as this term had been defined by modernity (Jameson 313–318.) A postmodern society recognizes itself as contradictory and enjoys the possibilities and the combinations of challenging roles. George Yúdice (17) rejected Jameson's premise that every "Third World" text is a national allegory, and I agree with Yúdice. It seems that my position coincides with Jameson. But there are two problems: (1) "Third World" is a static term; it imposes the imperialist vision of not letting the colony move without the permission of the metropolis, and (2) the structure of the synecdoche does not allow the allegory.

But the truth is that the indigenous population is at the bottom of society. The difference, according to *Duerme*, is that in the times of the colony certain wisdom was still alive and could give some hope to the so-called Indian people, while currently, again, a new transvestism has occurred, and the main goal of the indigenous population is to be part of Western society, destroying the remnants of their native cultures (Bonfil Batalla 23). According to Guillermo Bonfil Batalla:

Desindianización [the eradication of indigenous cultures] . . . is a historical process by which populations that had originally possessed a distinct identity of their own, based on their own culture, are forced to renounce this identity. . . . This is not the result of biological miscegenation, but rather the action of ethnic forces that end up impeding the historical continuity of a community as a socially and differentiated entity. (42, my translation)

This is why the action of the novel is in 1571 because at that moment the first wave of *desindianización* has already been completed. With the creation of Clara, the travesty, Boullosa problematizes the identity of the new Mexican/ New Spaniard. Claire's body has been presented as the representation of Mexico because of its lack of closure. Her body is not a normative telos, and as will be seen later when wounds are studied, Claire's body is a place of pollution.

The male costumes of the sixteenth century were about to be surpassed in ornaments by those of the seventeenth century, which would bring the concept of manhood to the point of collapse. An excess in accessories would be seen as feminine, and there are many testimonies regretting the lack of manhood in the overdressed men of the time. It is in this fashion that Clara does not have to prove her manhood when dressed as the count, but she has to do so when dressed as a woman or as a soldier. When Claire is dressed as an Indian, she is assaulted by soldiers who want to gang rape her: "I am totally overpowered by his arms. I try to encircle him, grabbing his sword with my left hand and raising it to stop its blade I shout: 'If any of you make a move, I'll kill him'" (60). She encounters the same soldier later: "I challenge you with the sword. If you win, I'll be yours, as many times as you like but no more than six. If I win, you will leave me alone. . . . And you would be a coward if you didn't accept, since you are a man, a soldier, strong, and I am just an Indian and a woman" (83). There are other testimonies: "And in spite of being a woman, I strive as hard as a man in the Viceroy's service" (93); "She and only she gave the orders, and we obeyed only her, enchanted by her grace and courage, dominated by the secret of her beauty" (97).

SEX AND EROTICISM

In the previous section, the reader finds Claire taking firm hold of the sword. I want to return to Garber and her concept of fetishism. In a chapter called "Fetish Envy" (118–127) she addresses this matter. Reading *Duerme*, the reader notices that although Claire has some sexual encounters with different men and women, and she is the object of desire of both men and women, either indigenous or European, she shows dissimilar degrees of interest in these sexual encounters. I already quoted Claire's loss of her virginity when she was raped by the colonel as well as the episode when she avoided the attempt to be raped by the Spanish soldiers. She is also raped by the count: "He makes me turn towards him on the horse. He lifts my blouse, he bares my breasts, I want to get loose, the servants hold my legs and arms, my wound and breasts are exposed. . . . He opens his breeches, lifts my petticoat, and takes me" (53). But there are two moments in the novel that are revealing: "Never, not even when I was a whore had I spent a night with so many caresses. Besides, this time, I am a man, rich, well-dressed, I am Count Urquiza. I am happy" (43); "The truth is that I have never loved. I have never seen what love does to people because I have never loved" (114). The first quote, page 43, is the night the female Indians are keeping vigil over the count's body (Claire), and they are caressing him/her. It should be noted that in the original Spanish "I am happy" is expressed as "*estoy feliz*" rather than "*soy feliz*." The second quote is recalled by Claire while another woman is caressing her, and Claire is letting her do so. What is clear in the first quote is that Claire is happy when dressed as a very rich man. When she is undressed the first time, she thinks: "I want to cry. The only son I could ever have wanted is dead, they have killed him in my own body. They put me to sleep so I could not defend my own offspring: me, yes, I am my own son, Claire as a man" (19).

Garber notices how classical psychoanalysis has not been able to conceptualize the possibility of female fetishism, especially the clothing fetish. Robert J. Stoller explained that women who wear men's clothes "suffer from the perfectly understandable desire to be men" (Garber 118). For Freud the only fetish possible for women was the penis. Recall the quote by Eugénie Lemoine-Luccioni opening this chapter, which corresponds to what I have called the other transvestites: Those who wore very expensive clothes with plenty of ornaments. But the concept of phallus brings Jacques Lacan to our equation. For Lacan, only the lesbian can have something analogous to fetishism. Garber argues: "That fetishism is a kind of theater of display—and, indeed, that theater represents an enactment of the fetishistic scenario. Thus Freud's 'penis,' the anatomical object, though understood through Lacan's 'phallus,' the structuring mark of desire, becomes re-literalized as a stage prop, a detachable object. No one has the phallus" (120). This is obvious in Claire's case: What sexually excites her is herself dressed as a rich man. The medical and psychoanalytical establishment of Western society (de Lauretis 222–226) has invested a significant amount of ideology in denying women the possibility of the structure of the fetish, unless the fetish is the envy for the penis; that becomes to Freud the wish for a baby. Then, according to Freud, women will develop a neurosis (a vacuum) that will be changed for the wish of a man; a man that has a penis (Garber 119). Boullosa's idea is a clever one: to write a novel in which the protagonist is a fetishistic lesbian who knows that the phallus, like the sword she can rob from men and use, is detachable. And she also knows of the theatricality of the fetish, of the public display necessary to develop it. But this is just the first step. As Teresa de Lauretis affirms:

The masquerade of masculinity in the mannish drag or the contemporary butch persona, although it operates as a fetish, is not a phallic symbol, a substitute for the penis, or a pretentious claim to the paternal phallus. A fetish-object and signifier of desire, it is constituted through the disavowal of castration, but with the fundamental specification that in lesbian subjectivity the ultimate meaning of castration as narcissistic wound is not the lack of a penis but the *loss of the female body*. (275, emphasis added)

This is how Claire challenges the patriarchal and the hierarchical society and how her body is constituted as Mexico's synecdoche. Her body, like Mexico, is in danger of being lost, castrated by the Western fathers.

Claire's narcissistic wounds do not represent the lack of the penis but the theatrical display of the female body. Carlos Fuentes refers to the border between the United States and Mexico as a scar. The wounds and the scars are reminders of the violence that produced them.

She undresses me, she lifts my head, *looking at my body,* and thrusts the obsidian knife with all her might into my nude breast, the left one. This Indian woman wants to skin me, as they do with the people of her race. . . . In the open wound she pours water from the pitcher. After opening me with the knife, my red blood flowed abundantly along my skin, without haste, at lukewarm speed. Now, with her fingers she opens the wound, pulling the edges towards opposite extremes, she pours water into it, and in spite of the violence exerted on the deep wound, I stop bleeding. (20)

Claire's wound is again exposed when she is raped by the count. After that, Claire is wounded for a second time with a machete that was on the floor: "I stoop and I can see the edge of my flesh. I move my foot back, a piece of flesh is dragging. I lift it. It hurts a lot. I do not bleed" (71).

When Clara is the captain of the soldiers fighting against an Indian chief, they are attacked, and Claire cannot defend herself because she is in a cathartic state. After she was bled by the medicine woman, far from Mexico City, she loses her life. Claire is immortal but she has to stay close to the city:

Whoever it was who had his sword against her opened her clothes from top to bottom, and what the sword could not do, was done by curiosity and the help of the hands; tearing off the clothes, leaving the body exposed. Looking at her two female breasts and a chest that even wounded was not bleeding, the Indian, their leader, Yuguey, shouted in his dialect God knows what, he called them to regroup and they fled. . . . Clara Flor was in the worst state of all of us, her naked chest, full of cuts, provoked pity and fear. (98–99)

The fetishistic scenario of the wounds is feminine, since men do not fetishize wounds (De Lauretis 267). The issue here is the absence of the phallus in Claire's castrations. Neither Claire's father nor his phallus are present in the novel. What is key in the De Lauretis interpretation that I am following is that in her reading of desire, of course, perverse desire, "the mediating term, the signifier of desire, is not the paternal phallus but the fetish" (289). Claire's own desire is mediated by her clothes, and Claire (like Mexico) is the fetish of the other's desire, the European desire.

What Boullosa does in her elaboration of Claire to explain Mexico's past and present is to try to avoid the normative and closed masculine historiography. This is very important in a country where official histories have systematically been imposed by different governments. There is another moment in the novel when Claire thinks: "Pedro de Ocejo, speaking, was seductive and convincing, since he had not been undressed" (107). According to Claire, Pedro's fetish is his voice, his words, not his forgettable penis.

With Claire as a fetish, as an object of desire representing Mexico, Boullosa can put in literary language the scenario of rape described by Octavio Paz in *El laberinto de la soledad* [*The Labyrinth of Solitude*](1950), but without male epistemology. At the same time, the travesty dissolves the antagonistic divisions of an epistemology based on very distinct binary oppositions. One of the means Boullosa has to challenge the *machista* Mexican society is by creating a queer territory within the novel, a same sex space, a lesbian gap that can attack the hierarchy established in Mexico between men and women, hierarchy that existed during the so-called hierarchical society and which still exists in Mexico today. Maravall notices that the picaresque novel is one of violence between the sexes. He finds "irrelevance or lack of love" and "love replaced by a dull agression from both sides" (673). Rosalyn Costantino quotes Boullosa affirming the following: "I believe . . . that if violence is present in most of my books it is due, precisely, to the fact that I am a woman. This element, however, is not the product of a moral, spiritual, or political decision, it's just there" (173–174).

The key moment in *Duerme* is nearly at the end of the novel, when, in a moment of anagnorisis, Claire asks: "And me, am I not also a daughter of the race? The only French woman with water in her veins, the woman of artificial life, the one who can only live on Mexican land" (125). At this moment in the adventure, Claire has become Mexican. It is not a process of naturalization, but an elaborate process. Nonetheless, *artificial* is the key word. Claire becomes a *mestiza*, a white *mestiza* like the *mestizas* desired by José Vasconcelos for his cosmic race, a French *mestiza*, the desire of the Mexican intellectual elite after the 1910 revolution. Claire is the fantasy, the mirage of a white Mexico, the object of the other's (Mexican) desire: "The [Indian] with lukewarm hands undresses me one garment at a time . . . we are alone and she touches me slowly and deliberately" (118). I had said previously that there are two revealing moments about Claire. There is a third one, with "*la italiana*," an actress:

"Are you of age?"

I [Claire] told her, "You are the most beautiful woman on earth."
She looked into my eyes. She took my chin and placed a kiss on my lips.

"After many years, I have learned to hide my expressions of affection. . . . I have learned other things, but not to love, that is perhaps what I should learn."

She had just uttered this last word when she began to undress herself: it puzzled me a little, but I did not want to say anything. The Italian wanted to become Aphrodite. . . . Once naked, she came with me to the bed. . . . She was very careful not to hurt my open wounds with her hands. Although where she put her hands can be considered an open wound. In my case it does not bleed anymore, but the excessive flow of red is not necessary to say that it is an ever-open wound in any body. . . . Color had returned to my face. (113–114)

Neither love nor need have to be present to perform the sexual act; the only condition is desire. The threat of castration of the narcissistic wound brought the loss of the female body and the loss of the country. To recuperate both, the body and the country, the sexual act is needed—the lesbian sexual act—because it is the fulfillment of desire. When Claire's body is raped by European men either when she is in Europe or in Mexico, her body is denied of any entity. She usurps honor to regain her body through her transvestism as the mannish drag, and her body is recognized as a totality when it cannot be castrated in a homosexual relation. Octavio Paz popularized the image of Mexico as a raped and Oedipized country; Boullosa has used this notion to create a fetishistic scenario to open up the possibilities for other interpretations or modes of writing/reading/conceiving/perceiving of history. The image produced is that Mexico became a Western nation, forgetting its indigenous past and present. But Mexico is limited by its indigenous blood/water, it cannot survive out of Mexico. A *mestizo* community, then, has to be developed. A true *mestizo* country, not the white mirage of the Vasconcelista movement, has to be built, and it has to be a feminist country. The lesbian scenarios invalidate the Mexican *machismo*, the phallus does not have to be present to start a riot against the metropolis, and the new democratic Mexico will have to be a "nonphallic" country. But Boullosa's story is not based on stable binary categories. My reading is not the only possible one, and other readings will be necessary to discuss Mexico's past, present, and future using the always challenging works by Boullosa.

NOTE

1. All translations from Spanish are mine.

REFERENCES

Adamson, Joseph. "Différance/différence." *Encyclopedia of Contemporary Literary Theory: Approaches, Scholars, Terms.* Ed. Irena R. Makaryk. Toronto: U of Toronto P, 1993.

Bonfil Batalla, Guillermo. *México profundo: una civilización negada.* Mexico: Grijalbo, 1990.

Boullosa, Carmen. *Duerme.* Madrid: Alfaguara, 1994.

Bullough, Vern L., and Bonnie Bullough. *Cross-Dressing, Sex, and Gender.* Philadelphia: U of Pennsylvania P, 1993.

Butler, Judith. *Gender Trouble: Feminism and the Subversion of Identity.* New York: Routledge, 1990.

Clark, Robert L. A., and Claire M. Sponsler. "Queer Play: The Cultural Work of Crossdressing in Medieval Drama." (Unpublished work).

Costantino, Roselyn. "Resistant Creativity: Interpretative Strategies and Gender Representation in Contemporary Women's Writing in Mexico." Diss. Arizona State U, 1992. 169–230.

Dekker, Rudolph M., and Lotte C. van de Pol. *The Tradition of Female Transvestism in Early Modern Europe.* New York: St. Martin's, 1989.

De Lauretis, Teresa. *The Practice of Love: Lesbian Sexuality and Perverse Desire.* Bloomington: Indiana UP, 1994.

Garber, Marjorie. *Vested Interests: Cross-Dressing & Cultural Anxiety.* New York: Routledge, 1992.

Jameson, Fredric. "Cultural Reification and the Relief of the Postmodern." *Postmodernism or, The Cultural Logic of Late Capitalism.* Durham, NC: Duke UP, 1992. 313–318.

Kandell, Jonathan. *La Capital: The Biography of Mexico.* New York: Owl, 1990.

Maravall, José Antonio. *La literatura picaresca desde la historia social (Siglos XVI y XVII).* Madrid: Taurus, 1987.

Paz, Octavio. *El laberinto de la soledad.* Mexico: Fondo de Cultura Económica, 1959.

Vega, Lope de. *Fuenteovejuna.* Barcelona: Plaza and Janes, 1984.

Webster's New World Dictionary. Compact Ed. New York: Simon and Schuster, 1982.

Yúdice, George. "Postmodernity and Transnational Capitalism in Latin America." *On Edge: The Crisis of Contemporary Latin American Culture.* Eds. George Yúdice, Jean Franco, and Juan Flores. Minneapolis: U of Minnesota P, 1992. 1–28.

cation, the author must effect a means of transtextual appropriation that at once inscribes and recontextualizes the parent text. Such parody, Hutcheon affirms, should be considered an ironic "inversion" or "transcontextualization," not necessarily at the expense of the parodied text (*A Theory of Parody* 6). By appropriating the resources of magic realism, Esquivel has consciously selected a mode that has become so much a part of the canon that it would be easily recognized by anyone even remotely familiar with contemporary Spanish American literature. Thus, although the hyperbolic episodes of magic realism that appear throughout *Como agua para chocolate* may indeed be indebted to *Cien años de soledad,* there is a marked difference in perspective between the two novels. While García Márquez's narrative centers on a re-examination of broad historical trends, Esquivel's work produces a meaning independent from the original text by concentrating on the individual experience in relation to history; rather than emphasizing issues of sexual domination and violence[3] upon which the Americas were founded, Esquivel "feminizes" her novel by presenting a community of women sustained through an activity—the preparation of food—that transcends social barriers of class, race, and generation (Leonardi 342).[4]

That Tita's personal record of her life is posited as an *alternate version* to the events recorded by canonized discourse is exemplified by the chapter in which her sister Gertrudis escapes with a revolutionary. In this episode, Pedro presents Tita with a bouquet of roses, which she holds so tightly to her chest that their petals mix with her blood. When she uses the bloodstained roses to prepare their meal, Gertrudis becomes so sexually aroused that her overheated body sets the shower on fire. Running nude through the fields, she is intercepted by a *villista* on horseback: "Without slowing his gallop, so as not to waste a moment, he leaned over, put his arm around her waist, and lifted her onto the horse in front of him, face to face, and carried her away" (55–56/60–61).[5] Endowed with incredible sexual prowess, the couple makes love in the saddle, as the horse continues to gallop. Later, in a parodic inversion of roles, Gertrudis finds that no one man can satisfy her and must spend time in a brothel on the border to placate her prodigious sexual appetite (133); subsequently she distinguishes herself on the battlefield and becomes a revolutionary general (180). This incident marks a turning point in the novel because it inspires Tita to begin to write *her version* of events. From Tita's perspective, the romantic encounter is more important than the events taking place on the battlefield, even though she is aware that official history will remember the incident differently (60). By recontextualizing such episodes from a female point of view, Esquivel effects a re-evaluation of official discourse, since the history that has been recorded does not always conform to the fantastic nature of perceived reality. At the same time, the parodic nature of the episode differentiates the novel from its literary precursors as well, as Esquivel plays not only with the supernatural sexual potency that García Márquez and others have imagined for their protagonists[6] but also the consecrated—and highly masculine—tradition of the literature (and cinema) of the Mexican Revolution.

As for Pedro and Tita's first sexual encounter, although the "explosiveness" of their passion lights the sky, the narrator does not pause for specific details: "Pedro . . . pulled her to a brass bed . . . and, throwing himself upon her, caused her to lose her virginity and learn of true love" (158/161). Although the violent prelude to this encounter is again reminiscent of similar scenes from the male canon, the narrator's reticence to enumerate physical details, as well as other romanticized elements of their relation, would seem more typical of women's popular romances.[7] This is consistent with the text's structure as a whole, which, as Carmen Ramos Escandón notes, is a conscious re-elaboration of the tradition of women's magazines that came into vogue during the mid-nineteenth century. These periodicals, sometimes called *"calendarios por señoritas,"* included, like Esquivel's novel, recipes, home remedies, and, often, sentimental novels in monthly installments (45).

The appropriation of popular discourse, with its emphasis on such "feminine" values as nurturing and selflessness, is a means of undermining the patriarchal system (Showalter 131). Moreover, since both the *novela rosa* and related genres such as the *folletín* and the *telenovela* are forms of discourse often written *by* women and *for* a female public, Esquivel reinforces the idea of a community of women. Just as the rituals associated with cooking provide Tita with a sense of security (15), the fact that these popular genres often rely on formulae provides women with an order and a control that may not exist in their everyday world. Thus, the kitchen, from which men are traditionally excluded, is an area in which women may assert a small measure of control.[8] Furthermore, as with her appropriation of magic realism, Esquivel has chosen to use conventions from popular discourse that will be easily recognized by the reader: Tita, treated like a servant in her own home, is denied marriage to the man she loves due to the social sanctions represented by her mother; there is a growing tension between the lovers prior to the consummation of their relation; a series of impediments and tragedies including the death of Pedro's son and Tita's subsequent emotional crisis; Tita's rescue by a kindly older man (the fact that he is North American makes him particularly innocuous) whose selfless love cannot be reciprocated; the obligatory (false) pregnancy; and even a scene in which she swoons. In short, like the archetypal romantic heroine, Tita must go through difficult trials but is ultimately rewarded at the end as love triumphs. In addition, as is typical of serial discourse, there is a continual play in the novel of climax/anti-climax as each crisis is resolved and a new one takes its place, as well as a tendency to fall into melodramatic and overwrought prose: "Damn good manners! Damn Carreño's etiquette manual! Both were to blame that her body was hopelessly destined to wither away, little by little. . . . And damn Pedro, so decent, so proper, so manly, so . . . lovable!" (58/61–62; ellipsis in original, translation revised).

As Jean Franco points out, one of the common themes of the romance and the *telenovela* is that of a woman faced by "rules she has not made and over which she has no control" ("The Incorporation of Women" 123). Likewise, Tita, unable to marry the man she loves due to an outdated rule of conduct, battles throughout the novel with imposed conventions and her own desires: "[S]he couldn't resist the temptation to violate the oh-so-rigid rules her mother imposed in the kitchen . . . and in life" (198/199–200, ellipsis in original). Thus, although it relies on set formulae, the emphasis on individual desire over social propriety in such popular genres positions such discourse as a kind of alternate "formula" that lies outside the "recipes" dictated by society. Janice Radway has shown that popular romances share many characteristics with oral literature (25), which reinforces a connection to the orally transmitted traditions of cooking and household remedies that structure the novel. Similarly, both the *novela rosa* and the *telenovela* emphasize the notion of pleasure in storytelling, a pleasure that Radway considers utopian (207). Esquivel invites the reader to reassess conventional approaches to literature and to experience this pleasure, through flagrant sight-gags, such as when Tita drops the apricots on Pedro's head (38), and, especially, through the sensorial stimuli—the scents, tastes, colors, and textures—induced by food. Food functions as a narrative device in the novel: Like a cinematic montage, bridging both temporal and spatial displacements, it transports both the characters and the reader into a sensual dimension of reality. Obviously, the taste and scent of food as a device to stimulate memory is not unique. However, Esquivel again approaches the subject playfully, as Tita compares her emotional and physical state in terms of ludicrous culinary metaphors that question both the "seriousness" of canonized discourse and the time-worn metaphors of popular literature: "[I]t was then that she understood how dough feels when it is plunged into boiling oil" (16/21–22); "She felt so lost and lonely! One last chile in walnut sauce left on the platter after a fancy dinner couldn't feel any worse than she did" (57–58/61); "At thirty-nine she was still as sharp and fresh as a cucumber that had just been cut" (236/236). The narrator's means of expression is humorous but at the same time concrete; it transcends abstract notions of femininity and returns them to immediate experience.

Clearly, then, the novel's culinary metaphors suggest an approach to reality that emphasizes what is tangible over what is abstract and theoretical.[9] At the same time, however, the re-evaluation of *written texts* in the novel forces the reader to reconsider not only the previous texts but also the context in which they were written. Thus, the fact that Esquivel situates her novel at the time of the revolution suggests a specific historical moment in which the nineteenth-century values of the Porfiriato were overturned.[10] Indeed, although the women's magazines of this era represent, as Ramos Escandón asserts, an alternate space for female discourse,[11] they also fostered an attitude toward women that actually further circumscribed their role, since, as Bridget Aldaraca notes: "Women were instructed in minute detail on how to be and act, what to do and think, and, especially, what they as superior beings might never aspire to. . . The ideology of domesticity, which limited a woman's social existence to a sphere of activity within the family institution, gained in strength throughout the nineteenth century" (63). During this time, writers, both male and female, promulgated what Kathryn Rabuzzi calls the "sentimentalization of womanhood" (48). However, this notion of domesticity actually proved antithetical to the home: "Whether it is through false words, false behaviors, or false interiors . . . sentimental beliefs in Happily Ever After distort, trivialize, and artificially sweeten Home so that it loses its full meaning" (87). In *Como agua para chocolate*, the superficiality of this cult of domesticity is typified by Elena and Rosaura, who, although by all appearances conform to the marriage plot, become caricatures due to their blind acceptance of the imposed regulations on female behavior. Elena, who rules her home with an iron fist, is more concerned with the "proper" way of performing tasks than with the actual creativity involved in making the product (18–19). For her part, although she is genuinely upset when Pedro refuses to make love to her, Rosaura's primary concern is with the appearance of decency (215).

Significantly, as Marquet notes, both Rosaura and Elena's estrangement from their essential "female" nature is underscored by their inability to care for their own children and, especially, by their unnatural relations to food (60–62). Rosaura becomes a monstrous aberration who expands to enormous proportions after each child she bears, yet can neither nurse them nor care for them, and is ultimately forced to renounce her matrimonial responsibilities as well due to her huge size, halitosis, and flatulence, which in the end kill her. For her part, Elena's bitterness toward Tita leads her to taste poison in everything she eats; although she finally consents to let Tita prepare her meals, she secretly expels the food from her body with syrup of ipecac and eventually dies from vomiting (140). Tita, in contrast, is so closely attuned to her "feminine" nature that even though she is not yet sexually active, she is able to nurse her infant nephew (81). Clearly, the narration privileges the ancient oral tradition of female knowledge bequeathed to Tita by Nacha (53) over the artificial rules of conduct, upheld by Mamá Elena and reproduced by Rosaura.[12] That Tita feels circumscribed, precisely, by this textually mediated tradition, is indicated by her vehement rejection of Manuel Antonio Carreño's *Manual de urbanidad y buenas maneras*, a popular manual on etiquette that demarcates proper behaviors in every detail of human activity.[13] Although love triumphs at the end of the novel, by uniting the lovers in death, *Como agua para chocolate* further challenges the sentimental canon as it negates the formulaic "happy ending"—at least in a traditional sense.[14]

A close reading of Esquivel's text reveals that although the novel replicates popular forms on the surface, a deliberate inversion of roles has been effected that allows the author to appropriate this genre and challenge it at the same time. One obvious variation from the norm is that, unlike the characters in standard romance fiction, in which passivity is considered a virtue (Butler Flora 65–66),[15] in Esquivel's novel the female characters are stronger and more decisive than their male counterparts. The head of the family is a woman, one of the sisters becomes a general in the revolution, and it is Tita, not Pedro, who eventually dares to stand up to her mother and to Rosaura as well. Indeed, even before her rebellion, Tita wields an underground power through the strange effects produced by her cooking. In a subtle linguistic inversion, it is Tita who "penetrates" her beloved through the sensual power of her culinary creations: "It was as if a strange alchemical process had dissolved her entire being in the rose petal sauce, in the tender flesh of the quails, in the wine, and in each and every one of the meal's aromas. In this way she penetrated Pedro's body, hot, voluptuous, aromatic, totally sensuous" (52/57, translation revised).[16] Pedro, in contrast, is portrayed as weak and indecisive and, even as an adult, is subject to petty jealousies. Although he loves Tita, he does not challenge her mother's decision that Rosaura be his bride. As if there were any doubt that the facetious inversion of masculine and feminine characteristics is intentional, Pedro refuses to consummate his relation with Rosaura until months after their wedding, and when he finally relents, he recites: "Lord, this is not lust nor lewdness, but to make a child to serve you" (40/45). John also incarnates certain characteristics more generally associated with women: He is patient, nurturing and long-suffering. His intuition surprises Tita on more than one occasion (120, 222), and like the stereotypical self-sacrificing woman, he waits a lifetime for Tita only to ultimately give her up to Pedro. Even in the traditionally female domain of the kitchen, Esquivel questions the rigidity of conventional roles. Since recipes are a code to which only women normally have access, Ramos Escandón maintains that we may speak of a "female language" suggested by culinary discourse (45). Nonetheless, Esquivel is careful to note that such language is not biologically *determined* but *learned* through oral tradition. Thus, when Gertrudis attempts to read a recipe, although she is a woman she is unable to decipher its code: "Gertrudis read the recipe as if she were reading hieroglyphics" (192/194). Moreover, in a further inversion of anticipated gender roles, it is a man, Sargent Treviño, who manages to decode the words and successfully prepare the desired product (197–199).

As Marquet notes, the male characters in *Como agua para chocolate* are of such secondary importance that they are never described in physical detail, whereas the female body is frequently lauded (65–66). The fact that details of male anatomy are excluded from the narration is perhaps consistent with a more feminine vision of romance that conventionally has privileged idealistic or spiritual attraction over graphic explicitness (von Franz 179, 188). A careful reading of the text, moreover, reveals that every instance in which the female body is described in hyperbolic detail represents a moment in which the focalization of the episode has shifted to a male character. In such passages, Esquivel evokes the male gaze by which *a woman* is converted into *Woman*,[17] and her parody of the overwrought nineteenth-century prose is at its most exaggerated at these times. For example, it is through Juan's gaze that the nude Gertrudis is evoked as "an angel and devil in one woman" (55/59), and when Pedro inadvertently walks in on a bare-breasted Tita nursing his child, it is *his* vision that transforms her into "Ceres herself, goddess of plenty" (76/82). Aldaraca notes that one of the results of the sentimentalization of womanhood during the nineteenth century was, precisely, that women became "often perceived not as an individual but as a *genre*" (66). Hence, far from a "banal" imitation or of a female "egotism" that symbolically castrates the male characters—as Marquet suggests (66)—Esquivel has adroitly taken this tradition and used it to differentiate between the textually mediated archetypes of Woman and the real experiences of women. Each of the female characters has an individual identity that does not necessarily fit into the rigid dichotomies imposed by patriarchal thought. Furthermore, just as women are not Woman in Esquivel's novel, nor are men expected to represent Man, there are no superhuman qualities about them, and therefore no need to describe in detail their extraordinary sexual potencies. In short, *Como agua para chocolate* portrays women and men as individuals, not as allegorical Others. Real women, the novel shows us, may have "masculine" attributes such as strength and courage, just as real men may show "feminine," nurturing sides.

The use of traditional resources has the potential to become revolutionary when reorganized from the vantage point of women or any other marginalized group. The fact that Esquivel has chosen discourses not just outside the canon but specifically associated with women's values and experiences allows her to set forth an alternative to the hegemonic standard, based upon real women's lives. As Teresa de Lauretis affirms, such an integration of everyday experiences into creative practice may serve to displace both aesthetic hierarchies and generic categories (10). In the canon, male voice and focalization are often privileged as the source of power. By humorously deconstructing this gaze and proclaiming women as a source of energy in their own right, the absolutes of the dominant order are undermined and an alternate order is posited. While reaffirming the traditional roles of women, Esquivel asserts their value with a project based on—*but not duplicating*—such roles. By dissolving the borders between canonized and popular literatures, between oral and written discourses, the hierarchy governing such distinctions is subverted as well.[18]

NOTES

1. In McMurray's defense, his critique of the novel is limited to a brief book review; therefore, he does not examine this transtextual relation at length. Marquet's virulent denigration of the novel is a fascinating study in misreading, with examples too numerous to enumerate here. Essentially, for Marquet, the central themes of the novel are matricide and the sadistic annihilation of maternal figures; he further asserts that the novel's main purpose is to satisfy "feminine sexual fantasies" such as prostitution and exhibitionism (64–65). Fadanelli's analysis, while less sophisticated, surpasses that of Marquet in its misogynous undercurrent as he concludes: "Elena Poniatowska has celebrated the publication of *Como agua para chocolate* . . . [and] has promised . . . to run out to cook alongside Laura Esquivel. I hope, and have no doubt, that both of them will get indigestion from their cooking and from their literatures" (4,

my translation).

2. As Naomi Schor notes in her discussion of the female critic's relation to patriarchal theoretical discourse, it is important to recognize the *playful* nature of this appropriation. This process, which Schorr terms "patriody" and which may also to be applied to narrative, refers to "a linguistic act of *repetition and difference* that hovers between *parody* and *parricide*" (xii, emphasis added). Similarly, as Beatriz González Stephan notes, Esquivel's appropriation of popular discourse *fluctuates* between parody of and homage to precursor texts (210). Kathleen Glenn's analysis also interprets the novel as a parodic text.

3. Significantly, this shift in focus is consistent with the differences that have been discerned between male and female humor. Gender-based studies on humor by Leigh Marlowe and Mary Crawford note that men's sexual humor typically "uses the symbolism of *domination* and *power*, not seduction and sensuality. *Exaggerations of male sexual prowess* and/or lack of same, abound, *with women almost invariably victims or butts of male sexuality*. The obvious conclusion is that sexual joking is a male privilege, emphasizing a sense of male community and male norms among the jokers" (Marlowe 149, emphasis added). Women's humor, Crawford suggests, "supports a goal of greater intimacy by being supportive and healing, while men's humor reinforces 'performance' goals of competition, the establishment of hierarchal relationships, and self-aggrandizement" (161).

4. As Leonardi points out, the act of foodmaking as a collaborative activity implicates the reader as well since the nature of sharing recipes has "some interesting relationships to both reading and writing. . . . Even the root of *recipe*—the Latin *recipere*—implies an exchange, a giver and a receiver" (340). Indeed, as Leonardi observes, the receiver of the recipe is *encouraged* to reproduce it (344); thus, recipes by their very nature demand active readers.

5. Unless otherwise noted, I use the translation of Carol and Thomas Christensen. The first set of page numbers in parenthesis corresponds to this translation; the second, to the original Spanish text.

6. Examples of hyperbolic sexuality abound both in the "boom" novels and in postboom narrative as well. *Cien años de soledad*, by Gabriel García Márquez, José Arcadio is so magnificently endowed that even Úrsula becomes aroused at the sight of her son (36); in an episode reminiscent of D. H. Lawrence in Carlos Fuentes's *Gringo viejo*, Harriet Winslow marvels over Tomás Arroyo's genitalia, which she describes in almost spiritual terms (120). García Márquez and Fuentes are, of course, playing with the institution of *machismo*; nonetheless such descriptions perpetuate certain stereotypes by retaining the use of the devotional female gaze to convey a masculine message. As a consequence of this male-centered consciousness and, in the case of García Márquez, by the categorization of female characters through archetypal conventions, the female experience is trivialized.

7. I am reminded of the scene in *Cien años de soledad* in which José Arcadio "draws and quarters" the virgin Rebeca (88).

8. This is true both in the preparation and of the consumption of food, since the act of eating becomes, for many women, an act of will, as only she may decide when to deny or provide for herself. The connection between food and expression is underscored in the novel as Tita refuses to eat *and to speak* following her emotional breakdown.

9. As Deane Curtin observes, cooking is an activity in which practice is more important than theory, and this practice hinges on physical experience and contextual knowledge (10). Lisa Heldke calls this approach "bodily knowledge" because it is a kind of perception that transcends the subject/object dichotomy and admits an interrelationship between human subjects and food (218).

10. Although the names of North Americans in the novel (John and Mary Brown, for example) are contrived, the less common surnames of the principal characters, Tita de la Garza and Pedro Múzquiz, are likely borrowed from two historical figures from Coahuila, both associated with the revolution: Pablo de la Garza, attorney general under Venustiano Carranza and military commander of Nuevo León, and Rafael Múzquiz, one of Carranza's closest friends and a diplomat in the United States and Europe. Coincidentally, these names figure in a *female* version of the revolution, that of Leonor Villegas de Magnon. In the other hand, María Victoria García Serrano's charge that Gertrudis's advancement to the rank of *generala* does not coincide with the real-life experiences of *soldaderas* in Villa's forces (200) fails to take into account the playful recontextualization of stereotypes associated with literary and cinematic versions of the revolution. Indeed, readers familiar with Mexican literature and culture may detect in Gertrudis a rewriting of the disempowered mulata *coronela* in Francisco Rojas González's *La negra angustias* (1944), made into a well-known film and reprinted in the widely distributed Colección Popular of the Fondo de Cultura Económica in 1984.

11. In Mexico, literary production during the nineteenth century remained a predominantly male domain. Although, as Nora Pasternac has demonstrated, many contributors to these journals were female (399), Franco and Aldaraca's research suggests that both novels and journals designed for a female public were often published by men, thus permitting male ideals to control not only the public sphere but the private sphere as well (Franco *Plotting Women* 82, 90–91; Aldaraca 75). Jane Herrick also finds that most women's magazines in Mexico during the nineteenth century were published by men and that, in fact, advice on etiquette and such matters as keeping one's hands white took precedence over sections on the more everyday aspects of domestic life as recipes (141). Moreover, in the journals Herrick examined, those that did include recipes emphasized a bland foreign cuisine dominated by puddings and such exotic advances as colored gelatin (142).

12. A clear example in which orally transmitted knowledge is considered superior to textually mediated discourse is during the birth of Rosaura's first child. At a loss as to how to deliver a baby, Tita condemns her formal education as useless: "What good did it do her now to know the names of the planets and Carreño's manual from A to Z if her sister was practically dead and she couldn't help her" (71/78). Subsequently, however, she is able to revive the spirit of Nacha, whose *voice* successfully guides her through the process (79).

13. For a detailed discussion of the Carreño's *Manual* in Esquivel's novel, see Salvador Oropesa.

14. Rachel Blau DuPlessis notes that in the nineteenth-century European novel death is the prescribed ending for characters with an "inappropriate relation to the 'social script' or plot designed to contain her legally, economically, and sexually" (15). In women's fiction of the twentieth century, however, death becomes more explicitly identified as "the vehicle for affirming the necessity for *critique of the conventions governing women and narrative structures*" (53, emphasis added). In the final chapter of her novel, which begins with the description of a wedding, Esquivel makes clear that

she is playing with popular formulae, since she leads the reader to believe, erroneously, that the novel will end with the marriage of the main characters.

15. Butler further notes that not only is dependence conventionally seen as desirable in women (66) but the inability to take care of oneself is considered an "endearing feminine quality" (69).

16. After completing the first version of this chapter I came across an interview with Esquivel that supported my intuition that this inversion is by no means gratuitous: "Writing this book taught me something: that cooking inverts the traditional sexual order. Man is the passive recipient, while woman is the active transmitter" ("El arte de la novela" 5, my translation).

17. I am using the notion of the "gaze" as it is employed by Laura Mulvey, E. Ann Kaplan, and Teresa de Lauretis in their work on cinema. For more on the women/Woman distinction, see de Lauretis (*Alice Doesn't* 5).

18. An earlier version of the essay presented in this chapter was read at the Kentucky Foreign Language Conference in April 1994 and subsequently published in *Hispanic Review* 63.2 (1995).

REFERENCES

Aldaraca, Bridget. "El ángel del hogar: The cult of domesticity in nineteenth-century Spain." *Theory and Practice of Feminist Literary Criticism*. Eds. Gabriela Mora and Karen S. Van Hooft. Ypsilanti, MI: Bilingual Press, 1977. 63–87.

Butler Flora, Cornelia. "The Passive Female and Social Change: A Cross-Cultural Comparison of Women's Magazine Fiction." *Female and Male in Latin America: Essays*. Ed. Ann Pescatello. Pittsburgh: U of Pittsburgh P, 1979. 59–86.

Carreño, Manuel Antonio. *Manual de urbanidad y buenas maneras, para uso de la juventud de ambos sexos; en el cual se encuentran las principales reglas de civilidad y etiqueta que deben observarse en las diversas situaciones sociales*. New York: Appleton, 1854.

Crawford, Mary. "Humor in Conversational Context: Beyond Biases in the Study of Gender and Humor." *Representations: Social Constructions of Gender*. Ed. Rhoda K. Unger. Amityville, NY: Baywood, 1989. 155–166.

Curtin, Deane W. "Food/Body/Person." *Cooking, Eating, Thinking: Transformative Philosophies of Food*. Eds. Deane W. Curtin and Lisa M. Heldke. Bloomington: Indiana UP, 1992.

De Lauretis, Teresa. *Alice Doesn't: Feminism, Semiotics, Cinema*. Bloomington: Indiana UP, 1983.

_____. *Feminist Studies/Critical Studies*. Bloomington: Indiana UP, 1986.

DuPlessis, Rachel Blau. *Writing beyond the Ending: Narrative Strategies of Twentieth-Century Women Writers*. Bloomington: Indiana UP, 1985.

Esquivel, Laura. "El arte de la novela como una forma culinaria." With Alejandro Semo and Juan José Giovannini. *Excélsior* (8 abril 1990): 5.

_____. *Como agua para chocolate: Novela de entregas mensuales con recetas, amores y remedios caseros*. Mexico: Planeta, 1989.

_____. *Like Water for Chocolate: A Novel in Monthly Installments with Recipes, Romances and Home Remedies*. Trans. Carol and Thomas Christensen. New York: Doubleday, 1992.

Fadanelli, Guillermo. "La literatura a la que estamos condenados." *Unomásuno* (28 abril 1990): 4.

Franco, Jean. "The Incorporation of Women: A Comparison of North American and Mexican Popular Narrative." *Studies in Entertainment: Critical Approaches to Mass Culture*. Ed. Tania Modleski. Bloomington: Indiana UP, 1986. 119–138.

———. *Plotting Women: Gender and Representation in Mexico*. New York: Columbia UP, 1989.

Fuentes, Carlos. *Gringo viejo*. Mexico: Fondo de Cultura Económica, 1985.

García Márquez, Gabriel. *Cien años de soledad*. Buenos Aires: Sudamericana, 1981.

García Serrano, M[aría] Victoria. "*Como agua para chocolate* de Laura Esquivel: Apuntes para un debate." *Indiana Journal of Hispanic Literatures* 6–7 (1995): 185–206.

Glenn, Kathleen. "Postmodern Parody and Culinary-Narrative Art in Laura Esquivel's *Como agua para chocolate*." *Chasqui* 23.2 (1994): 39–47.

González Stephan, Beatriz. "Para comerte mejor: Cultura Calibanesca y formas literarias alternativas." *Nuevo Texto Crítico* V.9–10 (1993): 201–215.

Heldke, Lisa M. "Foodmaking as a Thoughtful Practice." *Cooking, Eating, Thinking: Transformative Philosophies of Food*. Eds. Deane W. Curtin and Lisa M. Heldke. Bloomington: Indiana UP, 1992.

Herrick, Jane. "Periodicals for Women in Mexico during the Nineteeth Century." *Americas* 14.2 (1957): 135–144.

Hutcheon, Linda. *A Poetics of Postmodernism: History, Theory, Fiction*. London: Routledge, 1988.

———. *A Theory of Parody*. New York: Methuen, 1985.

Kaplan, E. Ann. "Is the Gaze Male?" *Powers of Desire: the Politics of Sexuality*. Eds. Ann Snitow, et al. New York: Monthly Review, 1983. 309–327.

Leonardi, Susan J. "Recipes for Reading: Summer Pasta, Lobster à la Riseholme, and Key Lime Pie." *PMLA* 104.3 (1989): 340–347.

McMurray, George. "Two Mexican Feminist Writers." *Hispania* 73 (1990): 1035–1036.

Marlowe, Leigh. "A Sense of Humor." *Representations: Social Constructions of Gender*. Ed. Rhoda K. Unger. Amityville, NY: Baywood, 1989. 145–154.

Marquet, Antonio. "La receta de Laura Esquivel: ¿Cómo escribir un best-seller?" *Plural* 237 (1991): 58–67.

Mulvey, Laura. "Visual Pleasure and Narrative Cinema." *Visual and Other Pleasures*. Bloomington: Indiana UP, 1989. 14–28.

Oropesa, Salvador. "*Como agua para chocolate* de Laura Esquivel como lectura de *Manual de urbanidad y buenas costumbres* de Manuel Antonio Carreño." *Monographic Review/Revista Monográfica* 8 (1992): 252–260.

Pasternac, Nora. "El periodismo femenino en el siglo XIX: *Violetas de Anáhuac*." *Las voces olvidadas: Antología crítica de narradoras mexicanas nacidas en el siglo XIX*. Eds. Ana Rosa Domatella y Nora Pasternac. Mexico: Colegio de México, 1991.

Rabuzzi, Kathryn Allen. *The Sacred and the Feminine: Toward a Theology of Housework*. New York: Seabury, 1982.

Radway, Janice. *Reading the Romance: Women, Patriarchy and Popular Literature*. Durham: U of North Carolina P, 1984.

Ramos Escandón, Carmen. "Receta y femineidad en *Como agua para chocolate*." *Fem* 15.102 (1991): 45–48.

Schor, Naomi. *Breaking the Chain: Women, Theory, and French Realist Fiction*. New York: Columbia UP, 1985.

Showalter, Elaine. "Toward a Feminist Poetics." *The New Feminist Criticism: Essays on Women, Literature, and Theory*. New York: Pantheon, 1985. 125–143.

Villegas de Magnon, Leonor. *The Rebel*. Ed. Clara Lomas. Houston, TX: Arte Público, 1994.

Von Franz, M[arie]-L[ouise]. "The Process of Individuation." *Man and His Symbols*. Eds. Carl G. Jung and M. L. von Franz. London: Aldus, 1964. 158–229.

10

STORYTELLING IN LAURA ESQUIVEL'S
COMO AGUA PARA CHOCOLATE

Yael Halevi-Wise

The integration of plot with culinary events in Laura Esquivel's *Como agua para chocolate* (*Like Water for Chocolate*, 1989) generates a complex sense of literary, historical, and textual perspective. This sense of perspective enhances the characters's fictional depth by building their private histories at the same time as it constructs a general sense of folkloric and historical depth through placement within the context of the Mexican Revolution and through ongoing references to traditional Mexican cuisine and home remedies. The intimate association of recipes with Tita's experiences, memories, and thoughts provides the main chronological and causal basis for the construction of her character, while the seasonal Mexican dishes in the background establish a historical sense of national tradition and culture.[1] Yet, in addition to the obvious use of recipes as a main structural device, Esquivel employs character storytelling as a more subtle narrative strategy. Her stories within the novel engender a distinct view of character and, without explicitly appearing to do so, contribute greatly to this sense of perspective. When one character tells a story to another, the reader evaluates both the teller and the listener's performance, comparing their distinctive features even if the story itself does not contain direct information about any of the characters. However, a story within a novel often includes valuable information about the novel's characters and frequently functions as an ingenious device to impel the plot forward.

In *Como agua para chocolate*, the ability to tell stories goes hand in hand with the propensity to give of oneself to, and care for, others. Mama Elena and Rosaura, who can bring children to the world but cannot nurse them, are conspicuously incapable of telling tales. Nacha, Chencha, the American doctor John Brown, his grandmother Luz del Amanecer, and Tita in her own special way are the storytellers in this novel. Pedro is not a storyteller, and his inability to disregard social conventions and Mama Elena's rules in order to fully love and give himself to Tita constitutes the real obstacle in the plot. Gertrudis lies in the middle of the storytelling versus nurturing spectrum. She is an occasional storyteller and, accordingly, is capable of loving and caring for others to a limited extent; but Gertrudis is more selfish than the rest of the storytelling characters. Her tales are centered upon herself: She has so many things to tell Tita about her adventures in the revolution "that she could talk day and night for a month without running out of conversation" (10.187) and without paying attention to her sister's grave problems. John Brown and Nacha's stories, on the other hand, are geared almost entirely towards the emotional benefit of their listeners.[2]

The first, although not necessarily the most important, level of storytelling in *Como agua para chocolate* corresponds to its narrator. To use Gérard Genette's terminology, the narrator here is extra-heterodiegetical, meaning that she refers to the events from an external vantage point and is not directly included in the action (203–225, 238–260). In this case, however, the narrator is to some extent relating her own history, since she is the protagonist's great niece.[3] Her sources of information (other than an apparently omniscient imagination) are a wealth of family stories and a recipe book/diary that her great aunt Tita composed in an attempt to attain some degree of self-expression. Occasionally, the narrator addresses the reader directly with remarks such as "take care to chop the onion fine. To keep from crying when you chop it . . . I suggest you place a little bit on your head" (1.5). These direct addresses are concentrated at the beginning and end of the novel, where the narrator speaks in the first person. By and large, however, the narrator uses a third-person mode to describe the life and culinary expertise of Tita. Tita is not a distinguished verbal storyteller, and, as we shall see further on, she often represses retorts and fails to express her thoughts aloud. Yet, Tita's reception and transmission of recipes can be regarded as a creative form of communication analogous to the art of telling, and in this sense, she is the novel's primary "storyteller." This connection between words and recipes is made explicit in the text when, following a description of Tita's most prolific and enthusiastic period as a cook, we are told that she played with the ingredients and quantities of traditional recipes "just as a poet plays with words" (4.69). Considered in this light, the art of storytelling acquires a wider anthropological and sociological dimension in this novel.

Storytelling experiences are portrayed on a variety of levels and in several narrative dimensions in *Como agua para chocolate*. The tales told by Chencha and John Brown function as a means to characterize them and those to whom they tell their stories: Chencha lies in order to elicit attention or avoid getting into a confrontation with her severe employer; John Brown uses his Native American grandmother's tales as a subtle form of psychotherapy that reaches beyond Tita's otherwise impermeable grief. The embedded stories also function as a tactic that either complicates or advances the plot and, occasionally, as a unifying device that ties imagery with plot, even as the magical power of Tita's recipes bind the novel both internally (thematically and symbolically) and externally (structurally).

Tita learns to express herself by adapting to her own needs and possibilities the modes of expression used by the storytellers who surround her. She learns primarily from Nacha, Chencha, and John Brown. From Nacha, she learns how to cook, and the succulent tastes of prehispanic and Spanish dishes continue to exist through these women's re-enactment of traditional recipes: "Tita was the last link in a chain of cooks who had been passing culinary secrets from generation to generation since ancient times" (3.48). But Tita takes Nacha's traditional mode of expression a step further. At first she merely follows the set recipes and is as surprised as everyone else is when her repressed emotions manifest themselves magically in the meals she prepares. But once she realizes that her emotions surface involuntarily in her cooking despite honest attempts to submit to the discipline of a cruel mother, Tita consciously harnesses the magic of her cookery to communicate with Pedro through it. Cooking then becomes Tita's unique form of expression and her only channel of communication.

The transition between routinely making food for the family and cooking as a conscious form of communication and self-expression occurs when Pedro gives Tita a bouquet of roses and instead of throwing them out as her mother orders, Tita employs them in the preparation of an exquisite lunch of quails in rose petals. The excitement and joy experienced by Tita when she receives the meaningful gift from her would-be-lover is transmitted through the food to Tita's unmarried sister: "Tita was the transmitter, Pedro the receiver, and poor Gertrudis the medium, the conducting body through which the singular sexual message was passed" (3.52). Gertrudis is affected by it to such an extent that the bathhouse burns down from the heat of her passion, and a revolutionary soldier—who from far away smells the sexual desire emanating from Gertrudis's skin—rides into the ranch and carries the naked woman away on his horse. Tita and Pedro witness this passionate scene, wishing that they were in the place of the couple already copulating for the first time as they ride away. A moment later, however, Tita is faced with the necessity of informing her mother that Gertrudis is missing and the bathhouse is on fire. But rather than tell her mother the true details of Gertrudis's scandalous action, Tita decides to alter the information to suit her own taste and needs. First of all, she cannot admit to Mama Elena that her own bottled up passion impelled her sister to run away with a soldier, and, furthermore, she favors the soldiers of the revolutionary against those of the federal army.

Seeking a less controversial explanation, Tita opts for an imitation of Chencha's typically deceptive tales. The vivacious Chencha tells stories about anything and everything. When Tita was a child, she would frighten her with "stories of La Llorona, the witch who sucks little children's blood, or the boogeyman, or other scary stories." Later on, she would describe "hangings, shootings, dismemberments, decapitations, and even sacrifices in which the victim's heart was cut out—in the heat of battle!" (4.68). Tita takes Chencha's stories with a grain of salt, for she "knew Chencha sometimes exaggerated and distorted things" (1.14).[4] Yet part of Tita longs to believe these stories. And similarly, when Tita tells her mother that "the Federal troops, which Tita hated, had swooped down on the ranch, set fire to the bathroom, and kidnapped Gertrudis," Mama Elena uncharacteristically swallows Tita's version of the events (3.58). From the afternoon in which she prepares the aphrodisiac rose sauce, watches her sister run off naked with a handsome soldier, and lies to Mama Elena for the first time, Tita begins to seek new channels of self-expression. That night she begins to write the cookbook/diary that constitutes the fictional basis of the novel. Her first entry describes the preparation of "quails in rose petals" and concludes with the terse observation that "[t]oday while we were eating this dish, Gertrudis ran away" (3.60). From this time onward, Tita dares to transform old recipes and invent new ones in order to recapture "the connection that flowed between [Pedro and Tita] through the food she prepared" (4.69). Cooking becomes a full-fledged creative outlet, and her primary means of communication with Pedro.

It takes Tita a long time to confront her mother face to face, and even when she does so, the cumulative years of fear and self-repression lead to a nervous breakdown. From this state, Dr. Brown patiently nurses her back to health. To do so, he relies to a great extent upon the wisdom and tales of his Kikapu grandmother, whose match-theory is useful as a metaphor for the state of Tita's psyche. In terms of length and beauty, this tale is the most substantial of the stories embedded in *Como agua para chocolate*. In this passage, Dr. Brown—whose Spanish is excellent but somewhat peculiar—gently explains to Tita that, according to his grandmother, "each of us is born with a box of matches inside us but we can't strike them all by ourselves . . . we need oxygen and a candle to help. In this case, the oxygen, for example, would come from the breath of the person you love; the candle could be any kind of food, music, caress, word, or sound that engenders the explosion that lights one of the matches." The problem is that if the matches are not ignited, the box of matches dampens, and "not a single match will ever be lighted. . . . If that happens, the soul flees from the body and goes to wander among the deepest shades, trying in vain to find food to nourish itself, unaware that only the body it left behind, cold and defenseless, is capable of providing that food." Yet Dr. Brown assures his patient that all is not lost for the sad individual whose matches have dampened. There are many ways to dry out these inner matchboxes. However, if all of the matches are ignited at once "they would produce a splendor so dazzling that it would illuminate far beyond what we can normally see; and then a brilliant tunnel would appear before our eyes, revealing the path we forgot the moment we were born, and summoning us to regain the divine origin we had lost. The soul ever longs to return to the place from which it came, leaving the body lifeless" (6.115–117).

John Brown tells Tita this exemplary story as they sit in his laboratory, their situation paralleling John's years as a child and adolescent in his grandmother's laboratory, and Tita's years of apprenticeship with Nacha in the kitchen. Tita, who at the time of the telling of this story is still in a state of shock, remains silent during the entire scene, having uttered no word, in fact, since Dr. Brown brought her to his house instead of to a mental hospital as Mama Elena requested. Tita slowly regains her mental health through frequent contact with this kind and intelligent doctor. And inspired by the suggestive metaphors implicit in stories such as the tale of the matches, she learns to dissociate her will and needs from those of her mother.[5] John's metaphorical story encapsulates the novel's entire plot. Like the phosphorus that waits for oxygen and heat to kindle it, Tita waits for the consummation of her passion to free her as an individual and as a woman. Although the novel's title refers explicitly to a state of anger rather than to sexual passion—"Tita was literally 'like water for chocolate'—she was on the verge of boiling over. How irritable she was!" (8.151)—one can easily equate the image of water about to boil over with Tita's imminent sexuality. Dr. Brown expresses this idea in terms of a match ready and meant to be kindled. The match's potential radiance can be dampened, though, as Tita's life has been by Mama Elena's selfish abuse.[6] Tita recognizes her own situation in Dr. Brown's metaphorical tale, and in his oblique explanations, she finds the beginnings of solutions to her problems. Soon she is physically and mentally strong enough to consciously free herself from Mama Elena's stifling influence. For the first time in her life, Tita is able to make (and subsequently change) decisions regarding her future. Eventually she gives free rein to her passion for Pedro,[7] who is not mentioned explicitly in connection to the initial context of John Brown's tale but is evidently the subject of Tita's inner admission that "the saddest thing was that she knew what set off her explosions, but each time she had managed to light a match, it had persistently been blown out" (6.116). Nonetheless, at the end of the one-sided conversation with John Brown—which is accompanied in the narration by a description of Tita's silent thoughts—Tita considers the possibility that the doctor might be her detonator. In subsequent months Tita tests the idea that John Brown's proximity would give life to her soul. Charmed by his kindness and deep-felt interest, Tita nearly marries him. At the end, however, she falls prey to the man who at the age of sixteen had made her feel like "dough feels when it is plunged into boiling oil" (1.16). Eventually, Pedro and Tita do act upon their mutual attraction, but only after Mama Elena's death. And even then they are able to indulge in sexual relations only stealthily and in a random manner because Rosaura (who knows about it) stipulates that the outward appearance of her marriage with Pedro must be maintained and that the innocence of her little daughter must be protected.

Many years later, following Rosaura's death and her daughter's marriage, Pedro and Tita are freed for the first time to make love to each other in complete privacy and in an unrestrained manner. But at this point, Pedro's excitement is so overwhelming that he dies in Tita's arms. Tita then realizes that she should have warned him about the matchlike properties of one's emotions: She should have told him the match story just as John Brown had once told it to her. Moments prior to Pedro's death, Tita prevents her own demise thanks to a timely recollection of Dr. Brown's words. His tale comes back to her like a prophesy:

"If a strong emotion suddenly lights all the candles we carry inside ourselves, it creates a brightness that shines far beyond our normal vision and then a splendid tunnel appears that shows us the way that we forgot when we were born and calls us to recover our lost divine origin. The soul longs to return to the place it came from, leaving the body lifeless." . . . Tita checked her passion. . . . She didn't want to die. She wanted to explore these emotions many more times. This was just the beginning. (12.244)

Unfortunately, Tita's insight arrives too late to prevent the death of her lover. To a certain extent, the fact that Pedro dies from the power of his first unrestrained sexual contact with Tita goes to prove that his interest in her was genuine all along. Yet better communication between them could have prevented his death, which likewise proves that their relationship was essentially flawed. Moreover, had Pedro been truly aware of Tita's needs, he would have satisfied them much earlier. As it is, for all practical purposes, he was Mama Elena's accomplice in castrating the motherly and otherwise creative Tita. Ultimately, Tita never marries nor has a child of her own. Conversely, had Tita warned Pedro of the dangerous properties of stifled emotions, he, too, might have taken care to pace his own and lived to fully enjoy the free lovelife that had finally become possible for them.

Tita's relationship with Pedro, as well as with her mother, is characterized by what she *does not* say. She never shares the match story with Pedro, and although when Gertrudis runs off, Tita almost asks Pedro to run away with her, she never actually suggests it because "[t]he words formed a lump in her throat and were choked one after another as they tried to escape" (3.57). A few moments later Tita is able to tell her mother a Chencha type of story about Gertrudis's disappearance. Yet she entirely ceases to speak when, after years of repressing clever retorts to Mama Elena's orders, she finally rebels, blaming her mother for the death of Pedro and Rosaura's son.[8] Although during their confrontation Mama Elena hits her daughter so hard that Tita's nose breaks, this time Tita retreats into silence but does not submit. She runs up to the pigeon house, where John Brown finds her almost a day later: "naked, her nose broken, her whole body covered with pigeon droppings" (5.100). This is the lowest point in Tita's trajectory toward freedom and self-expression. Her first act of self-expression occurs immediately after the match story, when Dr. Brown asks her to write down her reasons for not speaking. Tita writes: "Because I don't want to." With this bold declaration, written with phosphorus on the wall, she takes "her first step towards freedom" (117).

The most salient manifestation of Tita's characteristic *lack* of expression resides in the magical properties of the foods she prepares. Since she is denied the most basic channels of communication and is furthermore compelled to live under the same roof as her would-be lover and his lawful wife, Tita is obliged to somehow block her strong emotions in order to survive. These blocked emotions nonetheless find their way into the meals she prepares, affecting others with the feelings she tries to suppress. Her emotions consequently function as a detonator of the inner matches of those who eat what she cooks under the influence of a certain mood: The wedding guests suffer intense nostalgia (and vomit profusely) when they taste Rosaura's wedding cake; the aphrodisiac effect of the quail in rose petals affects Gertrudis as described previously, the smoked sausages, whose preparation is interrupted by the drastic rupture between Tita and her mother, become infested with worms. Initially, these inexplicable manifestations of Tita's emotions constitute her only mode of expression; they flow out of her and map her private story. Her identity and social relations subsequently develop through an awareness of other forms of communication, many of which are stories or styles of storytelling which she learns from, imitates, and generally uses in her own particular manner.

Como agua para chocolate is built from various interlocking modes and styles of communication.[9] Nacha's transmission and Tita's idiosyncratic production of recipes constitute the most obvious narratological and structural device of the novel, one which in many ways can be regarded as a mode of communication analogous to the art of storytelling. Spice is added by Chencha's spontaneous and picaresque interpretations of the world; like Tita's, Chencha's character is founded upon the personal search for creative forms of self-expression. John Brown's match story gives the novel a mythical and metaphorical dimension that holds together the various facets of Tita's tragic struggle for freedom and self-expression. Although the recipe for matches is technically the only one not involving food, at the end of the novel Tita consumes Dr. Brown's symbolic matches in what is a supreme literary fusion of recipe, characterization, plot, myth, and embedded storytelling.

NOTES

1. The association of recipes with milestones in the protagonist's life relies on the technique of magic realism in a way that Kristine Ibsen and Kathleen Glenn identify as a parodic subversion of this popular Latin American style. Ibsen describes Esquivel's approach in terms of a feminized appropriation of magic realism and thus as a far cry from the mere imitation of García Márquez suggested by George McMurray (Ibsen 134–135; McMurray 1035–1036). From a similar point of view, Glenn surveys various forms of popular and elitist literature recuperated and parodied by Esquivel, whose magic realism can be read as an essentially feminine vision of history, gender, and popular literary styles.

2. Translations are from published version by Carol and Thomas Christensen. Chapter numbers have been included with page references.

3. Since ultimately this narrator is a direct issue of the events she describes, her degree of involvement in them can be qualified to a certain extent. Her introductory words already anticipate crucial information given toward the end of the novel, in the very least because her existence testifies to the resolution of a number of forces at tension throughout it. See Shlomith Rimmon-Kenan for a fine-tuned discussion of the nuances distinguishing various examples of a narrator's participation in a story (94–96).

4. Chencha's process of producing stories is described in detail when she is forced to devise an explanation for meeting Tita against Mama Elena's orders: "Nervous, she twisted her rebozo around and around, trying to squeeze out the best of her lies for this situation. It never failed. When the rebozo was turned a hundred times, a tale that fit the occasion always came to her. For her, lying was a survival skill that she had picked up as soon as she had arrived at the ranch" (7.127). Chencha is a rogue and, like all picaresque characters, she tells lies to survive in a hostile world. As Glenn notes in relation to this particular story, "Chencha never manages to tell Mama Elena the tear-jerker of a story she has concocted about Tita because before she can do so, bandits attack the ranch, rape Chencha, and while Mama Elena is trying to defend her honor deliver such a blow to her spine that she is left paralyzed from the waist down" (43).

5. Antonio Marquet notes that Tita is a modern Cinderella complete with Nacha in the role of fairy godmother (62). Building upon Marquet's observation, Glenn discusses Esquivel's parodic use of fairy tales (44–45).

6. The narrator—possibly echoing Tita's own thoughts—refers to Mama Elena as "the castrating woman" (7.139), an epithet developed on a symbolic level earlier on, when Mama Elena forces Tita to castrate the fowls to be served at her sister's wedding (2.25–26).

7. Tita's relationship with Pedro is ambiguous. The narrator leaves ample room to disbelieve the romantic explanation for his engagement to one sister when he came to seek the hand of another: Nacha reports to Tita that she overheard Pedro explaining that marriage to Rosaura would enable him to live as close as possible to his real beloved, but "How strange that Nacha, who was quite hard of hearing by that time, should have claimed to have heard this conversation [between Pedro and his father]." It is added, however, that Nacha may have simply verbalized the words that everyone else suppressed (1.15). Early on, Tita is ready to run away with Pedro, or at least have sexual relations with him, but this last happens only after Mama Elena dies and when Pedro becomes jealous of John Brown.

8. Tita constantly stifles her objections to Mama Elena's decisions, yet her mother punishes even the *potential* retorts. For instance, when forced to castrate the fowls for Rosaura's wedding, Tita longs to scream ironically that "when they had chosen something to be neutered, they'd made a mistake, they should have chosen her. At least then there would be some justification for not allowing her to marry and giving Rosaura her place beside the man she loved. Mama Elena read the look on her face and flew into a rage, giving Tita a tremendous slap that left her rolling in the dirt" (2.27).

9. This recalls Mikhail Bakhtin's characterization of the novel as a heteroglossic genre comprised of "subordinated, yet still relatively autonomous, unities . . . [combined] into the higher unity of the work as a whole" (262). The novel is described as heteroglossia that has been artistically and strategically "dialogized" (272).

REFERENCES

Bakhtin, Mikhail M. *The Dialogic Imagination*. Ed. Michael Holquist, trans. Carol Emerson and Michael Holquist. Austin: U of Texas P, 1981.

Esquivel, Laura. *Like Water for Chocolate: A Novel in Monthly Installments with Recipes, Romances and Home Remedies*. Trans. Carol Christensen and Thomas Christensen. New York: Doubleday, 1992. (Originally published in 1989 under the title of *Como agua para chocolate: Novela de entregas mensuales con recetas, amores y remedios caseros*.)

Genette, Gérard. *Figures III*. Paris: Seuil, 1972.

Glenn, Kathleen M. "Postmodern Parody and Culinary-Narrative Art in Laura Esquivel's *Como agua para chocolate*." *Chasqui* 23.2 (Nov. 1994): 39–47.

Ibsen, Kristine. "On Recipes, Reading and Revolution: Postboom Parody in *Como agua para chocolate*." *Hispanic Review* 63.2 (Spring 1995): 133–146.

Marquet, Antonio. "¿Cómo escribir un best-seller? La receta de Laura Esquivel." *Plural* 237 (1991): 58–67.

McMurray, George. "Two Mexican Feminist Writers." *Hispania* 73 (1990): 1035–1036.

Rimmon-Kenan, Shlomith. *Narrative Fiction: Contemporary Poetics*. London & New York: Routledge, 1983.

11

THE SOUND OF SILENCE:
VOICES OF THE MARGINALIZED
IN CRISTINA PACHECO'S NARRATIVE

Linda Egan

In her ceaseless visitation of the marginalized *barrios* of Mexico City, Cristina Pacheco gathers for her middle-class readers an astonishing variety of images of underprivileged citizens who somehow get on with life amid crushing poverty, violence, and neglect. Her stark descriptions of that world include frankly horrendous scenes, such as that of the murderously self-centered man who kills his wife by dragging her out of the hospital too soon or of the abused child-man taking revenge upon a mother whom age has at last placed in his power. The dramatism of these representations is of an archaic line, emoting the fixed rigidity of a ceremonial tableau or medieval woodcut. This is Mexican *Kabuki*, presenting highly stylized symbols of wretchedness as the still-and-always most genuine of national traits. Her characters, often unidentified, always interchangeable, offer the murmurs, sobs, and futile gestures of the living dead. In Pacheco, the changeless, eternal vitality of oppression and misery are transferred from the widowed town of Agustín Yáñez's *Al filo del agua* and the phantasmal village of Juan Rulfo's *Pedro Páramo* to the contemporary urban wasteland.

Pacheco primes our reception of this view of a paralyzed society. She states that she has "listened to the stories of the people, seen their heroic and ignored struggle, witnessed their oppression, marginalization and eternal hope" (back cover *SF*)[1]; informs that her stories emerge from the artful addition of her own experiences and imagination to journalistic testimony, and specifies her creative task as that of presenting "a show of solidarity with the people to whom I belong, a testimony of these difficult years and also a means of capturing the styles of life, the symbols, popular speech and last defenses of Mexican men and women who, ever more dispossessed and impoverished, can now feed themselves only with the traditional noodle soup" (back cover *SF*). Allied in spirit with the poor (*CA* note), she will paint word pictures based on "real images, observations, conversations, news and words overheard by chance in the street" (*PVA* 11). Her language will "recapture moments of Mexico City life, to preserve something of what occurs and is then lost" (11). Thus, she invites her readers, privileged outsiders by virtue of their capacity to "visit" a culture they can then turn their backs on, to take in a museum exhibition.

The images are so ugly they sometimes are painful to envision. What we witness can approach the obscene; at such moments Cristina Pacheco flips back the front of her coat to shock us with ghastly displays of child pornography and "snuff" art. As readers, we may want to avert our eyes from the picture of the eight-month-old baby, dead in a filthy hotel for transients, covered only with flies because there is no money to bury it (*UNT* 30–33); from the avid cockroach on the wall that remains as the only living being a mother has to alleviate her loneliness after her children burn to death while she is at work (*PVA* 13–16); from the horde of starving dogs that advances inexorably upon the prostrate body of a woman dying alone (*PVA* 81–87); from the equally quiroga-esque tableau of the old woman in an abandoned building who will be eaten by armies of cockroaches (*PVA* 125–128); from the horribly scarred face of a young man who mutilated himself as a child to escape an abusive grandmother (*CN* 45–50); from skinny little Chelina, the child who sneaks back home after an earthquake kills her cruel parents in order to tie herself to the tree the way her parents always had (*CN* 75–79); from the psychotically self-centered son who kills his mother because when she turned on the iron, static electricity interfered with his view of a televised soccer match (*PML* 103–106). Readers are outraged by the despicable macho husband who sneaks back into the home he abandoned in order to sell the television and abscond with the money, blaming the wife as he goes (*UNT* 55–58). We feel outrage when we see the man who slides back into the house like a thief after two months, his only purpose being to steal the money that the mother had painfully set aside to buy shoes for the abandoned daughter. On the way out, he chides the child for stupidly opening the door to what could have been a thief (*UNT* 63–66).[2]

With endless pornographic gestures such as these, Pacheco makes us focus on the most grotesque of the many obscenities of poverty: the cynical exploitation of the most helpless among the helpless, the children. A palimpsest oozes to the surface of our mind as we read Pacheco. Her Mexico is the ancient sacrificial society that so cannibalized itself that it was easily victimized by the outsiders who came from Spain. It is not so difficult to see in the cruelty of the Mexican middle class's indifference to today's self-sacrificing underclass an analogy to Cortes's savvy exploitation of the weaknesses of the masses that his small band overcame with such efficiency.

The social criticism and, even, the rebellion inherent in such a view of Pacheco's museum exhibition nonetheless arise virtually independent of her texts. The spirit of self-assertion is all but undetectable in her discourse. Pacheco's omniscient all-seeing eye seems an efficient choice to present this passive cosmos. An uninvolved god impersonally proffers dirty pictures to shock. And they do shock. Nonetheless, this reaction is limited by her choice of narrative mode, which offers the sole recourse of empathy or indifference. One can feel sorry for the victims of her world, turn a blind eye to their suffering, engage in a burst of sterile anger at "the way things are." In the end, though, the reader may feel as helpless as her characters. They do not change, and we cannot change them.

We glue our ears to the voluminous dialogue of the characters, common people who are here allowed to speak as themselves, with the cadences and colloquialisms that strengthen Pacheco's writing. We may find ourselves unconsciously hoping to hear someone yell, "I'm mad as hell and I'm not going to take it any more!" When something resembling a subversive attitude presents itself, it is so unexpected and so muted with lyrical pathos that it could easily be missed or mistaken for the same fatalistic acceptance detected in the other 98 percent of Pacheco's texts.

"Desnudo al amanecer" ["Naked at Sunrise"] (*UNT* 134–137), the account of a miners protest, is an example of the ambiguity that envelopes the rare act of independence in Pacheco. The only strength the miners have is their malformed and undernourished bodies. That, then, is the weapon they turn against the tyrannical exploitation killing them. One miner decides to strip naked at dawn in front of the foreman's office. He persuades his co-workers to join in. At first the wives protest such a crazy act. But when they see the emaciated bodies of their men glowing in the cold morning air and see them stand with simple, silent dignity in a plea to be seen and heard, the women quietly gather to stand by their men. Everything else we see in Pacheco's works persuades us that the protest will probably result only in a few fatal cases of pneumonia. Still, this story moves because its human victims engage in an autonomous act of self-assertion whose futility in no way signifies failure.

Pacheco says she wants above all "to give a voice to Mexico's poor, to its heroic and anonymous men and women" (*PVA* 11). With the aid of a tape recorder and the microphone that sends her street interviews onto a weekly television screen, the Mexican writer does indeed let us hear the unsung poor of her country.[3] An updated version of José Tomás de Cuéllar's nineteenth-century "Magic Lantern,"[4] Pacheco's journalistic investigations shine a light on the most ordinary of Mexicans in the most ordinary places doing what they ordinarily do. The selected incidents inform us that the most common activity of the average man and woman is to suffer. While Cuéllar wanted to catch people both laughing and crying, Pacheco's characters are uniformly solemn or grim. Their words, wails, tears, gaping wounds, haunted eyes, shredded psyches, and deep sighs of resignation cast them not in a "human comedy" like Cuéllar's but in a contemporary human tragedy.

A reader of Pacheco's collections of fiction might figuratively be able to tune in at random to any of the individuals speaking into a microphone. The tone and message of each voice blend into a massive symphony of suffering:

- "There are nights when one feels completely weak and alone in the capital." (*CN* 136)

- "Don't tell anyone you had another son [with AIDS] and how he died. . . . Remember, Zacarías never existed." (*PML* 15–16)

- "'Doctor . . . is there anything that can be done?' . . . 'Grieve.'" (*PVA* 38)

- "They're right: [the Pope] can't come here. This is too dirty and neglected; there are bums and crooks [who] could harm him, insult him, rob him." (*PVA* 56)

- "[The five orphaned girls] have no one. No family, no friends. They all died. The poor things have been sent here, there and everywhere because nobody knows what to do with them. May God forgive me, but I think He made a mistake leaving these girls [alive] and all alone, to suffer." (*ZD* 114)

- "I never went to school and so I've lived my life by asking questions. . . . If I had known how to read and write I would remember the street and address because I would have them jotted down. . . . In the mind, things get erased. They last longer on paper." (*CA* 25–26)

- "Get away, you stupid brat!" (*CA* 17)

- "Only when I die will I have a hole to call my own. . . . I'm even eager to go there . . . I'm serious: it wouldn't bother me to be buried. I've always lived in this basement, always been lower than others and it never bothered me, not even when I was a young girl. Now that I'm 72, do you think it's going to embarrass me to live a little lower still?" (*SF* 93).

The voices speak of their rejection, humiliation, death, and despair without a hint of outrage. They simply describe their isolated battles for survival in intensely private and painful hells that promise to endure forever. The generalized image of a paralyzed society extends to paradox if we view Pacheco's works from today's feminist stance on writings by women about women, especially writings by concerned women of the middle class about the exploited woman of the underclass. The seven collections I focus on in this chapter contain 236 short fiction pieces. At least 193 of them are centered on the experiences of women who are unlettered and/or impoverished; the rest include tangential references to women as part of the overall marginalized sector of Mexico City, home of the under- and unemployed; the lower middle class constantly threatened with loss of its recently won stature; street children victimized by abuse and abandonment; the unhoused aged, infirm and insane; and, always, the self-sacrificing woman who uses herself up to make it all work.

The intensely feminine subject of Pacheco's narrative, ironically, reinforces the rigidity of her emblematic world of misery. Here is the historically submissive little woman, virtually always placed in distressed relationships with children or men as the suffering mother, wife, common-law spouse, mistress, or daughter. This feminine subject most typically "takes up the challenge of loss in order to go on living," embraces pain as a virtue and is always seen as "capable of unsparing loss" (Cixous, "Castration or Decapitation" 490). If she complains, it is with the passive pathos of the interminably helpless, the victim who survives psychologically by falling love with her tormentor and convincing herself that "I'm happy even though . . . he beat me up" (*PML* 48) because his violence is a sign of love; the victim who relinquishes all aspiration to a better life: "If one is born poor, she never chooses nor is able to say anything. She makes do with what she has" (*CA* 34).

The predictably "feminine" situations of Pacheco's fictional woman reflect the hardships and injustices of her place in Mexican society. She searches for food, prepares food, sacrifices her share of food, "fills herself up with children," worries about child care, submits to being used by a man, cleans or tries to clean the habitation, carries water, and so on. Her lot in life is virtually never rewarding or rewarded. Her man beats, abandons, and misunderstands or ignores her as a matter of course. Her children ail, go bad, or die on her. The laundry that was taken in for money, scrubbed in precious buckets of water carried over long distances and hung to dry is instantly fouled when the rain carries a liquid mountain into the slum colony. She thinks sad thoughts in the chair placed in a doorway that becomes her residence after authorities condemn her shabby quarters. She jumps off a roof with her children and lives to be jailed for murdering her starving offspring. Sometimes she just curls up and dies of despair.

As a journalist who gathers the material for her fiction in the course of a workday, Pacheco can provide endless authenticating details to elaborate her mimetic portrait of the disadvantaged female side of late twentieth-century Mexico City. She has gone to the tiny shack where the woman who "corrects" her grandchildren by hanging them like trousers from the clothesline (*PML* 13) invites her to sit "on the bed that fills up most of the room" (*PML* 11). She has visited the gynecology ward of the hospital where a young mother is hysterical because, the husband says, she fears "that here in the hospital her child will be stolen" (*CN* 88). She has observed a neighbor pour a cup of tea for the woman who confesses she allows her husband to throw knives at her in the hope that she can deflect his violence from the children (*CA* 35). Although Pacheco's narrative technique hides her journalistic persona, we are easily persuaded to accept as lifelike the world that her omniscient narrator reveals. If these are not real women, they are credible reflections of the millions of mothers and wives who daily "perform every kind of miracle to support their families" (interview with author, July 8, 1991).[5]

Given her primordial interest in the marginalized woman of Mexico, it would be natural to assume, as María Elena de Valdés and Claudia Schaefer-Rodríguez evidently do, that Pacheco exploits her privileged middle-class position, her professional training, and her access to the media with the goal of promoting the education and emancipation of the oppressed women of her society. A critic approaching Pacheco's works might already have stacked an array of theoretical works next to the computer and begun to look for the telltale feminist aspects of her language. For the purpose of making this point, let us assume that the object of "feminist writing" is the search for and (re)construction of an autonomous feminine subjectivity within the patriarchal order (Alcoff); that to this end the feminist author seeks freedom from "the dictatorship of patriarchal speech" (Showalter 465) in order to "bring into being the symbolic weight of female consciousness, to make the invisible visible, to make the silent speak" (472); that the primordial front on this field of struggle is the man-woman relationship, which the writer must attempt to "deconstruct and transform" in order to change culture itself (Cixous, "Castration or Decapitation" 482); that a genuine "woman-text" is one that affirms "woman's . . . power, her potency, her ever-dreaded strength" (488) and, finally, that the voice of a feminist text is always tinged "with a certain kind of laughter [that] . . . breaks out, overflows [with] a humor no one would expect to find in women —which is nonetheless surely their greatest strength because it's a humor that sees man much further away than he has ever been seen" (490).

A feminist text, in other words, reaches for a technique that distances the narrator from the culture that falsifies her, a technique that teaches her how to laugh first at herself. Her self-directed irony—and that of her women characters—may be the black humor that seeks to turn the outrageous situations she describes into paradoxically humdrum events, a "bleak humor" that Bruce Jay Friedman considers indispensable to "good writing" (26). Or it may simply be the double-voiced discourse that attacks gender stereotypes and racial presumptions in order to reverse or dismantle them (Finney 8). Whatever the case, a common assumption today is that a woman writing is obligated "to break up the 'truth' with laughter" (Cixous, "The Laugh of the Medusa" 258). Because women authors are historically assumed in a patriarchal society to be incapable of humor, any time a feminine discourse avails itself of the comic, it breaks barriers with an unmistakably feminist gesture that is "essential to feminist political struggle" (McWhirter 189). In a more generic sense, Mikhail Bakhtin assures us that all "people have used . . . festive comic images to express their criticism, their deep distrust of official truth, and their highest hopes and aspirations" (269).

My intent here is not to suggest that Cristina Pacheco should include humor in her works, but to point out that its absence fastens a paradoxical "antifeminism" to her densely feminine discourse. Of the 236 texts I have scrutinized, I find outright laughter in none; I detect a slight irony struggling from between the lines of only seven.[6] The fact is, the reality Pacheco fictionalizes is still the tragic stuff of newspaper headlines. So far as her readers can tell, it is simply too soon to begin laughing at a situation as unyieldingly dire as the one her characters endure.

The author chooses not to distance herself from but identify with her characters. Her point of view is predominantly omniscient and uncritical; its tone matches that of the characters and situations. When she chooses to narrate in the first person, the reader is usually unable to detect from the slightest discursive variation whether it is Pacheco or a character speaking. The individuals in her stories do not laugh; Pacheco refrains from using language to suggest that the misery of the world she mimics is absurd and must, finally, be seen as absurd in order to move the masses, and individuals, toward improving their lives.

Her language instead venerates the abject stoicism with which Mexico's historical downtrodden survive, like flowers sprouting among the weeds that choke an abandoned street. A young rape victim engages in a "secret ceremony" with her mother ("Ceremonia secreta" *PVA* 57–60) to hide her loss of virginity from society. Made homeless by an earthquake, old Domitila goes to lie on her husband's disturbed grave (*PVA* 61–64). A widow with three children becomes a drunk who dances in a tattered Aztec costume for alms and trusts in God to save the soul of her husband, who committed suicide (*PVA* 85–89). A middle-class woman masked as a volunteer social worker uses food to bribe children into her religious classes, and then cruelly demands that they sacrifice that food to God (*SF* 15–18). A mother who has "made do" to support her daughter for months since the husband abandoned them hesitates no time at all before admitting the returned man to her bed while leaving the little girl locked outside in the rain (*SF* 51–54). The "wife and martyr" (*CA* 33) of an abusive husband agrees to let him throw knives at her in the dark, a sacrifice to save the children from his violence (33–36).

With the multisignifying title "Oficio de mujer" ["Woman's Work"] (*UNT* 47–50), we have the story of a married woman with children who silently ushers husband and kids outdoors when a client arrives to pay for the use of her body. Everyone in the family agrees to this obscene arrangement so they can eat while he is looking for work. In one mini-theater piece, a form Pacheco often uses, four middle-class women dialogue about women's liberation, the freedom of single women, and an aggressively feminist paper one will deliver at a conference, while revealing that in their real lives, they still live as prisoners of their macho men's whims (*CN* 99–105). Raquel, a widow, takes her crippled son with her on the daily job of combing the garbage dumps for dinner:

"Well, what are we being sad for? Things didn't go so bad for us . . . I found a head of lettuce that is almost whole. I'll scrub it up and give it to you as a salad." At night, mother and son will pray together to give thanks to God: he will be grateful for the lettuce leaves that satisfied his hunger and she [will pray] that they have the power to give her son rest [from his pain]. (*PML* 103)

If this is feminism of any sort, we might borrow Naomi Wolf's term to characterize it as "victim feminism." Part of her definition observes that it "stresses the evil done to . . . 'good' women as a way to petition for their rights" (xvii).[7] I do not propose to label Pacheco's discourse one way or the other. Under whichever critical label one reads her, a unified portrait emerges of the model Mexican citizen: silent, suffering, stoical.

Once in a while, that statuesque image wobbles on its pedestal. In some of the most effective narrative moments of her production, Pacheco tentatively prods the people she commiserates with toward change. "Sal y pimienta" ["Salt and Pepper"] (*PVA* 65–68) is a good-humored piece worthy of an anthology, about a female invasion of the historically male ranks of construction workers. The men, macho as can be, of course resist this unthinkable heresy. But then the women show up and gradually fill the "bitter silence" (68) with the winning presence of the feminine. There's Esperanza, "a bleached blonde wearing grape-colored lipstick" (67) and high heels; Altagracia, who keeps her dead husband's pants up with a rope, and "Colorina" of the red hair and clanking earrings. They have respected the men's resentment and worked diligently to show their workmates they have the right stuff: "'OK, ladies, you know the drill: no flirting and for sure no giving up on the job. Remember: we've come here to go for it. Let those guys see we mean business'" (67). At the lunch break, the men go their way and the women theirs. The lady hardhats set up a camp kitchen and begin to sing. And the men soon feel that the "song of the sirens" has conquered all their resistence. One by one, in silence, they walk toward the meadow where the women are cooking (68). The language is patriarchal. Despite the nontraditional role the women have assumed, their feminine traits are emphasized: bright clothes, jangling jewelry, inappropriate high heels, cooking, singing. These are precisely the age-old forces that persuade men to override their fear of the feminine. Still, a taboo of Mexican society appears here to have been successfully challenged. Significantly, Pacheco has presented this vignette of change with the efficient lightness of humor.

"Uniforme blanco" ["White Uniform"] (*CA* 19–20) is a brush-stroke of a story in which, for a white-hot instant, the eternally abnegated mother's temper flares. Her son's teacher complains that the child does not come to school with his uniform perfectly clean. The mother runs through the litany of explanations: Where they live there is no water, not even for drinking much less laundry; there is so much dust the clothes get dirty before they are hung on the line; there is no transportation, so the child must walk in the dust to school. To this, the insensitive teacher responds by the numbers: "'Well, I'm warning you that he'll continue to get bad grades'" (20). The sketch ends on a rebellious note as the mother fires back: "'Who should be getting bad grades are those who take away our water and steal the money that was meant for building streets'" (20). The story does not suggest that the woman, perhaps in solidarity with others of her *colonia*, will follow up her complaint with action against corrupt bureaucrats. But we have caught a glimpse of the rage that simmers inside Pacheco's stolid sufferers. That, too, is a part of the Eternal Mexico Pacheco depicts; the implicit threat that erupted in 1910 in a failed revolution that has placed at least the semblance of a brake on official corruption since, as well as guided relations between Mexico and the United States over sensitive issues such as the "escape valve" of illegal immigration. The latter theme flits ephemerally through only a handful of Pacheco's texts; her focus remains implacably fixed on the unjust social reality within Mexico, a reality that seldom bares its anger as literally as in the previously mentioned story "Desnudo al amanecer" ["Naked at Sunrise"].

We have seen that Pacheco's discourse, while being taken for granted as feminist because of its focus on social injustice and women, is in fact of a nature that resists such easy categorizing. In the same way, the variety of discursive types she uses to package her fiction might tempt one to view her as a member of the postmodern camp, so raucously multigeneric. But the postmodern writer is even more pointedly noted for scoffing at narrative convention through a gamut of metafictional tricks and most especially for a parodic approach that aggressively deconstructs attempts to apprehend a realistic and believable textual world.[8] With only isolated exception, Cristina Pacheco does not fragment her chronologies, obscure her characters's identities, or force her own presence into the texts. Her preferred narrative mode recreates a mimetic world of realistic speech and logical progression in time. In view of this and the multiple narrative forms she uses, I am inclined to associate her discourse with the late Victorian era, or the Porfirian, as her world is situated in Mexico.[9]

Through the nineteenth century, as the Mexican nation suffered an overlong gestation and a painful birth, its miniscule cadre of writers, virtually all of whom relied on the quick and relatively inexpensive newspaper as a publishing "house," depicted the society they sought to forge in diverse styles that registered the still predominantly oral culture inspiring them. There were testimonials, miniature theatrical sketches, metaphorical dialogues, epistolary commentary, vignettes of social types, allegories that might personify throughout an essay such things as a feast day or a lantern, outright fantasies, surprisingly sophisticated psychological studies, reformist critiques of such graphic impact that they could easily have been written by the frequently "gothic" Horacio Quiroga, brief biographies, lyric-symbolist evocations, tiny *micro-relatos*, confessions, sermons, and *exempla* (moral for-instances).[10] Pacheco draws on all of this "art of oral history" (Monsiváis) as she weekly communicates her latest views of life in Mexico City to mass readers and television viewers.

This rich variety of registers is delivered with an ear tuned precisely to the sound of the often-illiterate citizens she interviews, those forgotten Mexicans crammed into crumbling tenements on the outskirts of urban centers and in mud huts dotting the rural landscape. These are witnesses to a Mexico-out-of-time whose meager goods do not include books, much less a light to read them by. The popular speech around which Pacheco builds most of her narrative is as arrestingly genuine as any reproduced by much-named gatherers of testimony such as Carlos Monsiváis or Elena Poniatowska. A reader trying to "situate" her along the spectrum of Mexican literary works, then, would do well to cast an ear well back in history to writers such as Guillermo Prieto (1818-1897), José Tomás de Cuéllar (1830-1894) and Manuel Gutiérrez Nájera (1859-1895) (although the latter two include a great deal more humor and irony in their multifarious "journalism" pieces than Pacheco does in her narrative[11]). What in fact comes most insistently to mind, as one passes from one tragic moment to another in Pacheco, is the lament of the defeated Aztec nation issuing from Fray Bernardino de Sahagún's great chronicle.[12] The overall impression is of a world of human beings captured at a moment of tragic crisis by the daguerro-typist's pale art, their bodies and souls forever frozen in attitudes of grotesque pain, frustrated rage, endless sorrow, unconquerable resignation. In this Mexi-co, a man crazed by loneliness and rejection will for a time draw the attention of the curious, but the traces of his presence will finally be erased "like the silhouettes of a photograph consumed by the sun" (*PVA* 93). In this world, nothing ever goes right anywhere, not in the city nor in the countryside, and all it takes is a little drought to bring a Life barely standing on its feet down to its knees (*CA* 73-75). The sisyphean inhabitants of Pacheco's Mexico might suffer "La vida en 'El Caracol'" ["Life in 'Caracol'"] (*PML* 72-75), a colony to which capital bureacrats consign twenty families that have escaped from their dead lives in the countryside. Caracol, like so many other poor sectors of Mexico City, is "barely a little lost dot on the southern edge of the city" (75). When it storms, the "town" turns into a "ravine where the rain stagnates and grows putrid, the same as a promise" (75).

A citizen does not have to be a penniless immigrant to experience this Mexico. He might be a government functionary with aspirations of snagging a permanent hold on the elusive middle-class life. He might be promised a job with housing outside the capital in the state of Michoacán and with faith in his heart arrange for the wife and children to join him once he's established there. Only the promise of the "Mexican Miracle" stagnates and rots for him, too. There is neither house nor office for him in Michoacán, and because communi-cations are so uncertain, he arrives back in the capital before he can stop his family from traveling south. Eventually, their savings exhausted by futile travel, they're all stuck in Mexico City again, and forced to beg a small space in a parent's house for as long as it takes to regain independence (*PML*, "La saga de un emigrante" ["The Saga of an Emigrant"] 112-115).

Most Mexicans victimized by their society are not that fortunate. Untold thousands become like the street urchin who suffers on "a cross of wind" (*UNT* 114) the martyrdom of an anonymous Christ. "Scarred, wounded, weak, bro-ken," this hardy soul nevertheless does not collapse because, "immutable and silent as an idol, he is made of good clay and thus resists everything . . . like the prodigious insects that . . . emerge from the most remote antiquity and . . . walk toward the future" (114). Pacheco thus passes from the image of prehistoric evolution through the ancient Christian analogy to the symbolic reality of a modern-day Christianized Indian who believes that the miserable parody of an Aztec dance he offers for alms on the street will awaken the compassionate generosity of God (*UNT* 15). "El combate de las águilas" ["Combat of Eagles"] (*UNT* 15-17) places the hyper-real portrait of silent, ragged Chon like a prayer at our passing feet. As Pacheco details the look of his tattered costume, his lurching dance, and his stoic dignity, we are taken back in memory to the worm-infested streets of Tenochtitlan, where the ragged, starved survivors of Cortés's siege surrender their arms but not the cultural spirit that has kept them on their feet, staggering, bowed down, beaten, but not defeated, in all the centuries since. "Chon's dance has neither a beginning nor an end . . . [and] it continues eternally . . . to a rhythm that is like an ancient and mysterious lament" (16).

This is the enduring Mexico that refuses to fall down before any catastrophe. After the earthquake of 1985, buildings with broken backs were condemned by the authorities but nonetheless seized as homes by Mexicans who had literally nowhere else to find shelter. In one such building's ruined labyrinth of rooms, ninety families endure the incest, rape, unplanned births, hunger, gossip, and lack of privacy that such overcrowding automatically brings. Indomitable, the inhabitants muster enough faith to hang a white sheet from a second-floor window that silently, patiently demands "a dignified living space" (*ZD* 63). Underneath the sheet, a scarcely visible official seal announces: "Historic Monument" ["Monumento histórico"]. The pile of human misery that Pacheco points to with implacable persistence is the one true monument Mexico has erected, she seems to say. It stands for a society that does not believe in its government nor even in itself but in the miraculous "multiplication of bread, space and bodies" (64). Thus divided and multiplied, "the houses are sanctuaries of the daily miracle" of life in Mexico. Because her textual reality is sustained by the supernatural, Cristina Pacheco does not suggest to the reader or to her characters what to do to escape so much misery. She only reminds us that it is there, stagnated and rotten, under a scab of broken promises.

NOTES

1. I will cite in parentheses the seven collections I analyze in this study by their respective abbreviations: *PVA* (*Para vivir aquí* 1983); *SF* (*Sopita de fideo* 1984); *CA* (*Cuarto de azotea* 1986); *ZD* (*Zona de desastre* 1986); *UNT* (*La última noche del "Tigre"* 1987); *CN* (*El corazón de la noche* 1989); *PML* (*Para mirar a lo lejos* 1989). Pacheco is also author of a collection of nonfiction chronicles, *La rueda de la fortuna* (1993) and two collections of celebrity interviews, *La luz de México* (1988) and *Los dueños de la noche* (1990). All translations are my own.

2. Two versions of this story appear in Pacheco's collections. The first is "Monte de piedad," from *Zona de desastre*, 109-111 (1986). The one I cite is "Los pies de la niña," from *La última noche del "Tigre"* 63-66 (1987).

3. Pacheco publishes a weekly column called "Mar de historia." The pieces are fiction occupying the back page of the daily newspaper *La Jornada*. She also publishes regularly in such magazines as *Siempre!* and hosts a weekly television interview show

called "Aquí nos tocó vivir," for which she identifies a sector of the anonymous masses and an "issue of the day" before inviting the usually voiceless poor to express their views and woes.

4. José Tomás de Cuéllar participated in the end phase of a long period of romanticism in nineteenth-century Mexico. A journalist, as virtually all of Mexico's writers were then, he did as Cristina Pacheco does today: create fiction out of the news. He, too, concentrated on the poor and lower-middle class and, again like Pacheco, did his best to capture them in the midst of their ordinary lives. Thus, his series of volumes under the umbrella title *La linterna mágica*. This magic lantern was his imagination and creative talent, shining into kitchens, bedrooms, and workplaces to illuminate the authentic heart of Mexico. In the prologue to one of his collected works, Cuéllar says: "I have copied my characters by the light of my lantern, not in fantastic, extraordinary drama, but in the midst of the human comedy, in real life, surprisingly them at home, with the family, at work, in the field, in jail, and everywhere; some with laughter on their lips, others with tears in their eyes; but I have especially focused on the correction of those traits pertaining to vices and virtues" (xvii).

5. The comment is transcribed from a lengthy interview I conducted with Cristina Pacheco in her Mexico City office, July 8, 1991. The portion of that interview devoted specifically to her journalism career and the role of women in newspapers today has appeared in Spanish and English articles. See Linda Egan, "Entrevistas con periodistas mujeres" and "Feminine Perspectives on Journalism." For more on Pacheco's combination of journalism and fiction, see the interview with her in Pacheco, *Confrontaciones*.

6. I was looking for the distancing "otherness" of irony, or the frank lightness of subversive laughter. I could detect only slight evidence of either in seven pieces. See the delightful "Sal y pimienta" ["Salt and Pepper"] (*PVA* 65–68), as well as the subtle touches of irony in "La ciega y el ángel" ["The blind woman and the angel"] (*PVA* 95–98), "Un muchacho de fuego" ["A fire-eating boy"] (*PVA* 115–119), "El sábado de Gloria" ["Gloria's Saturday"] (*PVA* 133–36), "La guerra de los mundos" ["The War of the Worlds"] (*CN* 99–105), "La escena de la traición" ["The Scene of the Betrayal"] (*UNT* 40–43) and "Tomando té" ["Drinking Tea"] (*PML* 54–57). Overall, Pacheco's writing is virtually humorless.

7. I would have to agree with the judgment Wolf appends to her definition: "Victim feminist assumptions about universal female goodness and powerlessness, and male evil, are unhelpful in the new moment for they exalt what I've termed 'trousseau reflexes' —outdated attitudes women need least right now." The portion of her definition of "victim feminism" I choose not to apply to Pacheco's discourse "casts women as sexually pure and mystically nurturing" (xvii). Pacheco's women, even as young as 13, are not sexually pure, although many might surely wish to be. And, although they are certainly nurturing, I'm not persuaded that any of them, or Pacheco, would like to think of their daily sacrifices as "mystical." They are hard work and they hurt like hell.

8. Linda Hutcheon's *The Poetics of Postmodernism* continues to be an indispensable starting place for understanding the postmodern sensibility and style (see especially 105–221). Brian McHale provides an excellent summary of the textual "tics" that reveal the postmodernist at work. Patricia Waugh focuses with great clarity on the self-ironizing nature of postmodern discourse. With exceptions so rare and tentative they don't bear mentioning, Pacheco's texts are an anomaly from today's universal literary perspective.

Within her own culture, they demonstrate the persistent Mexican preference for brief texts in the mimetic mode. On that trait, see Boyd G. Carter (75).

9. Porfirio Díaz "kept the peace" in Mexico during an iron-fisted dictatorship that lasted more than thirty years (1876–1880, 1884–1911), until the outbreak of suppressed tensions in 1910 and his ouster in 1911.

10. To avoid a long bibliography of nineteenth-century works illustrating these dialogic genres, I refer my readers to Jean Franco's article, an analysis focused on Fernández de Lizardi's *El Periquillo sarniento* (1816), generally held to be Mexico's first novel. Her analysis identifies a host of the genres of nineteenth-century journalism and narrative that were inspired and sustained by oral culture.

11. The romantic Tomás de Cuéllar's innocent joking in various novels of *La linterna mágica* are still entertaining today, and modernist Gutiérrez Nájera frequently mixes black humor with his powerful lyricism.

12. Fray Bernardino de Sahagún, among the first Spanish missionaries to establish permanent relationships with the defeated Mexicans, interviewed survivors (principally of the commercial class) soon after the fall of Tenochtitlan. With the help of Indian assistants who had learned both Spanish and Latin, Sahagún recorded with painstaking accuracy and detail the long, long story of the origins of the Aztec nation, its customs, religion, social and political structures and, in general, its cultural spirit. A large segment of the missionary's monumental work (finished around 1577) transmits, verbatim, a series of lengthy prayers and orations. His *Historia general de las cosas de Nueva España* was first published in 1829.

REFERENCES

Alcoff, Linda. "Cultural Feminism versus Post-Structuralism: The Identity Crisis in Feminist Theory." *Signs: Journal of Women in Culture and Society* 13 (1988): 405–436.

Bakhtin, Mikhail. *Rabelais and His World*. Trans. Hélène Iswolsky. Bloomington: Indiana UP, 1984.

Carter, Boyd G. "Revistas literarias hispanoamericanas del siglo XIX." *Historia de la literatura hispanoamericana*. Vol. 2. Ed. Luis Iñigo Madrigal. Madrid: Cátedra, 1982. 75–85.

Cixous, Hélène. "Castration or Decapitation?" *Contemporary Literary Criticism: Literary and Cultural Studies*. 2nd ed. Eds. Robert Con Davis and Ronald Schleifer. New York: Longman, 1989. 479–491.

———. "The Laugh of the Medusa." Trans. Keith and Paula Cohen. *New French Feminisms*. Eds. Elaine Marks and Isabelle de Courtivron. New York: Schocken, 1981. 245–264.

Cuéllar, José Tomás de. *Ensalada de pollos/Baile y cochino*. Ed. Antonio Castro Leal. Mexico: Porrúa, 1946.

———. *La linterna mágica*. Ed. Mauricio Magdaleno. 12 vols. Mexico: U.N.A.M., 1973.

Egan, Linda. "Entrevistas con periodistas mujeres sobre la prensa mexicana." *Mexican Studies/Estudios Mexicanos* 9 (1993): 275–294.

———. "Feminine Perspectives on Journalism: Conversations with Eight Mexican Women." *Studies in Latin American Popular Culture* 12 (1993): 175–187.

Finney, Gail, ed. "Introduction." *Look Who's Laughing: Gender and Comedy.* Langhorne, PA: Gordon and Breach, 1994. 1–13.

Franco, Jean. "Escritura y control social en vísperas de la independencia mexicana." Two-part series. *La Cultura en México* (15 Feb. and 22 Feb. 1984): 38–41, 38–42.

Friedman, Bruce Jay. "Foreword, Black Humor." *Black Humor: Critical Essays.* Ed. Alan R. Pratt. New York and London: Garland, 1993. 19–26.

Hutcheon, Linda. *A Poetics of Postmodernism: History, Theory and Fiction.* New York: Routledge, 1989.

McHale, Brian. *Postmodernist Fiction.* New York: Methuen, 1987.

McWhirter, David. "Feminism/Gender/Comedy: Meredith, Woolf, and the Recon figuration of Comic Distance." *Look Who's Laughing: Gender and Comedy.* Ed. Gail Finney. Langhorne, PA: Gordon and Breach, 1994. 189–204.

Monsiváis, Carlos. "Cristina Pacheco: el arte de la historia oral." Prologue to *La luz de México: entrevistas con pintores y fotógrafos* by Cristina Pacheco. Guanajuato, Mexico: Gobierno del Estado de Guanajuato, 1990. 9–17.

Pacheco, Cristina. *Confrontaciones.* Azcapotzalco, Mexico: U.A.M., 1987.

———. *El corazón de la noche.* Mexico: El Caballito, 1989.

———. *Cuarto de azotea.* Mexico: Gernika/Secretaría de Educación Pública, 1986.

———. *Los dueños de la noche.* Mexico: Planeta, 1990.

———. *La luz de México: entrevistas con pintores y fotógrafos.* Prólogo Carlos Monsiváis. Guanajuato, Mexico: Gobierno del Estado de Guanajuato, 1990.

———. *Para mirar a lo lejos.* Tabasco, Mexico: Gobierno del Estado de Tabasco, 1989.

———. *Para vivir aquí.* Mexico: Grijalbo, 1983.

———. *La rueda de la fortuna.* Mexico: Era, 1993.

———. *Sopita de fideo.* Mexico: Aguilar, León y Cal, 1991.

———. *La última noche del "Tigre."* Mexico: Océano, 1987.

———. *Zona de desastre.* Mexico: Océano, 1986.

Rulfo, Juan. *Pedro Páramo.* 1955. Mexico: Fondo de Cultura Económica, 1993.

Sahagún, F. Bernardino de. *Historia general de las cosas de Nueva España.* 2 vols. Eds. Alfredo López Austin and Josefina García Quintana. 1829. Madrid: Alianza, 1988.

Schaefer-Rodríguez, Claudia. "Embedded Agendas: The Literary Journalism of Cristina Pacheco and Guadalupe Loaeza." *Latin American Literary Review* 19 (1991): 62–76.

Showalter, Elaine. "Feminist Criticism in the Wilderness." *Contemporary Literary Criticism: Literary and Cultural Studies.* 2nd ed. Eds. Robert Con Davis and Ronald Schleifer. New York: Longman, 1989. 457–478.

Valdés, María Elena de. "Feminist Testimonial Literature: Cristina Pacheco, Witness to Women." *Monographic Review/Revista Monográfica* 4 (1988): 150–162.

———. "La obra de Cristina Pacheco: ficción testimonial de la mujer mexicana." *Revista de Teoría y Crítica Literarias* 16 (1991): 271–279.

Waugh, Patricia. *Metafiction: The Theory and Practice of Self-Conscious Fiction.* New York: Methuen, 1984.

Wolf, Naomi. *Fire with Fire: The New Female Power and How It Will Change the 21st Century.* New York: Random House, 1993.

Yáñez, Agustín. *Al filo del agua.* 1947. Mexico: Porrúa, 1988.

12

THE TRANSFORMATION OF THE READER IN MARÍA LUISA PUGA'S *PÁNICO O PELIGRO*

Florence Moorhead-Rosenberg

> There is commonly sufficient space about us. Our horizon is never quite at our elbows. The thick wood is not just at our door, nor the pond, but somewhat always clearing, familiar and worn by us, appropriated and fenced in some way, and reclaimed from Nature.
>
> —Henry David Thoreau

> Nothing happens in the real world unless it first happens in the images in our heads.
>
> —Gloria Anzaldúa

Isabel Allende, in "The Woman's Voice in Latin American Literature," argues for a strong connection between language and reality. Throughout the interview she concretizes the relationship between her world and her literature. For Allende, literature is an apt tool for exorcising the demons of anger, where anger is defined as a rejection of the things we view as wrong or evil. Violence, brutality, militarism, racism, rape—all "negative energy," in Allende's words —are potential zones of transformation because through writing we may propose, try on, alternate visions of reality. This is not to say that anger is everywhere apparent, seeping out through the seams of women's fiction. In some cases it is. However, in many texts, and particularly in Hispanic women's narrative, the anger and frustration may be lovingly transformed into tales of growth, change, renewal, and possibility.

One such example of this loving transformation is María Luisa Puga's marvelously crafted *Pánico o peligro*, published in Mexico in 1983. This semi-epistolary novel narrates, among other things, the attempt of its narrator (Susana) to resist being the victim of linguistic colonization. As she recounts her life, Susana describes and defines the distance between rhetoric and reality, as well as the extreme distances that exist between people in differing societal contexts. Through a series of twelve notebooks to her current lover and potential husband, she takes up the narration of her life and that of three of her closest friends—Lola, Lourdes, and Socorro—each of whom represents a specific situation of/for women in Mexico City during the 1960s and 1970s. As Susana regains control of her life through this auto-narration, she evolves an authentic language, one that triumphantly bridges the gap between her previous lack of contact with reality and her rejection of the complex and, for her, colonizing language of Lourdes and her lover.

In the process of this narration, the extratextual or "real" reader must continually define him/herself in relation to a series of internal addressees. These may be Susana's lover and/or Lourdes, as Susana initiates a dialogue with them in which she, for the first time, takes control of the master narrative of her life. Hence, the real reader often finds him/herself located both inside and outside the narrative. As we concretize the text, we either internalize and accept the images and suggestions of alterity signified by the constant state of being in-relation-to the addressees, or we reject them outright and individuate from the text. In this chapter, I analyze the process of this identification and differentiation and its effect on textual concretization and our subsequent perception of alterity and the Other. A basic premise of the ensuing discussion is that, in *Pánico o peligro*, María Luisa Puga has constructed a blueprint for an authentically feminine/feminist linguistic space; a space that is essentially utopian in nature in that it nurtures and accepts difference as it simultaneously and passionately rejects the colonizing desire to transform the Other into a mirror image of ourSelves.[1]

Anne K. Mellor, in her article "On Feminist Utopias," divides the tendencies of utopian fiction into three categories, each of which then falls neatly into a binary classification of either "abstract" or "concrete." According to Mellor, "Feminist utopian writers . . . have explored three types of feminist utopias: all-female societies, biological androgyny, and genuinely egalitarian two-sex societies" (241).[2] It should be apparent almost instantly that the first two of these categories belong to the realm of abstract utopias in that they are "generated out of pure desire and function as wish-fulfillment" (242).[3] This may not be a negative characteristic, especially if we take into account that "utopian authors construct ideal space in order to subvert inequality and inevitability" (Pfaelzer 282). However, the third more concrete category seems pragmatically more desirable as an authentically feminist genre if we wish to designate concrete utopian discourse as potentially something more than an escapist narrative we read to momentarily elude the drudgery of our everyday lives. This is particularly true if we agree with Mellor that "concrete utopian thinking . . . is inherently revolutionary: it offers a vision of a better world which we are both morally obligated and technically able to bring into being" (243).

A key point underlying the current discussion is that there is a strong connection between concrete utopian fiction and the Latin American construct of committed literature (*literatura comprometida*). Committed literature seeks to alter reality by existing in dialogue with it. Practitioners of this genre believe there is a "significant utopian element in [the] view that speaking, reading and writing are subversive activities" (Pfaelzer 283). If we relate this concept to the idea that feminist theory is, at heart, utopian in nature, because it seeks to redress issues of "gender equality, a social equality between the sexes which [has] never existed in the historical past" (Mellor 243), then we must conclude that most feminist narrative is conceivably utopian in that it "both critique[s] the present world and attempt[s] to prophesy or determine the future" (243).[4] We might also add that this future is necessarily prophesied as being fundamentally different from both the historical past and the present that spawned it. I would like to suggest here that it is precisely this prophetic nature of *Pánico o peligro* that defines the text as belonging both to the genres of committed and utopian literature because, as Susana addresses her reality, she simultaneously offers a model for transforming it for the better.[5]

The novel begins with an invitation, a command really, to read at the level of internal addressee, in direct relation to the text, without intermediaries, without boundaries: "Imagine: it was just my father, my mother and myself" (7).[6] For a brief moment, we are given the impression that Susana is talking directly to us; that we form an integral part of her world, in short, that we may know her. This illusion breaks down moments later, however, when she states quite matter-of-factly: "You are always talking about change" (7). Whether or not we typically speak of change, from this point on, the text forces us to constantly define ourselves in terms of negation of and/or identification with this as yet undefined narratee, this Other whose reality we do not share.

Definition by means of negation is nothing new in literature. We inherit the terms to describe it—*ostraneniye* and defamiliarization—directly from Russian formalism (Shklovsky). Literature of the fantastic is founded on the strategy of defamiliarization in order to force us to see (experience) our reality differently. The process disrupts our automatic and habitual view of our circumstances, and then presents them to us in an altered context; a context that may compel us to examine both ourSelves and our surroundings in a new light. Utopian and/or feminist literature functions in much the same way: It defamiliarizes our environment in ways that may alter our perception. Therein lies the inherently transformative power of this type of literature. For, if we believe that, at least in part, our perception is a controlling or productive factor in the construction of reality, then we must conclude that if it is altered (in this case through concretization of a text), then the text (literature) has the potential to modify reality.[7] Wolfgang Iser, in *The Act of Reading*, highlights the connection between literature and reality as follows: "In general, literary texts constitute a reaction to contemporary situations, bringing about attention to the problems that are conditioned though not resolved by contemporary norms" (3).

Danny J. Anderson, in his article "Cultural Conversation and Constructions of Reality: Mexican Narrative and Literary Theories after 1968," documents a few of the "problems" of Mexican society and particularly of Mexican literary production addressed by Puga in *Pánico o peligro*. Of particular interest to the current discussion is Anderson's assertion that "Mexican fiction since 1968, and especially *Pánico o peligro*, has staked out positions in the cultural conversation that place in the foreground how languages can evoke, define, and even distort 'reality'" (18). In this sense, then, *Pánico o peligro* highlights the difficulties intrinsic to the totalizing and, in many cases, colonizing language of the intellectual class, represented in the text most specifically through Lourdes, Mateo, Arturo, and finally, by Susana's lover (*tú*) (20). Susana's essential problem with the highly refined metalanguages of her friend and lovers is that the plethora of linguistic levels inherent in their discourse(s) imply an inevitable distancing from the actual object of discussion. At times, the referent disappears completely, and Susana is left to untangle the meaning behind words that, for her, signify nothing, as they have no connection whatsoever with the reality they pretend to examine and analyze.

It is this process of distancing that Susana addresses when she questions her lover (*tú*) about the endless meetings he attends with his intellectual and political cronies:

What happens in your meetings, in my opinion? You all stand in front of one another to affirm your convictions, questions of identity and forms of power. The words are just a pretext. What you say to one another remains outside your language. It's a little like putting on some background music so you won't hear what's really being said. You don't listen to each other. You watch each other. You compare yourselves to one another. All right, if there's no other way to do this besides talking, ok, but why place such importance on that and not on what is actually happening? (129)

Susana, after her long trajectory as a victim of linguistic colonization, has finally come to terms with the fact that the highly intellectualized language of her primary interlocutors—Lourdes and her lover (*tú*), in particular—often places an artificial distance between them and the reality they so carefully wish to scrutinize. However, she also becomes aware that even though this distancing may be a direct consequence of utilizing an overly self-conscious rhetoric, on the other hand, too much simplification and superficiality arise from ignoring—for whatever reason—the existence of this rhetoric and its connections, however tenuous they may be, with the world it attempts to explain (or control). It is from this place of newfound knowledge (locus of power) that Susana searches for her own language: a language constructed "based on sensations . . . by force of looking out the window and listening to things name themselves, represent themselves" (194). It is also from this space that she recognizes that in the present of narration she now has "more words and, obviously, many more examples" (157).

This new linguistic space that Susana so laboriously creates represents a harmonious triumph over her previous (and only apparent) lack of contact with reality; a lack stimulated in part by the hermetic, complex, and unreal language of Lourdes and her internal addressee, as well as her inability to understand this same reality due to a dearth of authentic (personal) words to describe it. Seen from this perspective, Susana's primary achievement is that, through her writing, she has ceased to be the object of Lourdes's and her lover's language —and by extension that of the intellectual, leftist class in Mexico—and has instead moved on to an empowered space of equilibrium; a space from which she is able to define her own position of subject and hence take control of her life.[8]

Through her writing, and especially as the notebooks progress, Susana adamantly resists being colonized by both the rhetoric and ideology of others. Instead, as she writes, she makes a conscious choice to live with and through her own language and simultaneously rejects being invaded and invalidated by that of Lourdes and her lover (*tú*). In socio-economic terms, Susana epitomizes the Mexican middle class as she attempts to define her destiny while slogging through a multitude of interpretive signs superimposed on her reality from a variety of directions: (1) that of Lourdes, representing the middle class as it is socialized to aspire to form part of the intellectual "elite"; and (2) that of Susana's lover, signifying the upper class that has the luxury of entertaining itself with ideals and ideologies and then applying them at will to often mysterious others, usually without their consent. Lourdes and Susana's lover thus combine in their function as the intertextual addressee, both playing the role of favored interlocutor, as well as that of the colonizing force from which Susana so intensely wishes to individuate herSelf. The real (actual) reader finds him/herself in a similar situation throughout much of *Pánico o peligro*. As we read, it is necessary to individuate, by means of a process of continual identification and rejection, from the definition of this interdiegetic addressee (*tú*) formulated in Susana's notebooks. The text forces us to query how we define ourselves in relation to the various ideological "camps" it proposes. Does our own intellectual training keep us from seeing the world directly? Are we like Lourdes? Like Susana's lover? Each time we open the pages of this suggestive novel, we must confront and question our own identity and where we stand in relation to the identity-building processes of others. This process ultimately situates us (the real readers) in a highly charged zone of transformation as we attempt to define ourSelves in relation to the Other.

However, if Susana, as narrator/author of her own history, is transformed by its recounting, how does this change occur when her original intent was to effect change in her current lover? Susana provides a clue when she states: "I no longer think so much about what [the notebooks] will mean to you. For you. I stopped writing them for you a long time ago. They are for me, by me, obviously, and it is only once in a while that I remember that you're going to read them" (234). Borrowing, for a moment, from Gerald Prince, we may affirm that when "the narrator constitutes his own narratee, the latter is gradually and profoundly changed by the events he recounts for himself" (18). Hence, Susana has no choice but to gradually transform herself into another.

Bit by bit, through writing and thinking about her personal history (and that of her friends Lourdes, Lola, and Socorro), she becomes conscious of the fact that, in one way or another, she is actively seeking change: "Things are no longer as clear as they were initially and at times I would like to go back to the beginning, to read what I've written, but something keeps me from doing it: an urgency to continue, to arrive at the heart of something . . . to find my true identity or a more palpable perception of what you call reality" (140). Even Susana's lover is aware of the fact that reading the notebooks will affect him, or at least, he believes that is why Susana is writing them. At the outset of the story, Susana tells him that what has most challenged her in life has always been a suffocating silence. Now, in the present of narration, she wants her life to be different. She tells him she is writing to him so that in the future they will be able to communicate better (64). Thus, even though we never ascertain whether or not the notebooks achieve their end—because Susana never actually gives them to him in the course of the story—we would like to believe that, upon reading them, her lover arrives at a sincere and authentic dialogue with Susana and that both allow themselves to be transformed by the communicative process she initiates by writing her life story.

Furthermore, the fact that her lover is fully cognizant of Susana's project —because he awakens earlier than usual one morning and surprises her in the study as she writes (139)—automatically colors the reception of the notebooks with Susana's intentions. We know he is aware of her project. We surmise that he—and by extension, their relationship—will be transformed by it. This desire for transformation is the essential locus of utopian intent in Susana's discourse. In her attempt to change herSelf, her lover, and her world, she is able to recast her frustration and use it to nourish and engender change. In fact, Aralia López González, in her article "Nuevas formas de ser mujer en la narrativa contemporánea de escritoras mexicanas" ["New Images of Women in Contemporary Mexican Women's Narrative"], cites Susana's case as pointing to the fact that "marriage and motherhood, the traditional means of satisfying needs and establishing social identity, are no longer the only alternative" (6, my translation). In this sense, Susana, alongside Elena Poniatowska's Jesusa Palancares, signals possible new directions for women in Mexican society. As such, she represents a feminist utopian vision of future (hopefully not too distant) possibilities.

But what of the real reader in relation to the text? Where do we fall within this scheme of communication? Paradoxically, due to its epistolary nature, we relate to *Pánico o peligro* both inter- and extratextually simultaneously. This is so because literary texts do not describe reality. Instead, they create another with a somewhat less than empirical existence. This does not mean, however, that we do not participate in an active dialogue with narrative. On the contrary, a literary text "can only come into being by way of ideation, and so the structure of the text sets off a sequence of mental images which lead to the text translating itself into the reader's consciousness" (Iser 38). Therefore, instead of maintaining a strictly inter- or extratextual position, one would have to conclude that the fully concretized, ideated text is a product of our imagination and, thus, necessarily and ultimately resides within us. This process of translation of the text into the mind of the reader requires no small degree of reorganization of the latter, the result being shifts, slight or not, of perception. In this manner, reading may be described as an essential act of transformation; that of the ideation of the text in the mind of the reader and that of the reader into another.[9]

However, the real reader, as opposed to the internal addressee(s) of *Pánico o peligro*, may not necessarily be consciously aware of this process. Faced with any narrative work, the real reader must try, with all his/her expectations and experiences at play, to construct, understand, and accept the fictitious world of the text.[10] This confrontation between text and reader generates a tension; a tension that arises when the real reader realizes that there are differences between his/her world and that described by/in the text. Upon recognizing and/or naming this point of disjunction between the two realities, the reader must attempt to bridge the gap and smooth over the disjunctive spaces in order to reach an agreement with the text. This agreement may loosely be called personal interpretation. One further aspect of this tension is pertinent to the current discussion. The fact that the reader may need to take on a variety of roles in relation to the text is of tantamount importance, especially when we consider that these roles may often be conflictive in nature. These roles are (1) that created and offered up by the text; and/or (2) the reader's own personal predisposition. Within the boundaries of this conflict, in general "the role prescribed by the text will be the stronger, but the reader's own disposition will never disappear totally; it will tend instead to form the background to and a frame of reference for the act of grasping and comprehending" (Iser 37).

It is this aspect of tension that works so subtly and so effectively throughout *Pánico o peligro*. Because the discourse is obviously directed to an intertextual addressee (*tú*) who has no relation to the real reader, the latter must continually compare him/herself with the former and at the same time differentiate him/herself from him. Furthermore, due to a specific linguistic strategy utilized throughout—that of occasionally employing the impersonal (*el tú impersonal*)—the real reader finds him/herself in a perpetually fluid state of identification with and rejection of the textual Other, be he Susana's well-defined and delimited lover or a more amorphous, less defined entity that forms part of a universal "we." Furthermore, "you" ["*tú*"] may, at times, refer to Lourdes, or to Susana herself because—as in the seventh notebook when they discuss Socorro's death—the two friends occasionally speak directly to one another, serving as interlocutors at the level of story, but not at that of discourse. We, and this time "we" includes all of the interlocutors, must then penetrate one more level to participate in the communicative process initiated by and in the text. And, even though Susana is conscious of the fact that she is re-creating scenes when she states, "I'm talking to you about what I remember from the present, as I see it now. Perhaps these weren't the exact words" (219), the psychological effect on the reader is the same. If we are in agreement with the position posited for Susana's lover, we will identify with him. If not, we attempt to reject the vision (much in the same way that Susana resists the linguistic colonization of Lourdes) as not pertinent to our perception of the world or how it should be. If we are unsure of our own position, then we will momentarily reside in an ambiguous space: a space that will allow for our potential transformation. Hence, when Susana writes the following, there arises an implicit identification with the feelings expressed in the text:

Imagine any night in this city of 13, almost 14 million inhabitants, this city where anything can happen, imagine two people caught up by something as opaque and amorphous as those moments. You can also imagine, simultaneously, an unpleasant gesture, a malicious smile, a violent movement, a crazed anger; it terrified me to imagine someone, for example, being run over while getting off the bus . . . to imagine violence, period, unleashed violence in which everyone finds their enemy, their reasons for hating, their need to strike out. (92–93)

The use of the impersonal in this instance forces us to locate ourselves within the story so that we may imagine what it would be like to live in an environment completely saturated—permeated—with fear; fear of the police, of the government, of being disappeared, in short, of being Mexican and living in Mexico City after the events of Tlatelolco in 1968.

Whether or not the individual reader happens to be Mexican, and/or a contemporary of the narrative action, at an emotional level we cannot avoid the sensation of terror produced by the text. As we read Susana's narrative, we come to recognize that we intrinsically comprise part of the amorphous and universal referent signified by the word "you" ["*tú*"]. We can identify with the terror of encountering our own limits, our own borders of hate, because in the above instance, the situation proposed by the text includes us both emotionally and grammatically. On the other hand, when Susana asks, "Do you remember when you told me a while ago and not without some tenderness: it's a shame you don't know how to love. You don't understand what it feels like" (93), we must distance ourselves immediately from the story and subsequently reject the identity offered us by Susana's use of "you" because, in this case, the specificity of the internal narratee precludes our participation.

As previously stated, this oscillation between identification and rejection is established with the very first sentence of the text. Initially we may be unaware of precisely to whom Susana is directing herself, but it is logical to assume, because the text at this point offers up no other sign, that she is speaking directly to us. Moreover, the illocutive force of the verb requires its corresponding performative response. When the text commands us to do so, we instantly define ourselves in the position of addressee (object of the discourse) and begin to imagine. We do so very attentively, as if we were the only addressee, at least until we read the previously mentioned statement: "You are always talking about change" (7). Who speaks of change? The internal, intertextual addressee or us? On an emotional plane, the inescapable fact is that we must henceforth question our position in relation to the discourse, and this questioning initiates a rupture with the comfortable identification we were previously able to assume.

Fortunately, this rupture does not last long because, just a few sentences later, the text takes up the impersonal [*el tú impersonal*] and offers us the possibility of inclusion once more. This is apparent as Susana describes her experiences in school: "The street vendors would arrive at recess. You couldn't not buy something. If you were in class, and you remembered you had a bag of sugar-coated peanuts in your backpack, then the time passed much more quickly" (8). In this example, a perfect correspondence between the description offered up by the text and the personal history of the real reader is unnecessary. It is irrelevant whether we have eaten roasted or sugar-coated peanuts. The particulars are superfluous because, in this case what is highlighted are feelings and reactions common to all who have, at one time or another in their lives, attended school. Nearly everyone has experienced the anticipation of a child with something sweet in his/her pocket and who knows that recess is imminent and that they will soon escape the tortures of the classroom.

In this manner, the text forges an identification between the real reader and the textual addressee. We understand, if only intermittently, that Susana is attempting to foment these same reactions and in her lover (*tú*). Simultaneously, we recognize that we may be responding just as he might. As Georges Poulet points out, the words and the actions to which they refer are objects, "but subjectified objects. In short, since everything has become part of [our] mind, thanks to the intervention of language, the opposition between the subject and its objects has been considerably attenuated" (1214). In *Pánico o peligro*, this opposition has been attenuated but not entirely eliminated. Instead of suppressing or erasing it completely, the novel uses this subjective opposition to a thematic end: It creates a tension that obliges the real reader to continually question his/her state as both semiotic subject and object.

Throughout the work we (the real readers) pass from one intertextual point of view to another, choosing—not necessarily consciously—whether or not we can incorporate the perspectives offered by the internal addressees into our personal cosmovision. If so, this rearrangement of our repertoire can be quite transformative because, due to the constant perceptual shifting, the limits between ourselves and the intertextual addressees begin to cloud over. Who is this "you"? Do we know him/her? Do we know ourselves? In the end, we, like Susana, must conclude that we are distinct and that there are differences. Simultaneously, the tenuous bridges between ourSelves and the Other have been broken down. In this fashion, both the story and discourse of *Pánico o peligro* harmonize so the reader may participate in, construct, if you will, a new perspective of alterity, otherness; one that is less threatening and, hopefully, not simply novelistic. Furthermore, to the degree that we successfully incorporate this new vision of alterity into our personal repertoire, the world-building utopian subtext of the novel will have achieved its end. We, as well as Susana and her lover, may choose to resist colonizing impulses, and instead live in solidarity with this different-and-yet-the-same Other as a result of reading her notebooks.

NOTES

1. Puga has visited utopian territory previously in her little commented *Cuando el aire es azul*, published by Siglo Veintiuno in 1980. The text, a fictional auto-biography, describes a town in which the adults, as well as the children could "write about whatever sparked their curiosity" (10). In the town where the air is blue the newspapers publish a special section on dreams, and everyone reads, and writes, and has the freedom to put their ideas into practice (12).

2. Jean Pfaelzer cites essentially the same categories in her article, "The Changing of the Avant Garde: The Feminist Utopia." Her terminology differs, but the conceptual frameworks are similar: The categories are "monogendered," "gender-merged," and "dialectical androgyny" (285).

3. Marleen Barr, in "Working at Loving: The Postseparatist Feminist Utopia," distinguishes between the separatist feminist utopias of the 1970s, in which men were defined as "dangerous, subhuman and alien" (180), and the postseparatist feminist utopias that began springing up in the 1980s that defined women's work/words as necessary to "altering gender constructions to include love relationships characterized by equality and dignity for women as well as for men" (179).

4. Before undertaking the analysis of a specific example, I would like to make the following point: not all women's literature is necessarily feminist and, by extension, utopian. Romance novels (*novelas rosas*) come to mind, for example. In terms of the present discussion, I agree with Jane Flax, in her book *Thinking Fragments: Psychoanalysis, Feminism & Postmodernism in the Contemporary West*, when I state that for a work to be utopian in nature it must answer, or at least address, the fundamental question of "how shall we live?" (21).

5. Prophetic in that in her narrative Susana attempts to change both herself and her lover, and, by so doing, alter her future relationship with him.

6. All translations from Spanish are mine.

7. Stanley Fish, in his introduction to "How To Do Things with Austin and Searle," suggests something very similar (197–200). He describes the difference between constative and performative language and arrives at the conclusion that the distinction between the two is invalid because there is only one type of language, performative. He states: "What Austin discovers at the end of *How to Do Things with Words* is that all utterances are performative—produced and understood within the assumption of some socially conceived dimension of assessment—and that therefore all facts are institutional, are facts only by virtue of the prior institution of some such dimension" (198). Furthermore, Fish concludes that all fact is "discourse specific (since no fact is available apart from some dimension of assessment or another)" (199). In other words, to a certain extent we construct reality by enunciating it.

8. See Paulo Freire, *Pedagogy of the Oppressed*, for an informative description of the process of "educating" the "oppressed" so they may take control of their reality, reorganizing it in accordance with their own desires and needs, and not those of their

"oppressors." One important aspect of Freire's theory is recognizing the individual's inherent state as subject and not object, and then educating him/her from this perspective, thus empowering the individual with an authentic language. This language then becomes a way of describing and understanding one's own reality from one's own perspective, and not from the position of the ruling classes—the traditional "oppressors" within Freire's theorectical framework.

9. Shklovsky describes the metamorphosis as follows: "An image is not a permanent referent for those mutable complexities of life which are revealed through it; its purpose is not to make us perceive meaning, but to create a special perception of the object—*it creates a 'vision' of the object instead of serving as a means for knowing it*" (18).

10. Hans Robert Jauss, in *Aesthetic Experience and Literary Hermeneutics*, defines this process as follows: "Effect [is] the element that is conditioned by the text and reception [is] the element of concretization of meaning that is conditioned by the addressee" (xxxii).

REFERENCES

Anderson, Danny J. "Cultural Conversation and Constructions of Reality: Mexican Narrative and Literary Theories After 1968." *Siglo XX/20th Century* 8.1-2 (1990–1991): 11–30.

Barr, Marleen. "Working at Loving: The Postseparatist Feminist Utopia." *Eros: XI Congres Du Cerli*. Quebec: Université de Provence, 1990. 179–189.

Fish, Stanley. "How To Do Things with Austin and Searle." *Is There a Text in This Class?* Cambridge: Harvard UP, 1980. 197–245.

Flax, Jane. *Thinking Fragments: Psychoanalysis, Feminism, & Postmodernism in the Contemporary West*. Berkeley: U California P, 1990.

Freire, Paulo. *Pedagogy of the Oppressed*. Trans. Myra Bergman Ramos. New York: Continuum, 1982.

Isabel Allende: The Woman's Voice in Latin-American Literature. Princeton: Films for the Humanities #4239, 1994.

Iser, Wolfgang. *The Act of Reading: A Theory of Aesthetic Response*. Baltimore, MD: Johns Hopkins UP, 1978.

Jauss, Hans Robert. *Aesthetic Experience and Literary Hermeneutics*. Trans. Wlad Godzich. Minneapolis: U of Minnesota P, 1982.

———. *Toward an Aesthetic of Reception*. Trans. Timothy Bahti. Minneapolis: U Minnesota P, 1982.

López González, Aralia. "Nuevas formas de ser mujer en la narrativa contemporánea de escritoras mexicanas." *Casa de las Américas* 31.183 (1991): 3–8.

Mellor, Anne K. "On Feminist Utopias." *Women's Studies* 9 (1982): 241–262.

Pfaelzer, Jean. "The Changing of the Avant Garde: The Feminist Utopia." *Science Fiction Studies* 15 (1988): 282–294.

Poulet, Georges. "Phenomenology of Reading." *Critical Theory Since Plato*. Ed. Hazard Adams. New York: Harcourt Brace Jovanovich, 1971. 1212–1222.

Prince, Gerald. "Introduction to the Study of the Narratee." *Reader Response Criticism*. Ed. Jane P. Tompkins. Baltimore, MD: Johns Hopkins UP, 1980. 7–24.

Puga, María Luisa. *Cuando el aire es azul*. Mexico: Siglo XXI, 1980.

———. *La forma del silencio*. Mexico: Siglo XXI, 1987.

———. *Pánico o peligro*. Mexico: Siglo XXI, 1983.

13

GROWING UP JEWISH IN MEXICO:
SABINA BERMAN'S *LA BOBE*
AND ROSA NISSÁN'S *NOVIA QUE TE VEA*

Darrell B. Lockhart

Jewish literature in Mexico has its earliest roots in the colonial period with historical figures such as Luis de Carvajal y de la Cueva (1539–1591?), who together with his family suffered greatly at the hands of the Inquisition for Judaizing (Toro). Nevertheless, it is in the twentieth century that the story of Mexican Jewish literature begins to emerge with the large influx of immigrants. The majority of Jewish immigrants to Mexico were Russian and Eastern European who were fleeing the Russian Revolution and World War I, and whose ultimate goal was to reach the United States (Laiken Elkin 63–64; Krause 147–173; Seligson Berenfeld 107–129). Consequently, a relatively strong tradition of Yiddish literature developed in the late 1920s and lasted through the mid-1950s. The main proponents of this writing were Jacobo Glantz (1902–?), Yitzkhok Berliner (1899–1957), and Moshe Glicovsky (1904–?) (Liptzin 404–406). This literature, however, had little, if any, influence on Mexican literature in general, since it was written and read only within the Jewish community. In addition, few Yiddish writers were able to make the transition into Spanish. It is not, therefore, until the children of these immigrants started to write in Spanish that a discernible body of literature began to emerge. Indeed, the presence of Jewish writing as a socio-literary phenomenon in Mexico did not begin to manifest itself until the early 1970s. Second- and third-generation Spanish-language writers have contributed extensively to contemporary Mexican letters, and yet their names historically have been excluded from histories, bibliographies, anthologies, dictionaries, and encyclopedias of Mexican literature.[1] It is interesting to note that the overwhelming majority of Mexican Jewish authors are women, which may play a part in the continued marginalization of Jewish authors from the Mexican literary canon. These authors, nonetheless, have much to say regarding their marginal status not only within Mexican society but also within Jewish culture. In their texts, they often posit strong feminist standpoints through characters that seek to overcome their double marginalization.[2] Margo Glantz (1930), Esther Seligson (1941), Angelina Muñiz-Huberman (1936), Ethel Krauze (1954), Gloria Gervitz (1943), and more recently, Sabina Berman (1955), Rosa Nissán (1939), Myriam Moscona (1955), Sara Levi Calderón (1942): Their names sound familiar enough to those acquainted with Mexican literature because they have been widely read—at least in academic circles—, received numerous literary awards, and been translated into English, yet they remain curiously on the margins of what in general terms is called "Mexican" literature. There is a relevant factor to consider regarding what can be perceived as the ironic benefit of being a marginal, or postcolonial, literature. Poststructuralist theory and criticism has played a central role in providing a means by which marginal texts have begun to achieve a position of prominence. The deconstruction of traditional power structures (Foucault) as well as theoretical postulations of *différance* (Derrida) have effected an inversion of the hegemony maintained by colonial discourses. In Latin American literature, we see this inversion taking place as women's, gay and lesbian, black, and Jewish writing move gradually toward the center, heretofore occupied by the totalizing discourse of Hispanism.

In Mexico, as is the case throughout Latin America, the contemporary Jewish text exemplifies the emergence of a postcolonial discourse in which the values, language(s), and traits of the margin are superimposed on those of the center. The creation of multilingual (incorporation of Yiddish, Hebrew, or Ladino) texts by Mexican Jewish authors represents a marked resistance and challenge to canonical monolingual Hispanic works. Likewise, Latin American Jewish writing has been characterized as pertaining to post-boom, postmodernist Latin American fiction categorized by what Doris Sommer and George Yúdice define as the fragmentation of the canon by means of the dissemination of marginalia (200–203). In a similar manner, Norman Finkelstein has aptly described the influence of postmodernism on American Jewish intellectuals and writers. While it can often prove to be a dangerous and even disastrous practice to apply North American theoretical models to Latin American instances, many of Finkelstein's observations are relevant to the situation of contemporary Mexican Jewish writers and/or intellectuals. He begins his assessment by stating that postmodernism has failed to attract what he terms "self-conscious" Jewish writers and intellectuals—those who ascribe to a Jewish identity—because they tend to adhere to history and cultural metanarratives of Jewish tradition (15). Nonetheless, this fact, he goes on to describe, does not prevent Jewish intellectuals from being affected by the postmodern world in which they live and operate. Speaking of secular Jewish intellectual Jacques Derrida's concept of *différance*, Finkelstein points out that this fundamental component of postmodernist ideology "speaks directly to the Jewish intellectual's self-conception, their understanding of their obviously vexed Jewish identity and the role they play in the greater drama of culture at large" (16). If *différance* is to be understood as the production of differences, or divisions, the connotation of the divided nature of a sign or sign systems in which one understands that the subject can both differ and defer, then it is reasonable to accept postmodernism, as Finkelstein argues, as being central to the concept of Jewish identity in that such an identity is based on difference. This implies an active process of self-identification on the part of Jewish writers as not only being different, but using that difference to their advantage. Such a characterization is readily extended to encompass the postcolonial nature of contemporary Jewish texts in Mexico, and more to the point, those that are the focus of the present study.

The debate over exactly what the term "Jewish literature" means or should mean is ongoing.[3] This dilemma stems from the fact that there is no precise definition of what constitutes Jewish culture as a source for literary production. The argument revolves around whether or not Jewish literature is defined in terms of language, national boundaries, thematics, or religiosity. Some argue that such a category is neither valid or useful (Shechner 5). Hana Wirth-Nesher, embracing reader-response theory, proposes that the definition resides with the reader and the circumstances of a given text's reception (5). Conversely, the concept of Jewish literature has much to do with how an author perceives his or her own ethno-religious experience as a Jew and how that experience is then translated onto the written page. This leads to the question of Jewish identity, an even more complex issue than the previous. It should be made explicit from the onset that what is at issue here are not expressions of Judaism as a religious system, but expressions of Jewishness as a cultural identity based on shared historical, ethnic, linguistic, and religious experience. Stated differently, of concern are issues of Jewish assent as opposed to Jewish descent. By Jewish assent, one understands the characterization of an individual's Jewishness, whereas Jewish descent implies an individual's ethno-religious identification as a Jew (Krausz). The topic of a Latin American Jewish identity poses various inconsistencies to be dealt with. Saúl Sosnowski has eloquently written on this hyphenated or dual existence:

When in addition to Latin American one adds the defining term Jewish, it is easy to recall astonished gazes and conflicting images of the accepted and simple clichés for both. Without engaging in endless definitions of national or ethnic literatures, it may prove useful to consider that in many cases it is the explicitness of literary motifs that render a text "Latin American" and/or "Jewish." Jewish components are defined as such in order to mark the entrance into a realm where a new set of literary and cultural conflicts will emerge beyond the seemingly flat surface of the page. The need to accentuate identity imposes itself upon the reader who from the outset is forced to recognize that "Latin American" in itself is not sufficient to place a text that challenges partial definitions. Molds are broken when elements considered extraneous to dominant cultural patterns are challenged. New perceptions are broadened when into the very strict definition of nationality caveats are made for the different. (299–300)

The present discussion of two novels by Mexican Jewish women will center on this concept of cultural identification through literature. The novels by Sabina

Berman and Rosa Nissán are similar in a variety of ways. Aside from the obvious similarity of placing a specifically Jewish subject at the narrative core of the texts, both authors utilize child narrators as a method of communicating their own nostalgic reminiscence. They differ, however, in that they write from two distinct experiences—one Ashkenazic, the other Sephardic—as they seek to create a narrative of Mexican Jewish identity.

Sabina Berman is both a poet and a novelist, but she is best known in Mexico as a dramatist. She has received numerous awards for her plays, and she forms part of what Ronald Burgess calls a new generation of dramatists in Mexico (1–13). While Berman identifies herself as a Mexican Jewish writer (Berman "El intelecto como hacedor de fantasmas"; Glickman 13), she is at the same time reluctant to allow critical or public perceptions to see her as somehow less Mexican for it: "In other words, I have a perception of otherness because I'm part of a minority group. It's possible. But in my life I feel very much a part of Mexico, I'm completely integrated here" (Ramírez 27).[4] Indeed, Berman's literary corpus does not reflect an overriding concern to write the Jewish experience in Mexico. In contrast, her literature, most specifically her dramatic texts, are very much concerned with issues germane to contemporary Mexican culture, history, and society. Specifically Jewish themes appear in her work as evidence of only one facet of her identity, much like the lesbian sensibility that can be identified in her writing (Costantino). In the play *Herejía* (1984), Berman recounts the tribulations of the Carvajal family in colonial Mexico who were aggressively persecuted by the Inquisition. Berman is the first person to bring a Jewish theme to the Mexican stage and to present this famous episode from a Jewish perspective. In doing so, she establishes a Jewish presence in the country as an integral part of national history while bringing to the fore the diverse aspects of Mexican identity.[5]

Of concern for the present study is Berman's 1991 novel *La bobe*. The title would seem to indicate difference and set the text apart as a narration of the Other. "*Bobe*," a word that connotes endearment, is Yiddish for grandmother, and the novel is centered around the young narrator's reminiscence of her grandmother, an immigrant who arrived in Mexico fleeing the Nazi persecution of World War II. The novel follows no solid plot line but is rather a compilation of nostalgic vignettes covering a period of some twenty years (roughly 1950–1970), which the reader is led to believe are told by a young girl. The narrator's advanced language, however, betrays an adult author who recalls the past as opposed to a young girl who is living the present. There are, in fact, three distinct voices that make themselves heard in the text: the young narrator's, the mother's, and the grandmother's. The grandmother was a former member of high society who now finds herself displaced in Mexico and who resists assimilation into Mexican society by clinging on to religious orthodoxy and Jewish tradition. The mother, on the other hand, has completely acculturated to the point of rejecting virtually all aspects of Jewish identity, most vehemently religiosity, opting for psychoanalysis in lieu of Judaism. The mother's atheism and dismissal of Jewish belief is manifested in no uncertain terms:

That the Jewish people are the chosen people of God is what is called a miracle of the imagination. Imagine: we Jews are the most mistreated people in history: every fifty years some tyrant tries to exterminate us, every time a country wants to find a scapegoat for their woes, they blame the Jews, so the Jews, what do we do? We invent among ourselves that God, that invisible man, that hypothetical man (later we'll talk about what hypothetical means), God, now He adores us. As you'll see: pure insanity. (34)

The young narrator seeks to strike a balance in her own life between the two extremes. She discovers in her grandmother an intriguing mystical quality represented by the *Ein sof*, the eternal light that converts the quotidian into the sacred. From her mother she learns the pragmatism necessary for living a dual existence. Likewise, through the intercalation of Jewish linguistic registers (i.e., Yiddish and Hebrew) with typically Mexican scenes, the author consistently weaves an identity from both cultures.

A peculiar aspect of the novel is found in the grandmother's characterization of her nose as Sephardic and the narrator's consequent promise: "I promise myself not to forget that: The History of Grandmother's Nose" (63). Berman, like her characters, is Ashkenazic. The author's use of Sephardic lineage can be interpreted as being anything but gratuitous. Whether consciously or not, Berman makes use of a narrative strategy that enables her to present the characters in a light that makes them less different, less of an outsider in relation to the general population. Aside from presenting the *bobe* as having a Sephardic heritage, Berman also utilizes *La guía de los perplejos* [*The Guide for the Perplexed*]—the famous treatise by the Sephardic philosopher Maimónides (1135–1204)—as a *leitmotif*. These elements help to forge a common "Hispanic" bond between the two seemingly disparate elements of Jewish and Mexican identity by means of employing the discourse strategy of "*sefaradismo literario*" as defined by critic Edna Aizenberg.

Although Aizenberg cites the case of early twentieth-century Argentine authors, her proposal is equally applicable to Mexican writers. That is, that Ashkenazic authors living in Hispano-Catholic societies manipulate "the Sephardic heritage as a link with the Hispanic world in which they now found themselves living, as a means of access to society" (55).[6] This is, nevertheless, but a minor element in the novel that should not be considered as a significant ideological maneuver on the part of the author. If nothing else, the recurrent references to *La guía de los perplejos* serve to emphasize the fact that Jewish identity is itself a perplexing construct. *La bobe* does not present an overly idyllic view of Jewish tradition; on the contrary, Berman is often critical of stringent religious laws, especially those that constrain women's roles. What is most evident in the novel is the evolution of an identity based on religious orthodoxy and adherence to tradition (the grandmother), to one centered on secularism (the mother), with the third generation seeking a balance between

the two poles. The young narrator seeks to recuperate the Jewish cultural tradition and values of her ancestors but remains largely secularized and assimilated
to the Mexican way of life. These evolutionary stages are typical of immigrant
Jewish communities in the diaspora. The general tone of the novel is achieved
by the use of ironic and/or sardonic humor. This, coupled with the fact that
it is a story told by a supposedly adolescent narrator, enables the author to
distance herself from the events and topics presented in the novel.

Rosa Nissán was born in Mexico City to Sephardic parents who emigrated
to Mexico at the turn of the century. Nissán's novel is more strictly autobiographical than Berman's in that it closely follows her childhood experience
growing up within the Sephardic community of Mexico City, attending Jewish
schools, and participating in the activities of the Club Deportivo Israelita. *Novia
que te vea* (1992) is the author's first novel, and it has enjoyed both critical
and commercial success in Mexico. The novel carries an enthusiastic endorsement on the back cover from Elena Poniatowska, Nissán's acknowledged men-
tor. A film version of the novel, written by Nissán and Hugo Hiriat and produced by Guita Shyfter, was released in 1993. Much like *La bobe*, Nissán's
title, with its strange archaic syntax, signals to the reader a certain sense of
"otherness." *Novia que te vea* is derived from a traditional Sephardic song in
Ladino, the archaic Spanish language conserved by the Jews who were expelled
from Spain in the fifteenth century. In comparison to the young narrator in *La
bobe*, Oshinica, the narrator in *Novia*, is more credible as a child in both language and action as she relates the stories of her youth. One is given the
impression that the protagonist is living the present as opposed to reminiscing
the past. Again, the linguistic registers of Hebrew, as a liturgical language and
Ladino as a secular one are intermingled with very typically Mexican lexicon
and images. Nissán's novel provides a more detailed view of Jewish life in
Mexico during the 1950s and 1960s, specifically within the Sephardic community. In this sense, the text serves the purpose of constituting a valuable socio-
historic record. Ladino figures prominently in the text as entire dialogues and
letters are presented in that language:

Since my mother, may her soul rest in *Gan Eden*, had just passed away, I came to the
Americas with your mother and grandmother who lived next door to me. I'm going to
die in a foreign land, I thought, *amá*, my father was afraid I would marry a *burdequí*.
So I set off on my journey. They married us on the ship, in Veracruz, it was the only
way they would allow us to disembark, when I saw how young your uncle was, small
like this, I burst into tears. For my own good, I swear to you Oshinica, I wanted to run
away. (111–112)[7]

The novel follows a traditional plot structure that advances as Oshinica
leads the reader through one humorous experience to the next. Like Berman,
Nissán is also critical of orthodox tradition and portrays an identity based on
Jewish cultural experience as opposed to religious experience. To fill the void

caused by the absence of religion in her life, Oshinica turns to Zionism as an alternate expression of her Jewish identity. She becomes very much involved in fund raising activities for the edification of Eretz Israel. She develops a strong desire to live and work on a kibbutz, viewing such a lifestyle in idealistically utopic terms:

In school they showed us some marvelous slides of the *kibbutzim*: young people like us carrying baskets of fruit, sporting shorts and their skin tanned by the sun that beams health and happiness, young Jewish men slicing enormous, juicy apples, trees with broad palm leaves, ever-happy faces inviting us to live like them. It makes me long to be there, to dance the Hora holding hands and to warm ourselves and sing around the fire of the medurah. (69)

While she embraces her heritage and identity, at the same time Oshinica seeks to break away from the traditions that constrain her as a female: the possibility of pursuing an education, and marriage to the man she chooses instead of the marriage arranged for her by her parents. She finds the traditional roles of other women in her family unsatisfactory, and she looks to the men as role models:

To want to be like mama, grandmother, or my aunt? No, it's better to be like my grandfather, papa, or even my brother. Women are so boring, and dumb, too!; well, mama isn't dumb, but she certainly isn't any fun; my grandmother can't even go alone to Sears, just two blocks away. She sneaks away with Uba. The women are always at home, it doesn't even occur to them to go rowing. My papa is very nice; the husbands go out and the women stay behind to watch their kids or their brothers and sisters, like I have to do. (25–26)

While Oshinica dreams of an education and travel, her mother, grandmother, and aunts regularly meet to sew and prepare items for her hope chest. The novels ends with a scene of her traditional Sephardic wedding and someone whispering in her ear *"hisho que te nazca"* ("may a son be born to you").

These two novels are representative of a growing body of texts that is emerging as a subcategory within Mexican literature. Jewish authors in Mexico, as elsewhere, draw on a variety of cultural experiences with which they encode their writing. A determining factor in this literature is the writer's own relationship with tradition. As contemporary Jewish writers, Berman and Nissán rely on a nostalgic relationship with Jewish tradition as it existed prior to the Haskalah (Jewish Enlightenment).[8] Finkelstein explains this relationship as one that operates on the ideology of loss and absence that "enables secular authors to manipulate their relation to the past, writing out of their melancholy sense of temporal distance" (131). This is not to say that Berman, Nissán, or any other contemporary writer spends great lengths of time pondering their relationship with medieval Rabbinic tradition. The point that Finkelstein is making is that contemporary authors, whether consciously or not, are in part responsible for the continuance of Jewish identity in as much as their writing helps to ensure the survival of a collective Jewish memory.

In writing about identity, Jewish authors in Latin America often turn to memory as an act of both personal and collective identification (Senkman 107). Yosef Hayim Yerushalmi has succinctly delineated the development and importance of collective memory in his *Zakhor: Jewish History and Jewish Memory*. Furthermore, he identifies literature as playing a key role in its creation:

Many Jews today are in search of the past, but they patently do not want the past that is offered by the historian. Much has changed since the sixteenth century; one thing, curiously, remains. Now, as then, it would appear that even where Jews do not reject history out of hand, they are not prepared to confront it directly, but seem to await a new, metahistorical myth, for which the novel provides at least a temporary modern surrogate. (97–98)

In this sense, Berman and Nissán can be readily seen as engaged in a process of identity formation and perpetuation specific to the socio-cultural milieu of the Jewish experience(s) in Mexico. The generationally progressive move from religious orthodoxy to secularized Jewishness portrayed in both novels is indicative of how socially motivated change is reflected and preserved in literature.

What is unusual about *La bobe* and *Novia que te vea* is that both authors utilize a child narrator as a nostalgia-imbued strategy for approaching the topic of Mexican Jewish identity.[9] The fictional representation of a child's and/or adolescent's voice establishes an arena in which conflicting frames of reference interact. The voice of the child is often placed in direct contrast with that of adults, creating a oppositional situation in the text that posits the voice of the child as that of the Other. A child's voice commands less authority, yet it enjoys more freedom of expression. Children are seldom held responsible for what they say, since they merely repeat what they hear from adults. A major obstacle faced by the author is overcoming his or her own adult perspective and mature discourse in order to create an "authentic" child's voice that at the same time conveys adult ideas. This literary ventriloquism is useful as a subversive means of criticism. An adult author, speaking through the protective innocence of a child's voice, is able to portray events and circumstances in a manner not afforded by an adult narrator. While the representation of youthful narrators is not by any means unique to Jewish authors, Naomi B. Sokoloff effectively argues that such authors as Sholem Aleichem, Henry Roth, Jerzy Kosinski, and Aharon Applefeld, among others, have masterfully used them in creating singular narratives of Jewish identity. In *Imagining the Child in Modern Jewish Fiction*, Sokoloff contends that the child narrator holds a privileged position from which to speak critically about issues of modern Jewish identity: "The child not yet fully initiated into tradition nor fully understanding of Jewish obligation becomes an indirect spokesman for authors who themselves moved away from the orthodoxy of their early family life. Secularized adults, the writers sought out characters capable of seeing *otherwise* the religious definition of Jewishness" (9). She goes on to say that this strategy works in texts that have a "clear autobiographical component and attempt a nostalgic reconstruction of the past" (9). Certainly, this characterizes the ideological underpinnings of both Berman's and Nissán's novels in which the narrators express strong opinions that contradict the beliefs and/or values of their preceding generations. With youthful exuberance, they struggle to forge an identity that is right for them, rather than one to which they must conform. This is not to say that they do not respect and admire them, as is evident in the young narrator's description of her grandmother's resourcefulness in *La bobe*: "That's my grandmother to me: the woman that has her wisdom tooth opened up in order to hide a diamond and then, when the last resources have run out and no one knows anymore how we will continue our voyage, she takes out the diamond and asks: 'Will this help?'" (31).

Both authors undertake a process of describing the various elements that comprise the nature of contemporary Jewish identity in Mexico. Central to this identity is the continuity of the family and a clear conception of one's own place within it. The most obvious examples are texts in which an author directly reproduces her own family genealogy in the form of a novelized autobiography, including photographs.[10] For Berman and Nissán, this is achieved less conspicuously by incorporating the family as essential to the advancement of the narrative. Most of the action revolves around the family or how family members react to different situations. By concentrating on the depiction of three generations of women, Berman underscores the significant role they play in Jewish tradition, emphasizing the fact that Jewish identity is matrilineal.

On a more strictly textual level, one may turn to Mikhail Bakhtin's concept of the dialogic imagination to gain a better understanding of the discourse strategies operant in Berman's and Nissán's novels. The collision of different narrative voices, languages, points of view, and the semiotic connotations embedded in utterances contribute to the heteroglossia of a given text (301–331). The resultant relativization of novelistic discourse is regarded as being dialogic. That is to say, meaning is determined by the way in which the heteroglossic elements of a text are relativized by one another as competing discourses interact. Dialogism does not consist merely of the alternation of opinions voiced through a novel's characters that serve to advance the plot. At the core of Bakhtin's theory is the notion that language is the primary motivator of and vehicle for ideological posturing, which places context before text in novelistic discourse:

The plot itself is subordinated to the task of coordinating and exposing languages to each other. The novelistic plot must organize the exposure of social languages and ideologies, the exhibiting and experiencing of such languages: the experience of a discourse, a world view and an ideologically based act, or the exhibiting of the everyday life of social, historical and national worlds or micro-worlds . . . or of the socio-ideological worlds of epochs . . . or of age groups and generations linked with epochs and socio-ideological worlds. In a word, the novelistic plot serves to represent speaking persons and their ideological worlds. (365)

Dialogism is endemic, although not limited, to the literature of *galut* authors, those who live in the exile of the diaspora and whose writing reflects a dual or bicultural existence. *La bobe* and *Novia que te vea* serve as excellent examples of this type of literature that has counterparts in virtually every corner of the globe. There are a number of factors at work that contribute to the heteroglossia of such texts. Principally, these include Jewish multilingualism that results in multiple linguistic cultural encodements within a given text. Likewise, the conflicting voices of different generations, readily apparent in *La bobe* and *Novia que te vea*, constitute another heteroglossic stratum of the text. The novel provides a forum for interpreting the position of the Jew as Other. In Mexico, this has meant writing from the margins of a predominantly Hispano-Catholic, nonpluralistic society. Dialogue between the contrasting cultural traditions, therefore, is necessarily inherent to this literary production, and the novel provides ample space for such dialogue to occur.

An exemplary model of dialogic interaction is to be found in a brief episode of *La bobe* concerning the story of Moses and the parting of the Red Sea (33–36). Berman very effectively creates a situation in which the young narrator absorbs and reinterprets conflicting versions of the story as told to her by different adults, thus ingeniously revealing the guiding ideological foundations of the adult characters. The result is that the child not only is punished at school for her insolence, but more importantly she receives a mixed message from which she must glean her own truth and draw her own conclusions regarding Jewish tradition.

Novia que te vea is also replete with instances of polyphonic discourse. Nissán employs a variety of discourse styles as part of the overall structure of the novel. Her incorporation of letters, yearbook dedications, songs, and literary excerpts all contribute to the multiplicity of voices that interact in the novel. Oshinica operates on a truly bicultural level that could be considered as a type of double-voicing. Bakhtin defines double-voicing most strictly as the double meaning that a single utterance can hold, but he also states that "double-voicedness sinks its roots deep into a fundamental, socio-linguistic speech diversity and multi-languagedness" (325–326). Oshinica's social heteroglossia, a literary refraction of Nissán's own, is evident in the two different types of social language she manipulates. Mostly, Oshinica's narration consists of an eclectic collage of adolescent thoughts that bounce from one topic to the next with no apparent connection. Her mind races to express her every interpretation of the events that unfold around her. Her vocabulary is that typical of any Mexican youth, filled with slang and popular usage. Her language, however, changes dramatically when she speaks of circumstances specific to Jewish culture. For example her speech is filled with words like "*retefeo*" (52), "*híjoles*" (70), and "*qué padres*" (87), while at the same time she says things like "A friend of Andrés's from Shomer came to my house, she arrived with her tilvoshet on,

her anivah and a big smile" (121). This dialogic interaction of linguistic registers in a contemporary socio-cultural setting is one element that makes this
novel, as well as *La bobe*, texts that in no uncertain terms seek to bring Jewish
identity into mainstream Mexican literature in such a way as to enrich society
with ethnic diversity and promote cultural pluralism.

Such a project is obviously ideologically motivated, especially if one accepts
Fredric Jameson's proposition that all literature is influenced by a "political
unconscious." These novels may be seen as not merely being informed by
ideology, but more significantly as ideological acts in their own right (79). Both
novels may also be thought of as models of cultural mediation. By mediation
we understand the establishment of a dialectical relationship between the different levels of social reality. For example, the idea of culture and consciousness
as manifestations or expressions of the underlying socio-political and economic
conditions from which they arise (39–41). In simpler terms, and more in tune
with the subject at hand, Jules Chametzky argues that literature functions in
this sense as mediator and creator of culture, what he calls "a meaningful way
of being in the world" (58–59).

One consideration worth mentioning prior to concluding is the fact that
since the nineteenth century non-Jewish Mexican writers of the center have
written in/of the Jewish margins. Justo Sierra O'Reilly utilized the figure of
the marginal Jew in his serialized novel *La hija del judío* (1849), later published
in book form in 1874. He used the metaphor of the Jew-as-victim as a liberal,
anticlerical literary weapon against political conservatism. Contemporary authors
that immediately come to mind are Carlos Fuentes, Homero Aridjis, and José
Emilio Pacheco. Fuentes in his *Terra nostra* (1975) and Aridjis in his two-
volume epic, *1492: Vida y tiempos de Juan Cabezón de Castilla* (1985) and
Memorias del Nuevo Mundo (1988), both look back to the historical circumstances of the expulsion of the Jews from Spain in 1492. In *La cabeza de la
hidra* (1978) Fuentes, against the backdrop of the Israeli-Palestinian conflict,
creates a Jewish character out of such negative stereotypes that the novel
borders on literary anti-Semitism. Pacheco provides readers with a different
outlook, one that goes beyond the superficial in order to better understand the
Jewish cultural milieu that is part of contemporary (metropolitan) Mexican
society, although it remains foreign to the majority population. In his 1967
novel *Morirás lejos,* Pacheco creates an eloquent representation of Jewish
suffering through centuries of persecution. These texts are not outside the scope
of the discussion of dialogism, since they provide another optic and, on a larger
scale, participate in an intertextual dialogue of the issue of Jewish identity as
interpreted in Mexican literature.

Notwithstanding the previous statements, there is an important distinction
to be made. The dialogic interaction between Jewish and non-Jewish elements
in literature, as well as authors, differs greatly according to the origin of such
discourse. Non-Jewish writers like those mentioned, by virtue of their privileged
position at the center, subsume Jewish discourse into their own without losing

their status. In contrast, those relegated to the margins must utilize the centripetal force generated by their postcolonial quest for status at the center to chip away at the hegemony of the accepted canon. Again, it is a question of a marginal author mediating cultural and societal constructs. It is this process of mediation that determines the shape of Jewish literature in Mexico and makes novels like *La bobe* and *Novia que te vea* especially equipped as a laboratory of the dialogic imagination, which in turn reflects the dialogic identity of the Mexican Jew.

NOTES

1. An examination of recent scholarly publications on Mexican literature reveals the continuing absence of Jewish authors, although in some cases the situation is improving. In their studies Sara Sefchovich, David William Foster and Steven M. Bell do not mention a single Jewish author. Cynthia Steele mentions Margo Glantz (14–15) and Ethel Krauze (17) only in passing, and Jean Franco also briefly comments on Margo Glantz (183). Eladio Cortés includes Max Aub (who arguably may also be considered a Spanish writer), Sabina Berman, Gloria Gervitz, and Margo Glantz.

2. While in the United States Jewish feminism has become a topic of considerable debate on a national level (see for example Judith Plaskow and Susannah Heschel), in Latin America it has yet to emerge as force to be reckoned with. Nonetheless, the vast majority of Jewish women writers in Latin America do write from a feminist perspective, and they have come to be recognized on a global level (see Nora Glickman's "Jewish Women Writers in Latin America").

3. A recent and excellent example of this debate is to be found in Hana Wirth-Nesher. Conspicuously absent from the volume, unfortunately, is any discussion of Latin American Jewish literature.

4. All translations are my own.

5. For a detailed study of *Herejía* see Sandra M. Cypess, "Ethnic Identity in the Plays of Sabina Berman."

6. The most famous of these cases is to be found in Alberto Gerchunoff (1884–1950) who undertook a lifelong campaign to legitimize the Jewish presence in Argentina by emphasizing the Hispanic commonality between the Sephardic heritage and dominant Hispano-Catholic tradition of Argentina. See Leonardo Senkman's thorough analysis of Gerchunoff's work in his *La identidad judía en la literatura argentina* (17–57).

7. The original passage with Ladino text is as follows: "Como mi amá, que su alma esté en Gan Eden, acababa de morir, me vine a las Américas con tu madre y tu abuelita que vivían puerta a puerta con la mía. En tierras ayenas me vo a murir, pensí, amá, mi padre tenía miedo que me casara con un burdequí. Así que tomí camino en mano. Nos esposaron en el barco, en Veracruz, sólo ansi desharon abashar, cuando vi el boy que estaba tu tío, así de chiquitico, me metí en un lloro. Por mi sanedad, te lo yuro, Oshinica, me quería fuir presto."

8. The beginning of Haskalah, the term given to the Jewish social, spiritual, and literary movement of enlightenment, developed in Germany sometime in the late 1760s. It spread throughout central and eastern Europe and into Russia. Essentially a movement of emancipation from strict Jewish law and integration into the dominant society, it lasted

until the early 1880s when virulent persecution of Russian Jewry proved that efforts of social integration were not enough to solve the "Jewish problem." Haskalah did not come to an abrupt end, but rather entered a new phase as its ideals were assimilated into the emerging Zionist and Jewish socialist movements and massive immigration to the Americas. Enlightenment enabled Jews to expand their cultural horizons beyond the boundaries of Judaism, undermining the practice of Jewish exclusivism. Prior to Haskalah, Jews had remained segregated from society as a whole, as much by their own will as from external exclusionary efforts. Persecution in many ways was the glue that held Jewish communities together. There was no ideological common denominator between the Jew and the Gentile and no theological common ground. Within the confines of the Jewish community, there existed clear and concise models of Jewish identity and there were no occasions for crises of identity. Enlightenment was a double-edged sword. It allowed Jews to break free from the rigid principles of medieval Judaism, but at the same time, it tragically undermined Jewish commitments to religious and cultural traditions. It also created an ambiguous space wherein the question of identity became a major problem with which to reckon. Jews began to think of themselves not only as Jews but also as Germans, or French, etc.

9. Salomón Laiter is the only other Mexican Jewish author of whom I am aware that uses this technique, and he does so rather unconvincingly in his novel *David*. See my entry on Laiter in *Latin American Jewish Writers: A Critical Dictionary* (New York: Garland, forthcoming).

10. See, for example, *Las genealogías* (1981; translated as *The Family Tree*, 1991) by Margo Glantz; *Sagrada memoria: reminiscencias de una niña judía en Chile* (1994) (Only the English version, *A Cross and a Star: Memoirs of a Jewish Girl in Chile* (1995) includes photographs) by Chilean Marjorie Agosín; *Pequeña familia, pequeña historia* (1991) by Argentine Perla Chirom.

REFERENCES

Agosín, Marjorie. *A Cross and a Star: Memoirs of a Jewish Girl in Chile*. Albuquerque: U of New Mexico P, 1995.

———. *Sagrada memoria: reminiscencias de una niña judía en Chile*. Santiago: Cuarto Propio, 1994.

Aizenberg, Edna. "Las peripecias de una metáfora: el sefaradismo literario judeoargentino." *Noaj* 5.7–8 (1992): 54–59.

Aridjis, Homero. *Memorias del Nuevo Mundo*. Mexico: Diana, 1988.

———. *1492: Vida y tiempos de Juan Cabezón de Castilla*. Mexico: Siglo XXI, 1985.

Avni, Haim. *Mexico: Immigration and Refuge*. Washington, DC: The Wilson Center, 1989.

Bakhtin, Mikhail. *The Dialogic Imagination*. Trans. Caryl Emerson and Michael Holquist. Austin: U of Texas P, 1990.

Baskin, Judith R., ed. *Women of the Word: Jewish Women and Jewish Writing*. Detroit: Wayne State UP, 1994.

Bell, Steven M. "Mexico." *Handbook of Latin American Literature*. 2nd. ed. Ed. David William Foster. New York: Garland, 1992. 357–442.

Berman, Sabina. *La bobe*. Mexico: Planeta, 1991.

———. *Herejía. Teatro de Sabina Berman*. Mexico: Editores Mexicanos Unidos, 1985. 147–211.

_____. "El intelecto como hacedor de fantasmas." *Noaj* 4.5 (1990): 71–73.

Burgess, Ronald D. *The New Dramatists of Mexico, 1967–1985*. Lexington: UP of Kentucky, 1991.

Chametzky, Jules. *Our Decentralized Literature: Cultural Mediations in Selected Jewish and Southern Writers*. Amherst: U of Massachusetts P, 1986.

Chirom, Perla. *Pequeña familia, pequeña historia*. Buenos Aires: Milá, 1991.

Costantino, Roselyn. "Sabina Berman." *Latin American Writers on Gay and Lesbian Themes: A Bio-Critical Sourcebook*. Ed. David William Foster. Westport, CT: Greenwood Press, 1994. 59–63.

Cortés, Eladio. *Dictionary of Mexican Literature*. Westport, CT: Greenwood Press, 1993.

Cypess, Sandra M. "Ethnic Identity in the Plays of Sabina Berman." *Tradition and Innovation: Reflections on Latin American Jewish Writing*. Eds. Robert DiAntonio and Nora Glickman. New York: SUNY P, 1993. 165–177.

Elkin, Judith Laiken. *Jews of the Latin American Republics*. Chapel Hill, NC: U of North Carolina P, 1980.

Finkelstein, Norman. *The Ritual of New Creation: Jewish Tradition and Contemporary Literature*. New York: SUNY P, 1992.

Foster, Davis William. *Mexican Literature: A Bibliography of Secondary Sources*. Metuchen, NJ: Scarecrow Press, 1992.

_____, ed. *Mexican Literature: A History*. Austin: U of Texas P, 1994.

Franco, Jean. *Plotting Women: Gender and Representation in Mexico*. New York: Columbia UP, 1989.

Fuentes, Carlos. *La cabeza de la hidra*. Barcelona: Argos Vergara, 1979.

_____. *Terra nostra*. Barcelona: Seix Barral, 1975.

Glantz, Margo. *Las genealogías*. Mexico: Martín Casillas, 1981.

_____. *The Family Tree*. Trans. Susan Bassnet. London: Serpent's Tail, 1991.

Glickman, Nora. "Introduction II." *Tradition and Innovation: Reflections on Latin American Jewish Writing*. Eds. Robert DiAntonio and Nora Glickman. Albany, New York: SUNY P, 1993. 8–31.

Heschel, Susannah, ed. *On Being a Jewish Feminist: A Reader*. New York: Schocken Books, 1983.

Jameson, Fredric. *The Political Unconscious: Narrative as a Socially Symbolic Act*. Ithaca, NY: Cornell UP, 1982.

Krause, Corinne A. *Los judíos en México: una historia con énfasis especial en el período de 1857–1930*. Trans. Ariela Katz de Gugenheim. Mexico: U Iberoamericana, 1987.

Krausz, Michael. "On Being Jewish." *Jewish Identity*. Eds. David Theo Goldberg and Michael Krausz. Philadelphia: Temple UP, 1993. 264–278.

Laiter, Salomón. *David*. Mexico: Joaquín Mortiz, 1976.

Liptzin, Sol. "Yiddish in Latin America." *A History of Yiddish Literature*. Middle Village, NY: Jonathan David, 1985. 394–409.

Nissán, Rosa. *Novia que te vea*. Mexico: Planeta, 1992.

Pacheco, José Emilio. *Morirás lejos*. Mexico: Joaquín Mortiz, 1967.

Plaskow, Judith. *Standing Again at Sinai: Judaism from a Feminist Perspective*. San Francisco: Harper, 1991.

Ramírez, Luis Enrique. Interview with Sabina Berman. 2 parts. *La Jornada: Cultura* (22 Feb. 1995): 25; (23 Feb. 1995): 27.

Sefchovich, Sara. *México: país de ideas, país de novelas. Una sociología de la literatura mexicana.* Mexico: Grijalbo, 1987.

Seligson Berenfeld, Silvia. *Los judíos en México: un estudio preliminar.* Mexico: Cultura SEP, 1983.

Senkman, Leonardo. *La identidad judía en la literatura argentina.* Buenos Aires: Pardés, 1983.

———. "Una literatura de la memoria y el olvido." *El imaginario judío en la literatura de América Latina: Visión y realidad.* Eds. Patricia Finzi, Eliahu Toker and Marcos Faerman. Buenos Aires: Shalom, 1992. 106–111.

Shechner, Mark. "Jewish Writers." *Harvard Guide to Contemporary Writing.* Ed. Daniel Hoffman. Cambridge: Belknap, 1979. 191–239.

Sierra O'Reilly, Justo. *La hija del judío.* Mexico, 1874.

Sokoloff, Naomi B. *Imagining the Child in Modern Jewish Fiction.* Baltimore, MD: Johns Hopkins UP, 1992.

Sommer, Doris, and George Yúdice. "Latin American Literature from the 'Boom' On." *Postmodern Fiction: A Bio-Bibliographical Guide.* Ed. Larry McCaffery. Westport, CT: Greenwood, 1986. 189–214.

Sosnowski, Saúl. "Latin American-Jewish Writers: Protecting the Hyphen." *The Jewish Presence in Latin America.* Ed. Judith Laiken Elkin and Gilbert W. Merkx. Boston: Allen & Unwin, 1987. 297–323.

Steele, Cynthia. *Politics, Gender, and the Mexican Novel, 1968–1988: Beyond the Pyramid.* Austin: U of Texas P, 1992.

Toro, Alfonso. *La familia Carvajal.* Mexico: Patria, 1944.

Wirth-Nesher, Hana. "Defining the Undefinable: What Is Jewish Literature." *What Is Jewish Literature.* Ed. Hana Wirth-Nesher. Philadelphia: Jewish Publication Society, 1994. 3–12.

Yerushalmi, Yosef Hayim. *Zakhor: Jewish History and Jewish Memory.* New York: Schocken, 1989.

14

BÁRBARA JACOBS:
GENDERED SUBJECTIVITY
AND THE EPISTOLARY ESSAY

María Concepción Bados-Ciria

In "Rosario Castellanos: Ashes without a Face," Debra Castillo categorically denies that Latin American women write autobiographies. In her opinion, only those who come from, or are educated in the Western tradition escape such a hyperbolic statement. In any case, they compose a privileged minority, and she cites three contemporary Mexican writers—Elena Poniatowska, Margo Glantz and Bárbara Jacobs—as examples to support her thesis. However, as Castillo acknowledges, none of them subscribes to the synthetic and monologic style of the autobiographic genre established as such by the androcentric Western canon (242). With the publication of *Doce cuentos en contra* in 1982, Bárbara Jacobs inserts herself within the circle of contemporary women writers for whom the rhetorical rigidities and imagistic structures of the traditional auto-biography have no meaning. Instead, she affiliates herself with the heteroglossic possibilities inherent in the new ideology of subjectivity that, in Sidonie Smith's opinion, has been debated and flexibilized since the beginning of the twentieth century by such theories as marxism, structuralism, feminism, and post-modernism, among others (*Subjectivity, Identity and the Body* 53–64). Jacobs's work distances itself from monologic style and projects itself toward forms of joint narration and collaboration, allowing the inscription of multiple voices as occurs, for example, in her novel *Las hojas muertas* (1987, translated as *The Dead Leaves*, 1993). At the same time, her work employs rhetorical strategies that resist the narrator's absolute power while making possible empathy and identification with the "other," whether this "other" is the reader, the charac-ters, or a second narrator, as is the case in *Las siete fugas de Saab, alias el Rizos* (1992) and *Vida con mi amigo* (1994).

   The book analyzed in this chapter, *Escrito en el tiempo* (1985), is a textual space that allows Jacobs to put in practice the discursive flexibility characteristic of the letter and the essay in relation to the autobiographical. On the one hand, Jacobs represents herself as an identity shaped by the various readings that make up her cultural and literary baggage. On the other, she makes her body visible both through writing and reading, inscribing in that way a strongly emotional connotation to all the fifty-three epistolary essays addressed but not sent to the publishers of the American magazine *Time*. If the letter presents itself as an appropriate genre for a type of confidential message, the essay—in the opinion of a large part of feminist criticism—would be the genre most conducive to feminine sensibilities and attitudes. According to Ruth Ellen Boetcher and Elizabeth Mittman, the essay is a genre without borders, antisystematic, and spontaneous; it not only centers itself on personal experience, but also emphasizes the particularities intimately connected with the one who practices it. Moreover, it is a nonfiction genre that invites dialogue and conversation, which makes it attractive to women writers in whom ideas of marginality and not belonging to a place of one's own continue to be pertinent (19). Bárbara Jacobs, a Mexican woman writer shaped in diverse traditions and cultures is an example of the identity in search of representation of a subjectivity, whose expression is realized by choosing a textual space that allows an interchange of literary forms. This combination of genres, moreover, allows the writer to define antagonistic and allied addressees and to assume a voice of authority before them, not only as a historical subject, but also as a theoretical one. Thus, Jacobs resorts to literature, which is the world she knows best, to expound upon and write about certain aspects that affect her in her relation to her task as a writer. Nonetheless, her reflections are antidoctrinal from the outset, since almost all the texts begin with questions directed at the readers, and not one of these questions is solved in a definitive manner.

Essayistic and epistolary texts allow the inscription of personal and autobiographical discourses, since both are nonfictional genres that permit and create a physical presence, invite dialogue, and are nonsystematic and spontaneous. Jacobs does not attempt to expound truths or arrive at a single conclusion; rather, through the process of deciding to write a weekly letter, the author gradually portrays herself temporally and emotionally, ultimately creating a self-portrait. The fortieth essay captures Jacobs's physical body and her personal attitudes when she notes—through more than twenty-five definitions—what she considers her style of dressing, which turns out to be a metaphor for her way of life: "Here's a jigsaw puzzle for anyone who wants to solve it. . . . My style is the style of the road. It gets along with the rain, with the sea: from a boat or out of season. It is designed for trains, for the mountains, for bridges, for parks, for plazas. My style is of the city and of small towns; of villages and of grass, of trees and of houses" (101–102).[1]

The rhetorical strategy of multiple addressees allows Jacobs to situate her knowledge and authority of literary material as well as to manifest the anxiety of an audience that is both accomplice and friend. Although it appears respectful in the beginning, the apostrophe "*Señores*," with which the epistolary essays are headed, is slowly degraded through constant repetition and because it loses its value relative to the implicit addressees, who are multiple and continually receiving the attention and confidences of the emissary subject. The different questions at the beginning of the texts are directed toward all readers, who are invited to respond with one voice to the author, so that a personal, democratic, and friendly tone shapes the epistolary essays to note intimate aspects related with the task of writing.

In the same way, but with a different intention, Jacobs reveals her subjective reaction as she marks her anger in the presence of something she considers inappropriate to the pages of *Time*: "Sheffield's sentence is missing something. Its author needs to be revealed, since that is what it is about. . . . But *Time* quotes it as is, which not only makes it incomplete, disorganized and meaningless, but also contrary to what it proposes, badly written" (69). Such an antagonistic appeal contrasts with the model of peaceful and docile intersubjectivity, which one would suppose characteristic of a Mexican woman author before the directors of an internationally renowned magazine. Thus, the letter, inscribed historically as a feminine literary genre and officially degraded for being the carrier of amorous and private discourses, is transformed in Jacobs's work into a text of political intervention, destined to promote socio-cultural changes. The repeated invocation at the beginning of the letters—indispensable in the epistolary genre—not only allows a direct appeal to an absent receptor made present in the discourse, but also creates a form of ventriloquism through which the writer gives voice, life, and human form to the addressee, turning his/her silence into a mute response. At the same time, and as Shari Benstock notes, the apostrophe is turned into a symbol of pure feminine subjectivity, whose effects are the abrupt appeal of male addressees, subjugated and opaqued by the insistence of the emissary in showing herself as an authority before them (86–122).

As for the content of the epistolary essays, Jacobs covers all four types established by Graham Good in *The Observing Self* (xii). They all participate in the impulses that move personal narratives, although, again, the negotiation of the autobiographic "I" suggests the fluidity of different subject positions. The author shifts between first-, second-, and third-person pronouns, but all make reference to her experiences, her reflections, and her emotions. The travel essay and the one with a moralizing approach, the critical essay and the properly autobiographical, all are intertwined due, without a doubt, to the fact that these four divisions cover the author's preferred activities: travel, reflection, reading, and remembering.

In her travel essays, Jacobs insists upon representing herself, above all, as a tireless traveler willing to subject herself to the discipline required by the essayist genre, in spite of finding herself in the most diverse places. On occasion, she sees herself traveling metaphorically through reading and making use of the camera to focus on what she sees as most interesting in each text. She affirms: "A writer photographs what she likes in a trip as a way of noting it down in her diary, the writer's diary is an photo album: in its pages she pastes images one next to the other, and not only the images she likes in a trip, but also what she dislikes in life" (70). The celebration of the places that have contributed to her formation or that have enriched her experiences provides us with some clues to her cultural and personal identity. The house in Chimalistac, different European and American cities, and the multiple spaces from which Jacobs writes are pleasant refuges for the work of a writer. The thirtieth essay affectionately recuperates the familial space: "The front door is open, my sister goes up the five steps from the garden to the veranda, she sees me lose my balance behind her: my bare feet hanging without touching the floor at the dining table" (84).

In other texts, Jacobs communicates her observations and feelings, her personal experiences, and encounters in different cities: a restaurant in New York, a street in Paris, a stroll through New Orleans, a conversation in Livorno; all are of special significance for her because their recuperation affirms her identity. The bookstore, however, is a place of anxiety, as is the world that surrounds the publishing industry. In the thirty-fifth text, while making use of an impersonalized rhetorical subject, the physical presence of the author is implicated by an anonymous writer who in the solitude of her work dreams of a friendship with her publisher. Jacobs concludes by affirming the conflictive relations existing among writers and publishers:

Well, the writer says to himself in the solitude of his studio; the only thing left is to be the enemy of the publisher. He lifts the manuscript from the desk, with great steps reaches the publisher and, without knocking on the door, bursts into the editor's office. Without any sign of good manners he forcefully lets the manuscript fall in front of the editor. He doesn't bother to impress on him that it is an exceptional work. He demands that he publish and sell it, and, without another word, he leaves. (91)

The re-creation of certain smells, noises, and sensations illuminates the emotional level that Jacobs seeks to communicate to her readers. In the twenty-third text, Jacobs portrays herself in the space of a bookstore. She sees herself as a writer and recognizes that the scene brings to mind a nightmare that caused uneasiness and anguish: "I am the author of a yet unpublished book and I visit a bookstore. As in every good bad dream, this bookstore is small, but high, it is dark and full of dust . . . I am suffocated by a smell that I would not know how to recognize but that, I have no doubt, would taste bitter if I opened my mouth and tasted, even a little, the sort of smoke that surged around me" (64). Jacobs's voice manifests itself as the bearer of certain nuances, gradations or tones, depending on the point she is interested in reflecting. Thus, in the texts with a moralizing intention, Jacobs represents herself communicating her particular experience and her direct observations with respect to some inconsistencies of human behavior to offer her personal point of view, although she might inscribe it as "universally particular." In the forty-fourth text, for example, the supposed visit of Susan Cheever to her father's tomb provokes a digression on the subject of identification among human beings: "What happened to Susan happened to me the other day. And if it happened to Susan and me, I think the same must happen to everybody else. In what happened and happens to us, we are all the same; what makes us different is what we do after what happens to us happens. . . . And this business of being different is what makes us all the same" (110–113).

The assertion in the style of a philosophic maxim with which she concludes this essay affirms the sameness of the human condition and points to the solidarity and empathy between individuals in the world. The moral essay, based in the reflection of an aspect of the human beings centers, often, in some type of inconsistency, seen from the personal point of view of the author. In the thirteenth text, the author recalls seeing the movie *Mondo Cane* while next to her a female spectator was sobbing. In the pages that follow, Jacobs reflects upon that fact and comes to the conclusion that what made her cry was the vulgarity of human beings, represented in the movie by a group of American tourists in Hawaii dancing wildly, gracelessly, and without rhythm. Jacobs declares, "And finally, today, I know what made her cry, what the director of that documentary wanted to show in that scene in Hawaii was the absurdity of humanity, it was the absurd. Absurdity, the absurd, as one of the most incredible and dramatic truths of our 20th Century civilized world" (36). In any case, Jacobs's concerns focus on the problematics of living in a society, reflecting on some human vices and suggesting, at the same time, that, although coming from individuals, those vices are universal. Thus Jacobs, reflects about suicide in text twenty-four; the human questioning of solitude in number forty-five; misanthropy in relation to human relations in number fifty, and the generalized need to preserve some animal species in number thirty-one.

The circular processes in reading and writing are the themes shaped in the texts considered to be critical epistolary essays. Jacobs presents herself physically and mentally before her addressees, in a confidential and conversational tone, up to the point in which she "visualizes" herself reading in the moment when she takes the object of her reflection to the pages of *Time*: "When I read in the issue number 15 of the magazine" (40); in others she presents herself behind the information that will complete her study: "I searched, due to obsession or personal discipline, but today encouraged by Russell Lynes's essay, 'Look it up!', for quotes on thoughts about childhood" (37); frequently she evokes the spontaneous though disciplined process of her research: "Once I believed"; "Later I even questioned"; "Then I thought"; "And so, more intrigued than before, I read again"; "And it was in this way that I suddenly knew"; "And now . . . You will see why" (14).

The rhetoric of a confidential physical presence is constant in the process of creation in *Escrito en el tiempo*, since Jacobs models in her pages the possibility of a personal brand of criticism through sophisticated manipulation of a theoretical discourse. This makes visible the traces of her own body in the moment of reading as well as in the moment of writing, while at the same time inscribing the modes and attitudes of a rhetorical subjectivity that is strongly biographic or, even, to use Roland Barthes's term, "biographemic."[2] Thus, in the thirty-fifth text, in reference to the proliferation of computers and word processors in the market, Jacobs points to the incidence of these in the life of the writer, and she expounds a sensorial attraction to the displaced typewriter:

I like seeing it on my desk, hearing the sound of the keys, knowing what function each one of its parts has and how to use it. I like the paper: seeing it, touching it, smelling it, it is a matter of the senses. I like to straighten the sheet and put it through the carriage; I like the letters that the typewriters print on the white pages. I like to pull out the paper and to correct its surface with a pencil. I like to take my time with the corrections, to revise at different times and in different corners of my house and the world. (92)

Passion for reading and writing is set forth throughout *Escrito en el tiempo* by way of a doubled discourse: on the one hand, with a conversational, dialogic style, directed at all readers; on the other, with an antagonistic discourse facilitated by the irritating apostrophe "*Señores.*" Consequently, we witness a rhetorical display, marked by the personal and the emotional in relation to the analyses that Jacobs effects on the world of literature and her work as a writer, facilitating, inevitably, a critical intervention of resistance to the official male canon. Of particular importance on this point are the texts through which Jacobs puts in circulation or recovers the works of women obscured by dominant patriarchal ideology and only recognized by said ideology as wives, mothers, and sisters. She especially recognizes Dorothy Wordsworth as "the spring that gave rise to the poetry of her brother William" (50), noted as well as essential in the work of Coleridge, who "extracted a quatrain of *Christabel*" from Dorothy's diaries. Of exceptional intensity is Jacobs's speculation that Saint Teresa may have been the author of one of the master works of literature written in Spanish, *La vida de Lazarillo de Tormes*: "An ingenious woman with a goal and a project to reach it, is not stopped by anything: not governments, nor societies, nor its law nor its principles: there we have the woman author of *La vida de Lazarillo de Tormes y sus fortunas y adversidades* to demonstrate it to all posterity" (98). *Time* magazine offers her few female names in comparison with the male ones, but Jacobs's emphasis in noting these figures, and including those she considers pertinent—the case of Saint Teresa, the only representative of the Hispanic tradition, together with women like Isak Dinesen (13), Hilda Doolittle (13), Lillian Hellman (77), Susan Cheever (109), and Lady Antonia Fraser (97), among others—makes these texts representative of what Nancy K. Miller describes as "anxiety of feminine exhibition" (10-25).

The personal and the autobiographic are detailed as themes in the critical essays. This supposes that the writer has read the biographies and autobiographies of the authors to which she alludes throughout the fifty-three unsent letters. Essayists, poets, novelists, they are all recovered by Jacobs through the inscription of private anecdotes that humanize them and bring them closer to the readers. Conscious of the importance that readers give to knowledge of the details of the private lives of an author, Jacobs does not hesitate in asking herself: "How will I read T.S. Eliot now, after *T.S. Eliot: A Life,* a biography for which Peter Ackroyd dug up, one after another, details of the intimate life of the poet and in which he reveals them (according to the 49th issue of *Time* magazine with next Monday's date)?" (122).

The recovery of the past through the activation of memory is the discourse that runs through the epistolary essays considered truly autobiographical. Numbers twenty-three, twenty-eight, and thirty refer to situations, not only real, but also dreamt or imagined, in which Jacobs paints herself as the principal protagonist, both subject and object. The fictional signs that frame these texts, that is to say, the fictions of memory, of the "I" who is subject and object of the narration, of the implicit reader and of the actual story are textualized simultaneously or, in any case, in accord with a personalized and emotional subjectivity. The "autobiographical pact" that Philippe Lejeune considers an essential element in autobiographical production and that unites the reader and the writer in the fabulization of reality can be found, in a similar way, in every personalized act of writing (13–46). As the author's voice inscribes itself in the spectacle that presumes its own representation in the text, an alternative process of literary creation is produced, which includes, also, private exhibition as discourse of the desire for a response that goes beyond the speculative. The autobiographical voice brings together facets of an experience that remembers with its impressions, descriptions, and emotions. In this way, it manages to construct a narrative composed by the recovery of a past that, inevitably, is intensely related with the present moment. Without a doubt, the nightmare in which the author offers herself before the reader full of anguish and fear is a metaphor that Jacobs uses to present herself ambiguously. The artifice of the dream allows her to reveal her emotions through the description of her most intimate impressions, physical as well as psychic, when she is confronted with the reading of her own work: "I read the first pages, the first paragraph. Before finishing the first page I feel agitated. My breathing quickens, I'm afraid that it might be heard. That first page reminds me of something. I read the second page and the memory gets sharper; at the third page, the memory is the purest consciousness that I have of the present. The book I am reading is my book, my only book at that point, and for me still unpublished" (65).

In the same way, in the twenty-eighth text, Jacobs evokes her visit to a small restaurant in Little Italy, in Manhattan, and through the exercise of remembering, she describes an scene in which fiction and reality are mixed:

I am at a table of my memory, in front of green felt tablecloth, or a red and white checkered one, or a blue and white checkered one where I will not be seen by anything or anybody, and from here, I look at the door now and again, and I see Lillian Hellman come down . . . and here we both are, although I do not have in my hand a single line of hers directed to me, to me, and although her hand hasn't ever written my name and mine, on the other hand, has written Lillian Hellman an infinite number of times. (80)

The use of dramatic rhetorical artifices such as dreams and nightmares reveal information about the present and about how the author places herself in her own reality relative to the cultural ideology that surrounds her and the authors that preceded her and that she considers her "models."

The memories of childhood, suggested in the vision of an old photograph, are evoked in the fortieth text. As in the two texts mentioned previously, Jacobs offers a black and white vision of herself, an image that is fragmented and in *chiaroscuro*. The photographic image serves to recapture the familiar space of childhood with nostalgia:

Whenever I think about the subject of photography I remember that morning next to my sister, with our flowered bathing suits and I cannot distinguish, years and years later, if it is a memory of a moment or of a photograph, nor what else may be in the memory that the photograph doesn't manage to capture, apart from my desire to remain in the garden, the pleasure of doing nothing, the sensation of being glad, the awareness of being happy. (84)

Clearly, the sensation intimately exposed before her readers provokes Jacobs to protect herself, on occasion, through the rhetoric of an anonymous voice and the fictions of dreams, nightmares, and photography. The tension that the writer feels in inscribing herself as feminine subjectivity has much to do with this type of representation that mixes fiction and reality. On the one hand, she does not allude explicitly to her gender, but resorts to anonymity, a fact that reminds us of the woman writer who, in the past, disguised an essay in a letter to have access to the public space. On the other, she disperses her addressees in a crowd, and she excuses herself, moreover, for assuming the position of subject. In any case, Jacobs establishes a correspondence based on relationships of unequal power, and she succeeds in constructing a feminine subjectivity in the form of personal narrative.

That intention is clear from the beginning of the book, which starts with a preface entitled "Dos palabras." Textualized as a manifesto, it serves as a space in which the Mexican author inscribes herself as an identity that embodies an ideology that commits her to alternate modes of representation: In that way, she proposes herself as a subjectivity that questions and resists the dominant discourse. Jacobs declares:

I wrote the 53 letters that follow without sending a single one to *Time*: years before, I had sent them one (May 6th, 1980) in which I manifested my opposition to the political points of view supported in the magazine, and they, by means of a form letter signed by María Luisa Cisneros, had rejected its publication on their pages. To this moment, this incident represents my political stance, and its outcome makes me proud. (99)

Jacobs employs the epistolary essay to consciously undertake a public critique of the dominant culture represented in *Time* magazine. At the same time, she commits herself to a project of both private and personal character; in the first place, she represents herself as a historical subject when she inserts herself in the tradition that alludes to the woman as writer of personal letters; in the second place, she inscribes herself as a theoretical subject, since she not only appropriates the essayist genre—established as eminently masculine by the androcentric canon—but also marks it with inflections and tones that are personal and intimate. In this way, she problematizes the relationship the writer has with literal language, belonging to the letter, and literary language, belonging to the essay, the only one appropriate for publication.

By interchanging a genre considered nonfictional—as is the epistolary essay—with fiction Jacobs manages to show herself for what she is: a writer. Her preferences in terms of types of discourse, which are set forth through the use of autobiographical readings and practices, are inscribed in *Escrito en el tiempo* in a fragmentary, spontaneous, and ambiguous form. The ideology of identity that Jacobs pursues in this work is reflected in an exhibitionism of a professional type surrounded by confidences and intimate tones in relation to her literary preferences. What she is really interested in rescuing are her experiences in relation to her duty as a writer. This anxiety about speaking as such is inserted in the crisis of representation attributed to generations of the so-called postmodernity. There is no doubt that *Escrito en el tiempo* is a contemporary production that includes genre and theory as indispensable conditions at the time of authorizing a discourse dominated by micronarratives that represent a hybrid identity but is not for that reason unaware of the importance of its own position as subject and object of a personal discourse.

The ambulatory and peripatetic style of the Mexican author, as well as her tendency toward the spontaneous discipline that characterizes her writing, converge in the fifty-three epistolary essays, texts that participate in a form in process, dialogical and open, without a definitive solution, just as is suggested by the metaphor of the jigsaw puzzle, which defines her personal and professional inclinations:

My style follows its own laws. My style is that of solitary work. It rejects interferences, indifference, ignorance, lack of conscience and sensibility. My style is that of sunrises and of books. It knows about contemplation, it knows about clouds, it knows about smoke. My style installs itself in childhood and adolescence, in desires and hopes. My style is of yesterday, today and tomorrow. My style is that of terraces; patios, backyards, swings; of echoes, underground paths; of stairs, ropes, hallways; of bridges, of hammocks. My style is of the path, of the roads, streets, destiny; of the highways, of good-byes, of returns. My style is of the path: the path that begins and never ends. (102)

In *Escrito en el tiempo*, Bárbara Jacobs clearly suspends herself between the maternal and paternal narratives that preceded her and that shape her cultural identity. In this way, the author transforms herself into a rhetorical subject when she represents herself, that is to say, she becomes a product of the history of psychosexual phenomena that surround her and thus reveals both textual and contextual forces of meaning. In a creative gesture, Jacobs speaks from the margins—female and Mexican—but although these margins have their limits they also have advantages: They have multiple voices, distant from the centers of power and the conventions of the universal "I." Her narratives, which are characterized by disphoria, searching, and intranquility, anxieties of authorship and authority, promote expectations and enthusiasm in the readers due to their anticonventional traits. Her discourse releases rebellion, ambivalence and confusion; in sum, as Sidonie Smith asserts, the uncertainties of female desire (*A Poetics of Women's Autobiography* 18). Her texts always underline the personal, emotive, temperamental, and passionate voice of a woman speaking of the lives and works of other women and attempts to achieve a balance by reading the lives and works of the men and women that preceded her. Without a doubt, these mark, particularly, the poetics of the feminine autobiography and its narrative practices.

NOTES

1. All translations are mine.
2. Nancy K. Miller alludes to the "biographeme," a term introduced by Roland Barthes to refer to the meanings that are borne by certain nuances or inflections of tone and voice in the text. These would function as metonimic marks of a subject printed in a dispersed form throughout the text. Miller applies it to the writing of women as a mode of resistance and personalized criticism (26).

REFERENCES

Benstock, Shari, ed. *The Private Self: Theory and Practice of Women's Autobiographical Writing*. Chapel Hill: U of North Carolina, 1988.

Boetcher Joeres, Ruth Ellen, and Elizabeth Mittman, eds. *The Politics of the Essay: Feminist Perspectives*. Bloomington: Indiana UP, 1993.

Castillo, Debra. "Rosario Castellanos: 'Ashes without a Face.'" *De/Colonizing the Subject: The Politics of Gender in Women's Autobiography*. Eds. Sidonie Smith and Julia Watson. Minneapolis: Minnesota UP, 1992. 242–269.

Good, Graham. *The Observing Self*. New York: Routledge, 1988.

Jacobs, Bárbara. *Doce cuentos en contra*. Mexico: Martín Casillas, 1982.

———. *Escrito en el tiempo*. Mexico: Era, 1985.

———. *Las hojas muertas*. Mexico: Era, 1987.

———. *Las siete fugas de Saab, alias el Rizos*. Mexico: Alfaguara, 1992.

———. *Vida con mi amigo*. Madrid: Santanilla, 1994.

Lejeune, Philippe. *Le pacte autobiographique*. Paris: Seuil, 1988.

Miller, Nancy K. *Getting Personal. Feminist Occasions and other Autobiographical Acts*. New York: Routledge, 1991.

Smith, Sidonie. *Subjectivity, Identity, and the Body: Women's Autobiographical Prac-*

tices in the Twentieth Century. Bloomington: Indiana UP, 1993. 53–64.

_____. *A Poetics of Women's Autobiography. Marginality and the Fictions of Self-Representation*. Bloomington: Indiana UP, 1993.

SELECTED BIBLIOGRAPHY

WORKS CITED

Primary Sources

Berman, Sabina. *La bobe*. Mexico: Planeta, 1991.

Boullosa, Carmen. *Duerme*. Madrid: Alfaguara, 1994.

_____. *Son vacas, somos puercos*. Mexico: Era, 1991.

Esquivel, Laura. *Como agua para chocolate: Novela de entregas mensuales con recetas, amores y remedios caseros*. Mexico: Planeta, 1989.

_____. *Like Water for Chocolate: A Novel in Monthly Installments with Recipes, Romances and Home Remedies*. Trans. Carol and Thomas Christensen. New York: Doubleday, 1992.

Jacobs, Bárbara. *Escrito en el tiempo*. Mexico: Era, 1985.

Mastretta, Ángeles. *Arráncame la vida*. Mexico: Océano, 1985.

_____. *Mexican Bolero*. Trans. Ann Wright. London: Viking, 1989.

_____. *Mujeres de ojos grandes*. 1ra ed. Mexico: Cal y Arena, 1990.

Nissán, Rosa. *Novia que te vea*. Mexico: Planeta, 1992.

Pacheco, Cristina. *El corazón de la noche*. Mexico: El Caballito, 1989.

_____. *Cuarto de azotea*. Mexico: Gernika/Secretaría de Educación Pública, 1986.

_____. *Para mirar a lo lejos*. Tabasco, Mexico: Gobierno del Estado de Tabasco, 1989.

_____. *Para vivir aquí*. Mexico: Grijalbo, 1983.

_____. *Sopita de fideo*. Mexico: Aguilar, León y Cal, 1991.

_____. *La última noche del "Tigre."* Mexico: Océano, 1987.

_____. *Zona de desastre*. Mexico: Océano, 1986.

Poniatowska, Elena. *La "Flor de Lis."* Mexico: Era, 1988.

_____. *Tinísima*. Mexico: Era, 1992.

_____. *Tinísima*. Trans. Katherine Silver. New York: Farrar, Straus, Giroux, 1996.

Puga, María Luisa. *Pánico o peligro*. Mexico: Siglo XXI, 1983.

Selected Secondary Sources

Ahern, Maureen, ed. *A Rosario Castellanos Reader: An Anthology of Her Poetry, Short Fiction, Essays and Drama*. Austin: U of Texas P, 1988.

Anderson, Danny J. "Cultural Conversation and Constructions of Reality: Mexican Narrative and Literary Theories After 1968." *Siglo XX/20th Century* 8.1–2 (1990–1991): 11–30.

———. "Displacement: Strategies of Transformation in *Arráncame la vida*, by Angeles Mastretta." *The Journal of the Midwest Modern Language Association* 21.1 (1988): 15–27.

Bailey, Kay E. "El uso de silencios en *Arráncame la vida* por Angeles Mastretta." *Confluencia* 7.1 (1991): 135–142.

Berman, Sabina. "El intelecto como hacedor de fantasmas." *Noaj* 4.5 (1990): 71–73.

Burgess, Ronald D. *The New Dramatists of Mexico, 1967–1985*. Lexington: UP of Kentucky, 1991.

Castellanos, Rosario. *Mujer que sabe latín*. 1973. Rpt. Mexico: SepDiana, 1979.

Castillo, Debra. "Rosario Castellanos: 'Ashes without a Face.'" *De/Colonizing the Subject. The Politics of Gender in Women's Autobiography*. Eds. Sidonie Smith and Julia Watson. Minneapolis: Minnesota UP, 1992. 242–269.

———. *Talking Back: Toward a Latin American Feminist Literary Criticism*. Ithaca, NY: Cornell UP, 1993.

Costantino, Roselyn. "Resistant Creativity: Interpretative Strategies and Gender Representation in Contemporary Women's Writing in Mexico." Diss. Arizona State U, 1992. 169–230.

———. "Sabina Berman." *Latin American Writers on Gay and Lesbian Themes: A Bio-Critical Sourcebook*. Ed. David William Foster. Westport, CT: Greenwood Press, 1994. 59–63.

Cypess, Sandra M. "Ethnic Identity in the Plays of Sabina Berman." *Tradition and Innovation: Reflections on Latin American Jewish Writing*. Eds. Robert DiAntonio and Nora Glickman. New York: SUNY P, 1993. 165–177.

Egan, Linda. "Entrevistas con periodistas mujeres sobre la prensa mexicana." *Mexican Studies/Estudios Mexicanos* 9 (1993): 275–294.

———. "Feminine Perspectives on Journalism: Conversations with Eight Mexican Women." *Studies in Latin American Popular Culture* 12 (1993): 175–187.

Esquivel, Laura. "El arte de la novela como una forma culinaria." With Alejandro Semo and Juan José Giovannini. *Excélsior* (8 abril 1990): 5.

Fadanelli, Guillermo. "La literatura a la que estamos condenados." *Unomásuno* (28 abril 1990): 4.

Fornet, Jorge. "*Arráncame la vida* en la encrucijada." *Casa de las Américas* 178 (1990): 119–124.

Franco, Jean. "Going Public: Reinhabiting the Private." *On Edge: The Crisis of Contemporary Latin American Culture*. Ed. George Yúdice, et al. Minneapolis: U of Minnesota P, 1992.

———. *Plotting Women: Gender and Representation in Mexico*. New York: Columbia UP, 1989.

Gerendas, Judit. "Hacia una problematización de la escritura femenina" *Escritura* 31–32 (1991): 91–101.

Glantz, Margo. "Criadas, malinches, ¿esclavas?: algunas modalidades de escritura en la reciente narrativa mexicana." *América Latina: Palavra, Literatura e Cultura*. Vol. 3. Ed. Ana Pizarro. São Paulo: Fundação Memorial da América Latina, 1995. 603–620.

Glenn, Kathleen Mary. "Postmodern Parody and Culinary-Narrative Art in Laura Esquivel's *Como agua para chocolate*." *Chasqui* 23.2 (1994): 39–47.

Gold, Janet N. "*Arráncame la vida*: Textual Complicity and the Boundaries of Rebellion." *Chasqui* 17.2 (1988): 35–40.

Gómez, Anamari. "Ella encarnaba boleros." *Nexos* 91 (July 1985): 51–52.

González Stephan, Beatriz. "Para comerte mejor: Cultura calibanesca y forma literarias alternativas." *Nuevo Texto Crítico* 5.9–10 (1992): 201–215.

Ibsen, Kristine. "Entrevistas: Bárbara Jacobs/Carmen Boullosa." *Chasqui* 24 (1995): 46–63.

———. "On Recipes, Reading and Revolution: Postboom Parody in *Como agua para chocolate*." *Hispanic Review* 63.2 (1995): 133–146.

Jörgensen, Beth E. *The Writing of Elena Poniatowska: Engaging Dialogues*. Austin: U of Texas P, 1994.

Kushigian, Julia A. "Transgresión de la autobiografía y el Bildungsroman en *Hasta no verte, Jesús mío*." *Revista Iberoamericana* 53:140 (1987): 667–677.

León, Fidel de. "Arráncame la vida [review]." *Chasqui* 15.2–3 (1986): 96–97.

Llarena, Alicia. "*Arráncame la vida*, de Angeles Mastretta: El universo de la intimidad" *Revista Iberoamericana* 159 (1992): 465–475.

López González, Aralia. "Dos tendencias en la evolución de la narrativa contem poránea de escritoras mexicanas." *Mujer y literatura mexicana y chicana: Culturas en contacto*. Vol. 2. Eds. Aralia López González, et al. Mexico: Colegio de México, 1990. 21–24.

———. "Narradoras mexicanas: utopía creativa y acción." *Literatura Mexicana* 2.1 (1991): 89–107.

———. "Nuevas formas de ser mujer en la narrativa contemporánea de escritoras mexicanas." *Casa de las Américas* 31.183 (1991): 3–8.

McMurray, George. "Two Mexican Feminist Writers." *Hispania* 73 (1990): 1035–1036.

Marquet, Antonio. "La receta de Laura Esquivel: ¿Cómo escribir un best-seller?" *Plural* 237 (1991): 58–67.

Masiello, Francine. "Discurso de mujeres, lenguaje del poder: reflexiones sobre la crítica feminista a mediados de la década del 80." *Hispamérica* 15.45 (1986): 53–60.

Miller, Beth. "A Random Survey of the Ratio of Female Poets to Male in Antho logies." *Latin American Women Writers: Yesterday and Today*. Eds. Yvette Miller and Charles M. Tatum. Pittsburgh: Latin American Literary Review, 1977. 11–17.

Monsiváis, Carlos. "Cristina Pacheco: el arte de la historia oral." Prologue to *La luz de México: entrevistas con pintores y fotógrafos* by Cristina Pacheco. Guanajuato, Mexico: Gobierno del Estado de Guanajuato, 1990. 9–17.

Oropesa, Salvador. "*Como agua para chocolate* de Laura Esquivel como lectura del *Manual de urbanidad y buena costumbres* de Manuel Antonio Carreño." *Monographic Review/Revista Monográfica* 8 (1992): 252–260.

Peralta, Braulio. "Mi novela es una historia, no un ensayo feminista: Angeles Mastretta." *La Jornada* (11 June 1985): 25.

Poniatowska, Elena. "A Question Mark Engraved on My Eyelids." *The Writer and Her Work*. Ed. Janet Sternberg. New York: Norton, 1991. 82–96.

Pratt, Mary Louise. "'Don't Interrupt Me': The Gender Essay as Conversation and Countercanon." *Reinterpreting the Spanish American Essay: Women Writers of the 19th and 20th Centuries*. Ed. Doris Meyer. Austin: U of Texas P, 1995. 10–26.

Ramírez, Luis Enrique. Interview with Sabina Berman. 2 parts. *La Jornada: Cultura* (22 Feb., 1995): 25; (23 Feb., 1995): 27.

Ramos Escandón, Carmen. "Receta y femineidad en *Como agua para chocolate*." *Fem* 15.102 (1991): 45–48.

Reisz, Susana. "Hipótesis sobre el tema 'escritura feminina e hispanidad.'" *Tropelías* 1 (1990): 199–213.

Robles, Marta. *La sombra fugitiva: Escritoras en la cultura nacional*. 2 vols. Mexico: U.N.A.M., 1985; rev. ed. Diana, 1989.

Schaefer, Claudia. "Popular Music as the Nexus of History, Memory, and Desire in Angeles Mastretta's *Arráncame la vida*." *Textured Lives: Women, Art and Representation in Modern Mexico*. Tucson: U of Arizona P, 1992. 88–110.

Schaefer-Rodríguez, Claudia. "Embedded Agendas: The Literary Journalism of Cristina Pacheco and Guadalupe Loaeza." *Latin American Literary Review* 19 (1991): 62–76.

Sefchovich, Sara. *México: País de ideas, país de novelas (Una sociología de la literatura mexicana.)* Mexico: Grijalbo, 1987.

————. *Mujeres en espejo: Narradoras latinoamericanas, siglo XX*. 2 vols. Mexico: Folios Ediciones, 1983.

Shea, Maureen. "A Growing Awareness of Sexual Oppression in the Novels of Contemporary Latin American Women Writers." *Confluencia* 4.1 (1988): 53–59.

Teichmann, Reinhard. *De la onda en adelante: Conversaciones con 21 novelistas mexicanos*. Mexico: Posada, 1987.

Torres, Vicente Francisco. *Esta narrativa mexicana: Ensayos y entrevistas*. Mexico: Leega/U.A.M., 1991.

Valdés, María Elena de. "Feminist Testimonial Literature: Cristina Pacheco, Witness to Women." *Monographic Review/Revista Monográfica* 4 (1988): 150–162.

————. "La obra de Cristina Pacheco: ficción testimonial de la mujer mexicana." *Revista de Teoría y Crítica Literarias* 16 (1991): 271–279.

ADDITIONAL READING ON WOMEN'S NARRATIVE IN MEXICO

General Studies and Studies on More Than One Author

Aviles Valdez, Cecilia. "Escritoras mexicanas de los últimos tiempos." *Modernity and Tradition: The New Latin American and Caribbean Literature*. Ed. Nelly S. González. Austin: U of Texas, 1996. 41–53.

Bradu, Fabienne. *Señas particulares, escritora: Ensayos sobre escritoras mexicanas del siglo XX*. Mexico: Fondo de Cultura Económica, 1987.

De Beer, Gabriella. *Contemporary Mexican Women Writers: Five Voices.* Austin: U of Texas P, 1996.

————. "Mexican Women Writers of Today." *Review* 48 (1994): 6–9. Also in Spanish as "Escritoras mexicanas de hoy." *Nexos* XVII.199 (1994): 69–75.

Domecq, Brianda. "Las escritoras en la década de los 80." *Fem* 85 (1990): 7–9.

García, Kay S. *Broken Bars: New Perspectives from Mexican Women Writers.* Albuquerque: U of New Mexico P, 1994.

González, Patricia Elena, and Eliana Ortega, eds. *La sartén por el mango: Encuentro de escritoras latinoamericanas.* Río Piedras, Puerto Rico: Huracán, 1984.

López González, Aralia, ed. *Sin imágenes falsas, sin falsos espejos: Narradoras mexicanas del siglo XX.* Mexico: Colegio de México, 1995.

Marting, Diane, ed. *Spanish American Women Writers: A Bio-Bibliographical Guide.* Westport, CT: Greenwood, 1990. Rpt. in Spanish as *Escritoras de Hispanoamérica: Una guía bio-bibliográfica.* Mexico: Siglo XXI, 1990.

Miller, Beth. *26 autoras del México actual.* Mexico: Costa-Amic, 1978.

Minardi, Giovanna. "Encuentro con ocho escritoras mexicanas." *Hispamérica* 23.68 (1994): 61–71.

Molloy, Sylvia. "Female Textual Identities: The Strategies of Self-Figuration." *Women's Writing in Latin America: An Anthology.* Eds. Sara Castro-Klarén, et al. Boulder, CO: Westview Press, 1991.

Morales, Mariano, ed. *¡Por la literatura!: Mujeres y escritura en México.* Puebla: U Autónoma de Puebla, 1992.

Pfeiffer, Erna. *Entrevistas: Diez escritoras mexicanas desde bastidores.* Frankfurt: Vervuert Verlag, 1992.

Salvador, Alvaro. "Narrativa hispanoamericana: relatos de mujeres en los 80." *Revista de Crítica Literaria Latinoamericana* XXI.41 (1995): 165–175.

Schaefer, Claudia. *Textured Lives: Women, Art and Representation in Modern Mexico.* Tucson: U of Arizona P, 1992.

Urrutia, Elena, ed. *Imagen y realidad de la mujer.* Mexico: SepSetentas, 1975.

Vidal, Hernán, ed. *Cultural and Historical Grounding for Hispanic and Luso-Brazilian Feminist Literary Criticism.* Minneapolis, MN: Inst. for the Study of Ideologies and Literature, 1989.

Carmen Boullosa

Chorba, Carrie C. "The Actualization of a Distant Past: Carmen Boullosa's Historiographic Metafiction." *Inti* 42 (1995): 301–314.

Granados, Pedro. "Carmen Boullosa, el árbol y el remolino." *Inti* 39 (1994): 223–225.

Granados Salinas, Tomás. "Crónicas del engaño." *Quimera* 129 (1995): 57–61.

Muñoz, Mario. "Carmen Boullosa: *Son vacas, somos puercos.*" *Revista de Literatura Mexicana Contemporánea* 1.1 (1995): 75–77.

Vaughn, Jeanne. "'Las que auscultan el corazón de la noche': el deseo femenino y la búsqueda de representación." *Sin imágenes falsas, sin falsos espejos: Narradoras mexicanas del siglo XX.* Ed. Aralia López González. Mexico: Colegio de México, 1995. 607–629.

Laura Esquivel

Arredondo, Isabel. "¿Amarte para qué?: El mito del amor en *Como agua para chocolate.*" *Romance Languages Annual* 6 (1994): 413–416.

Beckman, Pierina. "Realidad y fantasía en el mundo culinario de Laura Esquivel." *Fem* 18.136 (1994): 37–40.

Lawless, Cecilia. "Experimental Cooking in *Como agua para chocolate.*" *Monographic Review/Revista Monográfica* 8 (1992): 261–272.

Lillo, Gaston and Monique Sarfati Arnaud. "*Como agua para chocolate*: Determinaciones de la lectura en el contexto posmoderno." *Revista Canadiense de Estudios Hispánicos* 18.3 (1994): 479–490.

López González, Aralia. "Ética y estética del fuego." *Sin imágenes falsas, sin falsos espejos: Narradoras mexicanas del siglo XX*. Ed. Aralia López González. Mexico: Colegio de México, 1995. 561-575.

Saltz, Joanne. "Laura Esquivel's *Como agua para chocolate*: The Questioning of Literary and Social Limits." *Chasqui* 24.1 (1995): 30–37.

Schmidt, Heide. "La risa: Etapas en la narrativa femenina en México y Alemania." *Escritura* 16.31–32 (1991): 247–257.

Spanos, Tony. "The Paradoxical Metaphors of the Kitchen in Laura Esquivel's *Like Water for Chocolate.*" *Letras Femeninas* 21.1–2 (1995): 29–36.

Valdés, María Elena de. "Verbal and Visual Representation of Women: *Como agua para chocolate/Like Water for Chocolate.*" *World Literature Today* 69.1 (1995): 78–82.

Bárbara Jacobs

Bados-Ciria, María Concepción. "Bárbara Jacobs: *Las siete fugas de Saab, Alias el Rizos.*" *Revista de Literatura Mexicana Contemporánea* 1.1 (1995): 75–77.

————. "El ensayo epistolar como práctica autobiográfica para Bárbara Jacobs." *Revista de Literatura Hispanoamericana* 31 (1995): 7–12.

Ibsen, Kristine. "Their Heart Belongs to Daddy: *Las hojas muertas* and the Disintegration of Patriarchal Authority." *Cincinnati Romance Review* XV (1996): 174–183.

Jiménez de Baez, Yvette. "Marginalidad e historia o tiempo de mujer en los relatos de Bárbara Jacobs." *Mujer y literatura mexicana y chicana: Culturas en contacto*. Vol. II. Eds. Aralia López González, Amelia Malagamba and Elena Urrutia. Mexico: Colegio de México, 1990. 127–137.

Rojas-Trempe, Lady. "La iniciación y el discurso de dos adolescentes en 'Carol dice' de Bárbara Jacobs." *Cuento contigo: La ficción en México*. Ed. Alfredo Pavón. Tlaxcala: U Autónoma de Tlaxcala, 1993. 117–127.

Ángeles Mastretta

Bailey, Kay E. "El uso de silencios en *Arráncame la vida* por Angeles Mastretta." *Confluencia* 7.1 (1991): 135–142.

Earle, Peter. "El tema del sacrificio en obras de Fernando del Paso, Elena Poniatowska y Angeles Mastretta." *Literatura Mexicana/Mexican Literature*. Ed. José Miguel Oviedo. Philadelphia: U of Pennsylvania P, 1993. 34–43.

Fornet, Jorge. "*Arráncame la vida* en la encrucijada." *Casa de las Américas* 30.178 (1990): 119–124.

Gerendas, Judit. "Hacia una problematización de la escritura femenina." *Escritura* 16.31–32 (1991): 91–101.

Gold, Janet. "*Arráncame la vida*: Textual Complicity and the Boundaries of Rebellion." *Chasqui* 17.2 (1988): 35–40.

González, Mirta Aurora. "Innovación en la actual novela feminista mexicana: Domecq, Mastretta y Sefchovich." *La mujer y su representación en las literaturas hispánicas. Actas de la Asociación Internacional de Hispanistas*. Vol II. Ed. Juan Villegas. Irvine: U of California, 1993. 220–227.

Llarena, Alicia. "*Arráncame la vida,* de Ángeles Mastretta: El universo desde la intimidad." *Revista Iberoamericana* 58.159 (1992): 465–475.

Martínez Echábal, Lourdes. "*Arráncame la vida*: crítica de una crítica." *Sin imágenes falsas, sin falsos espejos: Narradoras mexicanas del siglo XX*. Ed. Aralia López González. Mexico: Colegio de México, 1995. 545–558.

Oropesa, Salvador. "Popular Culture and Gender/Genre Construction in *Mexican Bolero* by Ángeles Mastretta." *Bodies and Biases: Sexualities in Hispanic Cultures and Literatures*. Eds. David William Foster and Roberto Reis. Minneapolis: U of Minnesota P, 1996. 137–164.

Elena Poniatowska

Aronson, Stacey L. Parker. "La textura del exilio: *Querido Diego, te abraza Quiela, Eva Luna, Crónica de una muerte anunciada*." *Chasqui* 22.2 (1993): 3–14.

Beckman, Pierina E. "Tina y Quiela: mujeres detrás de la cortina." *Fem* 18.131 (1994): 39–41.

Berry, John. "Invention, Convention, and Autobiography in Elena Poniatowska's *Querido Diego, te abraza Quiela*." *Confluencia* 3.2 (1988): 47–56.

Bruce-Novoa, Juan. "Subverting the Dominant Text: Elena Poniatowska's *Querido Diego*." *Knives and Angels: Women Writers in Latin America*. Ed. Susan Bassnett. London: Zed Books, 1990. 115–131.

———. "La búsqueda de la felicidad en *De noche vienes*." *Sin imágenes falsas, sin falsos espejos: Narradoras mexicanas del siglo XX*. Ed. Aralia López González. Mexico: Colegio de México, 1995. 379–392.

Bungard, Ana. "Identidad e historicidad. Los discursos del amor y la memoria en *Querido Diego, te abraza Quiela*." *Sin imágenes falsas, sin falsos espejos: Narradoras mexicanas del siglo XX*. Ed. Aralia López González. Mexico: Colegio de México, 1995. 369–378.

Capote Cruz, Zaida. "Biografía y ficción: El desafío de *Tinísima*." *Sin imágenes falsas, sin falsos espejos: Narradoras mexicanas del siglo XX*. Ed. Aralia López González. Mexico: Colegio de México, 1995. 405–412.

Castellevi Demoor, Magda. "*Querido Diego, te abraza Quiela* o la escritura de un texto femenino." *Alba de América* 10.18–19 (1992): 261–271.

Cella, Susana Beatriz. "Autobiografía e historia de vida en *Hasta no verte Jesús mío* de Elena Poniatowska." *Literatura Mexicana* 2.1 (1991): 149–156.

Chevigny, Bell Gale. "The Transformation of Privilege in the Work of Elena Poniatowska." *Latin American Literary Review* 13.26 (1985): 48–62. Rpt. in *Faith of a (Woman) Writer*. Eds. Alice Kessler Harris and William McBrien. Westport, CT: Greenwood, 1988. 209–220.

Davis, Lisa. "An Invitation to Understanding Among Poor Women of the Americas: *The Color Purple* and *Hasta no verte Jesús mío.*" *Reinventing the Americas: Comparative Studies of Literature of the United States and Spanish America*. Eds. Bell Gale Chevigny and Gari Laguardia. New York: Cambridge UP, 1986. 224–241.

Earle, Peter. "El tema del sacrificio en obras de Fernando del Paso, Elena Poniatowska y Angeles Mastretta." *Literatura Mexicana/Mexican Literature*. Ed. José Miguel Oviedo. Philadelphia: U of Pennsylvania P, 1993. 34–43.

Fiscal, María Rosa. "*De noche vienes* o el despertar de la conciencia social de Elena Poniatowska." *Latino America* 23 (1990): 197–219.

Flori, Mónica. "Visions of Women: Symbolic Physical Portrayal as Social Commentary in the Short Fiction of Elena Poniatowska." *Third Woman* 2.2 (1984): 77–83.

Fox-Lockert, Lucía. "Elena Poniatowska: *Hasta no verte Jesús mío.*" *Women Novelists in Spain and Latin America*. Metuchen, N.J.: Scarecrow P, 1979. 260–277.

Friedman, Edward. "The Marginated Narrator: *Hasta no verte Jesús mío* and the Eloquence of Repression." *The Antiheroine's Voice: Narrative Discourse and Transformations of the Picaresque*. Ed. Edward Friedman. Columbia: U of Missouri P, 1987. 170–187.

García, Kay S. "Elena Poniatowska: Search for the Voiceless." *A Dream of Light and Shadow: Portraits of Latin American Women Writers*. Ed. Marjorie Agosín. Albuquerque: U of New Mexico P, 1995. 237–251.

García Serrano, María Victoria. "Apropiación y transgresión en *Querido Diego, te abraza Quiela* de Elena Poniatowska." *Letras Femeninas* 17.1–2 (1991): 99–106.

Gertel, Zunilda. "La mujer y su discurso: conciencia y máscara." *Cambio social en México visto por autores contemporáneos*. Ed. José Anadón. Notre Dame: U of Notre Dame, 1984. 45–60.

Gnutzmann, Rita. "Tres ejemplos de escritura femenina en América Latina." *Letras de Deusto* 19.44 (1989): 91–104.

Gold, Janet. "Elena Poniatowska: The Search for Authentic Language." *Discurso Literario* 6.1 (1988): 181–191.

―――. "Feminine Space and the Discourse of Silence: Yolanda Oreamuno, Elena Poniatowska and Luisa Valenzuela." *In the Feminine Mode: Essays on Hispanic Women Writers*. Eds. Noel Valis and Carol Maier. Lewisburg, PA: Bucknell UP, 1990. 195–203.

González Lee, Teresa. "Jesusa Palancares, curandera espiritista o la patología de la pobreza." *Mujer y literatura mexicana y chicana: Culturas en contacto*. Vol. II. Eds. Aralia López González, Amelia Malagamba and Elena Urrutia. Mexico: Colegio de México, 1990. 93–97.

Hancock, Joel. "Elena Poniatowska's *Hasta no verte Jesús mío*: The Remaking of the Image of Woman." *Hispania* 66.3 (1983): 353–359.

Jaen, Didier T. "La neopicaresca en Mexico: Elena Poniatowska y Luis Zapata." *Tinta* 1.5 (1987): 23–29.

Jörgensen, Beth Ellen. "Perspectivas femeninas en *Hasta no verte, Jesús mío* y *La 'Flor de Lis'*." *Texto Crítico* 15.39 (1988): 110–123.

―――. "*Tinísima*: Elena Poniatowska's Tina Modotti." *Literatura Mexicana/Mexican Literature*. Ed. José Miguel Oviedo. Philadelphia: U of Pennsylvania P, 1993. 22–33.

―――. *The Writing of Elena Poniatowska: Engaging Dialogues*. Austin: U of Texas P, 1994.

Kaminsky, Amy K. "*Gaby Brimmer*: A Life in Three Voices." *Reading the Body Politic: Feminist Criticism and Latin American Women Writers*. Minneapolis: U of Minnesota P, 1993. 60–76.

Kerr, Lucille. "Gestures of Authorship: Lying to Tell the Truth in Elena Poniatowska's *Hasta no verte, Jesús mío*." *MLN* 106.2 (1991): 370–394. Also in *Reclaiming the Author: Figures and Fictions from Spanish America*. Durham, NC: Duke UP, 1992. 46–64.

Kuhnheim, Jill. "Un nacionalismo internacional: *Tinísima* de Elena Poniatowska." *Literatura Mexicana* V.2 (1994): 460–478.

Lagos–Pope, María Inés. "El testimonio creativo de *Hasta no verte, Jesús mío*." *Revista Iberoamericana* 56.160 (1990): 243–353.

Lemaître, Monique J. "La identidad asumida y el texto subversivo en *La 'Flor de Lis'* de Elena Poniatowska." *Explicación de Textos Literarios* 19.1 (1990–1991): 27–37.

―――. "Jesusa Palancares y la dialéctica de la emancipación femenina." *Hispamérica* 30 (1981): 131.135. Rpt. in *Revista Iberoamericana* 51.132–133 (1985): 751–763 and *Texturas* (Madrid: Oasis, 1986): 77–82.

Matthews, Irene. "Woman Watching Women, Watching." *Reinterpreting the Spanish American Essay: Women Writers of the 19th and 20th Centuries*. Ed. Doris Meyer. Austin: U of Texas P, 1995. 227–241.

Moorhead, Florence. "Escuchando las voces de los márgenes: *Hasta no verte Jesús mío*, de Elena Poniatowska." *El testimonio de mujeres: una estética contestaria*. Eds. Joy Logan and Emma Sepúlveda-Pulverenti. Santiago: Asterión, 1994.

―――. "Subversion with a Smile: Elena Poniatowska's 'The Night Visitor'." *Letras Femeninas* 20.1–2 (1994): 131–140.

Otero, José Manuel. "*Querido Diego, te abraza Quiela*: destrucción y reconstrucción de la personalidad; lengua, estructura, y símbolos del proceso." *Confluencia* 7.2 (1992): 75–83.

Paley de Francescato, Martha. "Elena Poniatowska: Convergencias en *La 'Flor de Lis'*." *Hispamérica* 21.62 (1992): 127–132.

Paul, Marcella L. "Letters and Desire: The Function of Marks on Paper in Elena Poniatowska's *Querido Diego, te abraza Quiela*." *Continental, Latin-American and Francophone Women Writers*. Vol. II. Eds. Ginette Adamson and Eunice Myers. Lanham, MD.: UP of America, 1987. 1–6.

Pérez Pisonero, Arturo. "La mujer en la narrativa mexicana contemporánea." *Cuadernos Hispanoamericanos* 498 (1991): 129–134.

Poot-Herrera, Sara. *"La 'Flor de Lis,'* códice y huella de Elena Poniatowska." *Mujer y literatura mexicana y chicana: Culturas en contacto.* Vol. II. Eds. Aralia López González, Amelia Malagamba and Elena Urrutia. Mexico: Colegio de México, 1990. 99–105.

————. "Tina Modotti y Elena Poniatowska: Dos mujeres, un libro." *Sin imágenes falsas, sin falsos espejos: Narradoras mexicanas del siglo XX.* Ed. Aralia López González. Mexico: Colegio de México, 1995. 393–404.

Richards, Katherine C. "A Note on Contrasts in Elena Poniatowska's *De noche vienes.*" *Letras Femeninas* 17.1–2 (1991): 107–111.

Rosengreen-Williams, Claudette. "Subtextuality in Elena Poniatowska's *Hasta no verte, Jesús mío.*" *Hispania* 77.2 (1994): 215–224.

Scott, Nina M. "The Fragmented Narrative Voice of Elena Poniatowska." *Discurso* 7.2 (1990): 411–420.

Shaw, Deborah. "Gender and Class Relations in *De noche vienes.*" *Bulletin of Hispanic Studies* LXXII.1 (1995): 111–121.

Starcevič, Elizabeth D. "Neglected by the boom: so what else is new?" *Requiem for the "boom"—premature?* Montclair, NJ: Montclair State College, 1980. 103–109.

Steele, Cynthia. "La creatividad y el deseo en *Querido Diego, te abraza Quiela* de Elena Poniatowska." *Hispamérica* 14.41 (1985): 17–28.

————. "Gender, Genre and Authority: *Hasta no verte, Jesús mío* (1969), by Elena Poniatowska." *Politics, Gender, and the Mexican Novel, 1968–1988: Beyond the Pyramid.* Austin: U of Texas P, 1992. 28–65.

————. "The Other Within: Class and Ethnicity in Mexican Women's Literature." *Cultural and Historical Grounding for Hispanic and Luso-Brazilian Feminist Literary Criticism.* Ed. Hernán Vidal. Minneapolis, MN: Inst. for the Study of Ideologies and Literature, 1989. 297–327.

————. "Retreat from the Phallus: *La 'Flor de Lis,'* by Elena Poniatowska." *Hispanic Culture on the Pacific Coast of the Americas.* Ed. Grinor Rojo. Long Beach: California State UP, 1993. 53–60.

————. "Testimonio y autor/idad en *Hasta no verte, Jesús mío* de Elena Poniatowska." *Revista de Crítica Literaria Latinoamericana* 18.36 (1992): 155–180. Also in *La voz del otro: Testimonio y veracidad narrativa/The Voice of the Other: Testimonio and Narrative Veracity.* Eds. Hugo Achúgar and John Beverly. Lima: Latinoamérica, 1991.

Tatum, Charles M. "Elena Poniatowska's *Hasta no verte, Jesús mío.*" *Latin American Women Writers: Yesterday and Today.* Eds. Yvette E. Killer and Charles M. Tatum. Pittsburgh, PA: Latin American Literary Review, 1977. 49–58.

Volek, Emil. "Las modalidades del testimonio y *Hasta no verte, Jesús mío* de Elena Poniatowska." *Literatura Mexicana/Mexican Literature.* Ed. José Miguel Oviedo. Philadelphia: U of Pennsylvania P, 1993. 44–67.

Zavala Alvarado, Lauro. "Humor, erotismo y lenguaje en tres cuentistas hispanoamericanas." *La Palabra y el Hombre* 92 (1994): 178–181.

Zielina, María. "La falsa percepción de la realidad en 'Cine Prado.'" *Mujer y literatura mexicana y chicana: Culturas en contacto.* Vol. II. Eds. Aralia López González, Amelia Malagamba and Elena Urrutia. Mexico: Colegio de México, 1990. 87–91.

María Luisa Puga

Acevedo Leal, Anabella. "El reconocimiento de la realidad a través de la alteridad en *Las posibilidades del odio.*" *Monographic Review/Revista Monográfica* 8 (1992): 223–228.

Domenella, Ana Rosa. "María Luisa Puga: Del colonialismo a la utopia." *Mujer y literatura mexicana y chicana: Culturas en contacto.* Eds. Aralia López González, Amelia Malagamba and Elena Urrutia. Vol. I. Mexico: Colegio de México, 1987. 239–250.

Guinazu, César Ulíses. "Elogio de María Luisa Puga." *Repertorio Latinoamericano* 5.39 (1979): 3–6.

López, Irma M. "María Luisa Puga: *La viuda.*" *Revista de Literatura Mexicana Contemporánea* 1.1 (1995): 99–104.

López González, Aralia. "Literatura de la diferencia." *Mujer y literatura mexicana y chicana: Culturas en contacto.* Eds. Aralia López González, Amelia Malagamba and Elena Urrutia. Vol. I. Mexico: Colegio de México, 1987. 251–258.

Pfeiffer, Erna. "El enfoque tercermundista en *Las posibilidades del odio* de María Luisa Puga." *Literatura del mundo hispánico*: *VIII Simposio Internacional de Literatura.* Ed. Juana Alcira Arancibia. Westminster, CA: Inst. Literario y Cultural Hispánico, 1992. 181–188.

Poniatowska, Elena. "Susana, Lourdes, Socorro y Lola." *Fem* 8.30 (1983): 62–63.

Reckley, Alice. "The Historical Referent as Metaphor." *Hispania* 71.3 (1988): 713–716.

Rodríguez Hernández, Raul. "María Luisa Puga: Aspectos de una nueva sensibilidad de narrar." *La escritora hispánica.* Eds. Nora Erro-Orthmann and Juan Cruz Mendizabal. Miami: Universal, 1990. 152–158.

Salcedo, Verónica. "La historia, dentro de la creación literaria de acuerdo a María Luisa Puga." *Dactylus* 10 (1990): 54–60.

Saltz, Joanne. "*Pánico o peligro* de María Luisa Puga: Reescribiendo la familia." *Kañina* 16.2 (1992): 101–104.

Smith, Susan M. "María Luisa Puga: Reflexiones sobre la identidad en *Las posibilidades del odio.*" *Chasqui* 23.1 (1994): 75–82.

Valdés, María Elena de. "Crítica feminista de la identidad en 'Inmóvil sol secreto.'" *Journal of Hispanic Research* 1 (1992–1993): 239–248.

INDEX

ABOUT THE CONTRIBUTORS

DANNY J. ANDERSON is author of *Vicente Leñero: The Novelist as Critic*, as well as numerous articles on contemporary Mexican literature. Currently an associate professor of Spanish at the University of Kansas, from which he also received his Ph.D., Anderson is presently completing a book on the social history of reading in twentieth-century Mexico, tentatively titled *Reading/Modernity/Culture: Literate Imaginings in Mexico, 1876–1992*.

MARÍA CONCEPCIÓN BADOS-CIRIA holds a Ph.D. from the University of Washington, Seattle, where she completed a dissertation on the works of Bárbara Jacobs. She has published articles on Latin American, Catalan, and Spanish literatures and is currently studying the works of Mexican photographers Cati Horna and Flor Garduño.

LINDA EGAN is an assistant professor at the University of California at Davis. In addition to numerous articles on Mexican literature, she is author of *Diosas, demonios y debate: las armas metafísicas de Sor Juana* and is currently completing a book-length monograph on Carlos Monsiváis. Egan is a graduate of the University of California at Santa Barbara.

CHARLOTTE EKLAND, who teaches at California State University at Chico, completed her dissertation on *Tinísima* at the University of California at Davis. She received her master's degree from the University of Rochester and bachelor's degree from Reed College.

YAEL HALEVI-WISE is currently completing her doctoral degree in Comparative Literature at Princeton University. Her publications include articles on Góngora and Dickens.

KRISTINE IBSEN received her doctoral degree from the University of California at Los Angeles. She is author of *Author, Text and Reader in the Novels of Carlos Fuentes*, as well as several articles on Spanish American literature. She is currently an assistant professor at the University of Notre Dame.

BETH E. JÖRGENSEN is an associate professor of Spanish and chair of the Department of Modern Languages and Culture at the University of Rochester. A graduate of the University of Wisconsin at Madison, Jörgensen is the author of the only book-length study to be published on Poniatowska to date, *Engaging Dialogues: The Writing of Elena Poniatowska*.

DARRELL B. LOCKHART, who teaches at the University of Arizona, received his doctoral degree in Latin American Literature with a minor in Jewish Studies from Arizona State University. He is author of *Latin American Jewish Literature*, and editor of *Latin American Jewish Writers: A Critical Dictionary*.

FLORENCE MOORHEAD-ROSENBERG is an associate professor of Modern Languages and director of the Spanish Program at Boise State University in Idaho. She received her doctorate from the University of California at Davis and specializes in Mexican and Chicano literatures.

DIANNA NIEBYLSKI received her Ph.D. from Brandeis University and presently works as an associate professor at Earlham College. Author of *The Poem on the Edge of the Word: The Limits of Language and the Uses of Silence in the Poetry of Mallarmé, Rilke and Vallejo*, she is currently completing a book on the subversive uses of humor in works by contemporary Latin American women authors.

SALVADOR OROPESA, an associate professor of Spanish and Latin American Studies at Kansas State University, received his doctorate from Arizona State University. He is author of a book: *La obra de Ariel Dorfman: ficción y crítica*, and numerous articles on women's writing both in Spain and Latin America.

CYNTHIA M. TOMPKINS holds a master's degree from the National University of Córdoba in Argentina and a Ph.D. from Penn State University. A professor of Women's Studies at Arizona State University, she is co-author of *Utopías, ojos azules, bocas suicidas: La narrativa de Alina Diaconú*, and has written numerous articles on women's writing in Latin America.

JEANNE VAUGHN is a doctoral candidate in Comparative Literature at the University of California at Santa Cruz who has lived and worked in Mexico City for several years. In 1987 she co-edited, with Sandra Pollack, *Politics of the Heart*.

ISBN 0-313-30180-8

90000>

EAN

9 780313 301803

HARDCOVER BAR CODE